AARON G. GREEN
ORGANIC ARCHITECTURE
BEYOND FRANK LLOYD WRIGHT

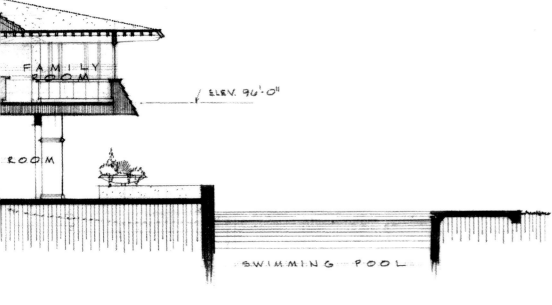

ELEV. 96'-0"

FAMILY
ROOM

ROOM

SWIMMING POOL

CTION

BY RANDOLPH C. HENNING

ORO
EDITIONS

EDITIONS

Publishers of Architecture, Art and Design
Gordon Goff: Publisher

www.oroeditions.com
info@oroeditions.com

Published by ORO Editions

Art direction and design: Allan Wright Green
Edited by Jan Novie and Allan Wright Green
Text by Randolph C. Henning
Managing Editor: Jake Anderson

10 9 8 7 6 5 4 3 2 1 First Edition

Library of Congress data available upon request.

ISBN: 978-1-939621-37-5

Color Separations and Printing: ORO Group Ltd.

Printed in China.

International Distribution: www.oroeditions.com/distribution

ORO Editions makes a continuous effort to minimize the overall carbon footprint of its publications. As part of this goal, ORO Editions, in association with Global ReLeaf, arranges to plant trees to replace those used in the manufacturing of the paper produced for its books. Global ReLeaf is an international campaign run by American Forests, one of the world's oldest nonprofit conservation organizations. Global ReLeaf is American Forests' education and action program that helps individuals, organizations, agencies, and corporations improve the local and global environment by planting and caring for trees.

TABLE OF CONTENTS

The history of Organic architecture is dominated by the titanic figure of Frank Lloyd Wright. Even Ludwig Mies van der Rohe, champion of the International Style's interpretation of Modern architecture, realized he stood within Wright's shadow: "he was like a majestic tree in a broad landscape which each succeeding year grows in the

FOREWORD

splendor of its foliage," wrote Mies for a 1940 exhibit on Wright. Architects closer to Wright than Mies often struggled to stand out from that shadow. Yet just as Organic architecture had a history before Wright in the work of Frank Furness and Louis Sullivan, so it had a dynamic life beyond Wright in the buildings of a host of excellent architects. Among these Aaron Green stands as a central figure. Though the diaspora of Organic architects was not as large as that of the followers of the International Style school, it was just as varied, innovative, and influential. They shared the same philosophy as Wright, but they applied those ideas in wide ranging ways. Some of these architects had worked directly with Wright at Taliesin before embarking on their own distinguished careers across the country and the world; others were influenced by Wright though they never studied with him. In the former group we see John Lautner's earthy forms and dynamic spaces, E. Fay Jones' delicate wood structures evoking metaphorical nature, and Paolo Soleri's visionary forms for sustainability, alongside other contributions by Alden Dow in Michigan, Foster Rhodes Jackson in Southern California, Sim Bruce Richards in San Diego, Blaine Drake in Arizona, Henry Klumb in Puerto Rico, and many others. In the latter group we see how Harwell Hamilton Harris's residential architecture built organically on his California roots while Alfred Browning Parker drew from Florida's materials and climate; larger firms (such as Anshen and Allen in San Francisco, MacKie and Kamrath in Texas, and Armét and Davis in Los Angeles) applied Organic principles to everything from high rise towers to coffee shop chain restaurants. Though each of these is distinctive, we can see the prominence of interior space, the interaction with natural settings, and references to nature's structural ideas that characterize Organic architecture.

In this notable group, Aaron Green is unique. He alone worked as Wright's business and building associate in their joint office, in San Francisco, imagining and building some of Wright's greatest accomplishments in the last decade of his life. Yet at the same time Green also had his own thriving architecture practice where he demonstrated his independent creative abilities.

These dual aspects of his career prove why this study of Aaron Green's career is important. He contributed to Organic architecture at both the macro and micro scale. At the broadest scale, Green addressed the major issues of the period through the lens of Organic ideas in a wide range of projects: public housing, high rise towers, schools, religious buildings, landscape, commercial buildings in growing suburbs, civic centers, mausoleums, and of course the single-family home. And at the scale of the individual building, Green's personal interpretation of Organic concepts lead to his own distinctive approach to design.

When he first went to Taliesin, Green already had an architectural education, at New York's Cooper Union, a condition that in Wright's eyes often disqualified young architects seeking to work with him; they were "spoiled" by conventionality. Yet Wright accepted Green; the fact that he brought with him a Usonian house commission probably did not hurt. Now we can see what Green did with that opportunity. Clearly Wright's ideas deeply inspired him. Though he stayed at Taliesin for only two years before enlisting in World War II, he remained in close contact with Wright for the rest of the latter's life.

With the self-assurance to open his own office after the war, Green moved first to Los Angeles and then settled in San Francisco. Both cities were attracting scores of talented, young Modern architects exploring a wide range of ideas, materials, and experiments: there was the Case Study House program of *Arts + Architecture* magazine, which gained international fame; Modern master Richard Neutra was active designing landmark homes and campuses; William Wurster was blending International Style ideas with the rich vernacular architecture of the region in homes and high rises. Even in that remarkably fertile period, Green's work bears comparison with the best of them.

Suburbia was presenting a new challenge for Modern residential design, and the Case Study Houses and the mass-produced Modern housing tracts of Jones & Emmons and Palmer & Krisel addressed them. So did Aaron Green. The Reif house (1950) in Glendale, California, for example, maximized both outdoor living space and privacy on a typically narrow 50 x 150-foot suburban lot.

Green's solution began with the oblique and complex three-dimensional geometries of Organic design. They contrasted sharply with the signature rectilinearity of the International Style. The Reif house is not a glass box like Charles Eames' famous Case Study House #8. There Eames made a point of using broad glass walls to open the house' living spaces to its eucalyptus grove setting; it nonetheless drew a distinct line between indoors and out. At the Reif house Green made a point of entirely erasing that line. The walls were mostly glass, but the complex geometries created dynamic, flowing spaces that allowed the plan and structure to zigzag and intertwine. Sight lines and circulation paths shifted imperceptibly from inside to outside. At the heart of the house a small atrium, open to the sky, reinforced this spatial concept. This is far from the universal space and minimalist details of International Style Modernism; Green expanded on Organic ideas to solve new problems, to articulate new spaces. The house is of the garden, not just in the garden

Green's use here of free geometries, natural wood, red brick, and the articulation of specific living room, kitchen, bedroom, and patio spaces places the design firmly in the realm of Organic architecture. It balances muscularity and delicacy with rich blends of textures. Yet at the Reif house Green also distinguished his approach from that of Wright. While Wright used compelling but often stringent hexagonal frameworks for his designs (at the Hanna house, for example), Green maintained order while allowing a more relaxed flow of spaces.

2

Aaron Green at home in San Francisco, c. 1985

design in the heart of the traditional city; the unbuilt Butterfly Wing bridge across San Francisco Bay blending dynamic engineering with graceful architectural design; and an early high-tech campus (unbuilt) for Lenkurt Electric Company that followed in the footsteps of Wright's revolutionary Larkin and Johnson Wax office buildings. And at the end of his illustrious career, Wright, always keenly aware of his place in history, entrusted Green to carry out the large and complex Marin County Civic Center project, the culminating proclamation of Wright's urbanist theories. Its lessons are still being learned.

Green's long career was well recognized in his time, with buildings published frequently in magazines such as *Sunset* and *House Beautiful*. But as we realize from the careers of countless other excellent but unheralded architects, contemporary fame is not enough to insure a mention in the history books. Too often Organic architects have been the victims of such neglect. The skilled publicists of International Style Modernism made sure that that their brand of Modernism was more widely promoted than Organic Modernism. It has taken years for John Lautner, Fay Jones, Alden Dow, Lloyd Wright, and others to achieve the attention they always deserved.

As more architectural archives are opened for study, the full panorama of Modern architecture in the mid-twentieth century is becoming ever more impressive. It is now clear that Organic design was a major force in that period with a wide-ranging spectrum of design ideas and buildings, and that Aaron Green played a major role in this through his long career. With this book he is happily reintroduced to us.

Alan Hess

And so it goes with original thinking throughout Aaron Green's career. In his Chapel of the Chimes columbarium addition (1955) he expanded Modernism by drawing on its affinities with Julia Morgan's original 1926 Romanesque and Gothic design without compromising either. In larger projects such as the major public housing project of Marin City (1957, with John Carl Warnecke and landscape architect Lawrence Halprin) Green applies Organic ideas in new ways. Like his many other projects, Marin City is, in effect, a piece of Broadacre City, Wright's idealized concept for the modern multi-nodal city blending with nature. Its multi-story structures are not, however, towers rising like trees in a meadow, but horizontal fins emerging gently from the sloping topography. Clustered two-story structures provide residents a close relationship with the ground, parks, and playgrounds. As suburbia developed, Green designed shopping centers, offices, medical buildings, churches, fire stations, civic centers, and cemeteries to further redefine the city in the image of the Organic city.

At the same time (and like few Wright protégés other than William Wesley Peters and John Howe) Green had a parallel career working closely with Wright. In 1951 Green and Wright became business and building associates in a joint San Francisco office. He collaborated on a string of Wright's most visionary masterpieces in the last decade of his career: the V.C. Morris gift shop proclaiming Organic

In October 1932, Frank Lloyd Wright and his wife Olgivanna opened a school for the training of young architects. Since their home Taliesin, in Wisconsin, was the base of operations for this new school they named it "The Taliesin Fellowship." Its general outline of work and study was unlike anything else in the nation at that time, or the

PREFACE

world, for that matter. Applicants who were accepted were not called "students" but "apprentices." Their education and training would be in the nature of apprenticeship to Mr. Wright, with a strong hands-on approach. The program was divided into three parts.

First, they would assist Mr. Wright in his work in the drafting room, each according to his or her capabilities. In the early years of the Taliesin Fellowship, with the nation still suffering under the Great Depression, there was little architectural work for Mr. Wright. But there was a great amount of work to be done in the second part of their apprenticeship training – building construction.

In 1932 Taliesin needed to be refitted to house the apprentices, and a quarter mile over the hill from Taliesin were the Hillside Home School buildings. This school was founded by his maternal aunts, Jane Lloyd Jones and Ellen Lloyd Jones, in 1886. The aunts were lovingly called "Aunt Jennie" and "Aunt Nell" and their system of education was way beyond its time, taking in boys and girls from age five to eighteen, to live in a home environment at the school. Their education consisted, among the usual training, of a strong diet of Transcendental Unitarian beliefs, dear to the entire Lloyd Jones family. By 1917 the school was closed and the aunts retired. They gave the buildings and the land to their nephew, exacting a promise from him that he would someday continue the school's mission of education. In 1932, Mr. Wright honored that promise, this time as education in the cause of architecture.

The Hillside buildings, neglected for fifteen years, had fallen into a sad state of disrepair and victim of vandalism. To repair them was the first task in this program of construction. Apprentices who had little or no experience along these lines soon found themselves cutting stone from neighboring quarries, felling trees in the forests to be turned into lumber, and then putting it all together to create new buildings or additions to the existing ones.

The third phase of their training was the community life within these buildings, keeping them clean, decorated with fresh flowers and branches, according to the season, and repairing them when necessary. Added to this, Mrs. Wright suggested that they hire no cooks, but encouraged the apprentices to learn how to prepare and serve meals. Soon music became an essential factor in the life of the Taliesin Fellowship and a chorus was formed. Apprentices who had musical training formed a chamber ensemble. The principle building of the Hillside Home School was simply called "Hillside," a building of sturdy sandstone and oak that Mr. Wright had designed for the aunts in 1902. With the formation of the Taliesin Fellowship, its wood shop became a new kitchen and dining room, while its gymnasium was converted into a playhouse/theater. Here musical events took place weekly, and cinema came into play, showcasing

films from around the world. Eventually a new, large drafting room was added to the north side of the building.

Midway between Taliesin and Hillside were the barns, called "Midway," for the cattle, hogs, and chickens. Farming, too, became an essential part of this apprenticeship training. During the Depression years, growing their own food was truly a hand-to-mouth affair, and a very necessary one with produce coming from the kitchen gardens at Hillside, as well as field crops. Vegetables and fruit, harvested in the season, were put down in a deep root cellar at Taliesin for winter provision. Even after those early hand-to-mouth days were over, work in the kitchen gardens and field crops remained a steady tradition at Taliesin. Consuming the produce that one raised on one's own soil was a powerfully contributing factor to good health.

This was the well-rounded life that the Wrights believed to be essential as a hands-on education that would develop strong young men and women ultimately to become architects. "We will have no armchair architects here," Mr. Wright avowed. Apprentices were learning not only how to design a building, but also how it was constructed, and how it was maintained. In work there was no segregation of the sexes at Taliesin. The young women were able to tend the concrete mixer to provide cement and mortar while the young men were able to tend the mixing bowl to provide bread and cakes.

In 1940, into this vigorous and exciting world of Mr. and Mrs. Wright and the Taliesin Fellowship came Aaron G. Green, a young man of twenty-three. At that time, neither Frank Lloyd Wright nor his work was new to Aaron. In 1938, while at the Cooper Union in New York, he came across the January issue of *The Architectural Forum*, which had recently featured a solo edition devoted to the work of Frank Lloyd Wright. At the same time Aaron read Frank Lloyd Wright's *An Autobiography* and became determined to join Mr. Wright. Returning to his home in Florence, Alabama, he met with his friends Mildred and Stanley Rosenbaum, who had recently heard of the Usonian home that Mr. Wright had designed for the Herbert Jacobs family in Madison, Wisconsin. The Rosenbaums decided they wanted a home along the same lines, and asked Aaron to design one for them. Aaron's reply was that if they desired a Usonian home, they should go directly to the source.

Thus Aaron, although a practicing architect by this time, graciously turned the commission over to Mr. Wright. This generosity would be a character feature of Aaron's that would endure during his entire life. On the first conceptual sketch of the Rosenbaum plan, Mr. Wright wrote, "House for client of A. G. Green." Following the production of the working drawings, or construction documents as they are called today, Aaron volunteered to supervise the construction of the house, a task for which he was well qualified. The concept of design of the Usonian House was an entirely innovative system of building construction, and most of the contractors whom clients selected to build found the drawings needed interpretation. To accommodate this need, Mr. Wright would send an apprentice, usually the one associated with the design of that particular house, to live with the client and supervise the construction. This practice went on all during the years of the Taliesin Fellowship. It was, naturally, a vital tool in the education of the apprentice as well as a way of getting the job constructed in the most economical fashion.

Upon completing the supervision of the Rosenbaum house, Aaron received an invitation to come to Taliesin. "Mr. Wright invited me to join him, which is of course the thing I had hoped for more than anything else. I went back to Florence and cleaned up my work." He described his initial visit to Taliesin as, "Everything about it was sort of a 'fairy-land.'" As for meeting Frank Lloyd Wright for the first time Aaron said, "I don't think anybody was ever disappointed in Frank Lloyd Wright as a human being—a remarkable human being! He was almost awesome in his genius, and personality and intellect."

In the beginning he had little contact with Mrs. Wright. But when he ran out of money and thought he should leave, Mrs. Wright heard about it and called him in. "'No, don't go,' she said. 'You can do your work here.' And she handed me fifteen dollars and said, 'I understand you're pressed for finances.' I was absolutely amazed! I was very emotional about it, that she was so sensitive to it. Fifteen dollars in those days would be like three hundred today."

When Aaron came to Taliesin in 1940, the early Depression years were over and architectural work was flourishing. The home of Edgar J. Kaufmann, "Fallingwater," was complete and widely published. The administration building for the S. C. Johnson Company had its grand opening in 1939 and was heralded as a spectacular new approach to an office building. Taliesin West, Mr. Wright's winter studio and residence on the Arizona desert, was in construction since 1938. Usonian homes were in construction from New England to California. Designs for the buildings for Florida Southern College were on the boards, and the Pfeiffer Chapel was in construction. This was indeed a most productive time and Aaron took a major part in it.

At the time of his arrival in 1940, Mr. Wright and the Taliesin Fellowship were intensely involved in the preparations for the forthcoming Frank Lloyd Wright Exhibition at the Museum of Modern Art in New York. For this show Mr. Wright wanted to have several new models made, especially of some of the Usonian houses. There had existed an earlier plaster model of the Press Building of 1912, but he had the apprentices make a new model, out of wood,

Aaron working al fresco *at Taliesin West, c. 1941.*

larger and in more detail. One of the buildings that particularly fascinated Aaron was the Ralph Jester house, and he suggested to Mr. Wright that he would like to make a model of it. Mr. Wright agreed. It was a hectic process since the deadline for materials going to New York was approaching. Yet Aaron persisted and the model was done in time.

In 1939 he had given his commission for the Rosenbaum house to Mr. Wright. In 1942 again his generosity prevailed, when two Michigan clients came to him for the Cooperative Homesteads and the Circle Pines Resort Camp. He turned both over to Mr. Wright, who remarked, "No other architect has ever done that – they're always trying to get work away from me." Aaron continued to bring work to Mr. Wright.

Aaron recollected "The last eight years of his life, we were—by his terminology—building associates and business associates. He asked me to open the office in San Francisco jointly with him, with both our names on the door. I took care of his work, and did my own as well. It happened this way: in the early part of 1951, I happened to be through Phoenix. Changing planes in those days took hours, so I took advantage of that. I went out to Taliesin and had lunch with the Wrights. As I was leaving, I told him I had decided to move my office, which I had recently opened in Los Angeles, to San Francisco. That's when he said, 'Well, I'm glad to hear that because I've got quite a bit of work there that needs taking care of better than it is. Why don't we jointly open an office?'"

When Aaron had made the plans for this new office, Mr. Wright sent him a four-inch square red tile with his initials in it,

his personal mark, to place beside the sign at the entrance. The red square had particular significance for Mr. Wright. When he was a boy of eleven, he had an encounter with the color red while he was working on his uncle's farm in Wisconsin. The encounter made such a lasting impression on the boy that he later wrote about it in his autobiography where he described his boyhood years in the third person singular.

"Wending his way along the ridges of the hills gay with Indian-pinks or shooting stars, across wide meadows carpeted thick with tall grass on which the flowers seemed to float. The field-lilies stood there above the grass like stars of flame. Always he was the one who knew where the tall, red lilies could be found afloat on tall meadow-grass. The spot of red made by a lily on the green always gave him an emotion. Later, the red square as spot of flame-red became the crest with which he signed his drawings and marked his buildings."

The first use of the red square can be found on the perspective drawing for the A. C. McAfee house in 1894, one year after he opened his own architectural practice. After 1932 his apprentices prepared his drawings with the use of the red square placed on either the right or left side of the perspective, and always on the lower right or left of the working drawings. When a drawing was finished Mr. Wright personally reviewed each one. He then signed the red square with his initials "FLLW." He also affixed the date of his signing as evidence of his approval.

In 1951 Mr. Wright visited the home of Aaron's mother-in-law, Jeannette Haber. As a way of signing not only the drawing but the actual building, Mrs. Haber and Mr. Wright came upon the

One of Aaron's first tasks at Taliesin was the construction of this model of the Ralph Jester residence.

solution of producing red square tiles, with his initials inscribed upon them. He took a sheet of paper, drew a square, initialed it, and handed it to Mrs. Haber. She then proceeded to manufacture the tiles, one at a time, by making a clay square, meticulously copying his initial in it, and firing it to come out flame red, what Mr. Wright identified as "Taliesin Red."

Now that Aaron was an associate, when he brought the large job of the Marin County Government Center to Mr. Wright in 1957, Mr. Wright split the fee with him 50/50.

Later in life when Aaron was asked once more about meeting the man he so deeply admired, he replied, "This was a wonderful human being, awesome in his genius, in his ability to respond to everything in life with a higher standard. I think that characterized a great deal of his reputation also, because he criticized lots of things, only because they weren't of the standard that he aspired to, that he saw his country should have, whether it be in architecture, whether in politics, economics, education, whatever. Working with him was really a fabulous privilege, it was a learning experience always, and it was a terrific, emotional experience to go back and realize what one had gained from this person. I think that Frank Lloyd Wright's basis of life and work was the same – it was based on principles, always the highest principles for everything he did. The principle was the high standard of beauty that man could attain, whether it was the way that the dining room table was set by his apprentices, whether it was the music that they performed, whether it was his dress, whether it was his buildings. His standards were so high, relative to principle from which he never varied."

Of all the holidays at Taliesin West, Easter was the most festive, second only to the celebration of Mr. Wright's birthday each June 8th. There could be upwards of 150 guests invited for the Easter brunch. The day began with the chorus performing sacred music in the Music Pavilion, followed by an egg hunt for children, and then breakfast outdoors on the Sunset terrace. Colorful balloons anchored all around floated high above. The breakfast menu was derived from Mrs. Wright's upbringing in Russia: a special bread called "Baba" was prepared, along with an equally special cheese called "Pashka," both in Russian tradition. Aaron was invited to each Easter during Mr. Wright's life and after his death. Following Mrs. Wright's passing, Aaron still observed this beautiful occasion. He customarily arrived a few days early to participate in the preparations. In his most beautiful calligraphy he wrote out the names of the guests on the place cards.

Even when Mr. Wright was no longer alive, Aaron's generosity and concern for the buildings of Taliesin West continued, including his funding for the restoration of Mr. Wright's office, the water tower, and the Frank Lloyd Wright archives. In 1991 he made possible the extension to the existing building to provide offices and a conference room for the staff of the archives. On the plate glass window a sign reads, "The Offices of the Frank Lloyd Wright Archives. The Gift of Aaron G. Green, 1991."

Shortly after Mr. Wright died, Aaron found an antique Asian bronze dragon, about three feet long, and presented it to Mrs. Wright. He said the former owner had used it as a fountain. But Mrs. Wright thought otherwise. Earlier, Mr. Wright had made several

changes to Taliesin West in order to make what was originally a desert camp into something more permanent in which to live and work. One of those changes was a most dramatic one. The advent of power lines beginning in 1950 to the south impeded the view of the valley and distant mountains. Mr. Wright remarked, "We are going to turn the building one hundred and eighty degrees around to face the mountains to the north!" What he meant by that was the *orientation* of the buildings. Originally a low stone wall ran along the north side, and the desert came up to the wall. He removed the desert growth, and made plans for gardens, with a citrus grove at the far end. The feature of this change, of course, was to bring the view of the Mc-Dowell Mountain Range into focus, what the Japanese call, "capture the landscape." Access to these gardens and grove was gained by a wide flight of concrete steps. On one side of the steps he had placed a six-foot-tall slender stone stele. This gave Mrs. Wright the idea of having the dragon perched on the top of the stone, and connected to a gas line, so that it would breathe fire and illuminate that area with its glorious flames at night. When she showed it to Aaron shortly after, she remarked, "No respectable dragon is going to spout water when it can breathe fire!"

From his first encounter with Taliesin in 1940, Aaron never lost a strong, personal connection to Mr. and Mrs. Wright and the Taliesin Fellowship. After Mr. Wright died, Mrs. Wright usually made at least one trip a year to San Francisco. Aaron was always there at the airport to greet her, help her get settled in the hotel, drive her wherever she wished to go, all the time leaving his work and devoting full time to assist her. After her passing, that strong connection continued with the members of the Taliesin Fellowship.

These were the salient features of Aaron's character – devotion, care, and generosity for those whom he admired and loved.

Even before meeting Frank Lloyd Wright and joining the Taliesin Fellowship, Aaron was strongly drawn to what the great architect had written about organic architecture. Any building conceived according to the principles of organic architecture was appropriate to time, place, and man. To time meant that it was built with the materials and technology of the current time, and derived its form accordingly, not harking back to past styles or eras. To place meant that it took into account where it was built; if in the landscape, it sought to blend with it and associate with any outstanding features, to bring the beautiful world of nature into the life of the people. If in the city, the building was designed to turn within itself, shielding its occupants from the surrounding city and creating, instead, a harmonious world within. To man, meaning mankind, the building provided along with shelter an inspiring place in which to worship, work, study, or live. The building was designed with human scale, casting aside the grandomania that crushed the individual rather than exalting him.

When Aaron struck out on his own in the practice of organic architecture, these principles are evident in all he designed. His work reflects his deep love for architecture in the service of humanity.

Bruce Brooks Pfeiffer

I have had the privilege of working directly with Aaron Green for almost thirty-five years during his lifetime, and, on a spiritual level, beyond. This book reveals his biography and signature body of work. I offer you here a glimpse into his character revealed from the perspective of his very special liturgical client, Father Daniel Danielson, pastor of St. Elizabeth

INTRODUCTION

Seton Catholic Church, which was the last of four churches Aaron designed for the Roman Catholic Diocese of Oakland.

We had a wonderful celebration for Father Padraig's twenty-fifth anniversary of Ordination. But I would have to say that I was somewhat distracted that day. It was the first time I had celebrated liturgy at St. Elizabeth Seton since I had heard about the death of its architect the previous week, Aaron Green, at age eighty-four. The first thing that anyone who knew this colleague of Frank Lloyd Wright would always say about him was 'He is a gentleman.' Things, during building, can from time to time get a little tense. People can disagree. Things can go wrong. In the midst of all of that, I never saw Aaron upset. I would get upset, but not him. He was always gracious, even in the face of unwarranted criticism or decisions he did not really approve of, occasionally by me.

Two weeks ago, I looked around our facilities of St. Elizabeth Seton Catholic Church and noticed again the many fine touches there that came directly from the mind and hands and talent of Aaron Green. The feel of the overall design of course is his, though following my original conceptual program. But the warmth of it, the organic beauty and quality of it is all his. I remain grateful permanently for the talent, the graciousness, and the beauty of this man who, while not a Christian himself, has served our community and our God so well.

Father Dan Danielson

I was involved in all phases of the project and can attest to the constant refining of each element and myriad of details until both Aaron and Father Dan were satisfied and the best possible solution was found. I hope the warm words of Father Danielson remain with you as you read about the many projects and reflect on the human equation that was the seed for each and every project.

Each client, program, and design revealed in this book was unique. What was not unique was the well-earned deep respect, admiration, and appreciation his clients felt towards their warm and engaging architect, whose all-encompassing desire was the fulfillment of their goals on every level. Each client received his complete devotion, attention, and the best of his refined ability to provide practical, beautiful, harmonious, and singular organic architectural design.

Over the years the office staff often included young apprentices from all over the world. Most remained as long as possible as they quickly learned that they could not have had a better role model for the profession than Aaron Green. The wide variety of projects in the office made it interesting and challenging. They were supervised not only by a staff member but also by Aaron himself. The harder they worked the more they learned, and the more experience they gained the more responsibility they were given. In return Aaron gave freely of himself to them. He made it clear that he was to be called Aaron, but he was held in such high esteem that it was difficult for them to break the *Mr. Green* pattern. Sooner or later they relented, and with a sigh of relief out came the word *Aaron*.

Aaron was very generous with his friends, staff, and associates. He always reached for the check for meals, no matter who he was with. He simply had to, as this generous gesture gave him immense personal pleasure. We often worked late as an office and he would always take us to a great place for dinner, usually in Chinatown. When you were with Aaron you were always his guest. We had a good time together often at diners, drive-ins, and dives. He was very sophisticated but had a well developed salt-of-the-earth side as well.

While serious most of the time, Aaron could also display a devilish sense of humor. Aaron and Wes Peters (Taliesin Associated Architects chief architect and a flamboyant fun-loving creative spirit) were great friends and often played practical jokes on each other, always attempting to raise the stakes. On April Fools Day in 1968, architect Bob Price was tapped to impersonate Sally Stanford's business manager. Sally was a well-known madam and owner of a restaurant called "Valhalla" in Sausalito. Aaron and his staff gathered around the speaker phone as the call was made. "Mr. Peters, I am Sally Stanford's business manager," said Bob. "Sally has selected you as the architect for a project she feels you would be perfectly suited for." Bob explained that a new bordello was to be built at the end of a pier extending out into San Francisco Bay, flanked by columns of mermaids leading to the bordello itself, which would be complete with mirrors on the ceilings of the rooms, etc. Bob asked Wes if he was interested in the job and could he be discreet. "Yes, yes and yes!" was his answer. The call ended and we all had a good laugh. A few hours later Aaron received a call from a very excited Wes Peters describing an amazing call he just had from Sally Stanford and wondering if he would joint venture with him on the project. Of course it ended with Aaron breaking the news that it was all in jest and Wes letting Aaron know he had better beware.

There is one more wonderful client memory I would like to share. Shortly after Aaron's passing Alan and Arlene Paul, for whom Aaron had designed a home over fifty years earlier, wrote a note saying: "Jan, you were very close to Aaron and if anyone has a pipeline to him it is you. Please let Aaron know that 'we thank him each and every day for giving us a little piece of heaven right here on earth.'" The Pauls were a renaissance couple. They had found their Thoreau in Aaron and he gave them their very own "Walden Pond."

Jan Novie

◼ AARON GREEN: HIS LIFE
◼

◼ Aaron Gus Green was born on Friday, May 4, 1917, a month after Woodrow Wilson, America's 28th president, had started his second term and the United States Congress declared war on Germany. However, the United States entering the Great War, later known as World War I, had little effect on Green's little known entrance into America's Deep South. He was born in Corinth, a small town in northeastern Mississippi with a population of approximately 5,000. Its northern boundary is the Tennessee state line and only twenty miles east is the Alabama state line.

Aaron's parents were Abraham Greenglass (1883–1946) and Rose Blunker (1892–1970). Abraham was born in Minsk, Russia, near the village where his parents, Joseph (1837–1934) and Ethel "Yetta" (1847–1933) lived and farmed. He immigrated to the United States at the age of fourteen and, upon arrival, his name was shortened to Green. Rose was born in New York. Her parents were Abraham Blunker (1873–1933) and Anna Goldstein (1875–1936). Abraham was the youngest of nine; Rose was one of six. Abraham originally trained as a painter, which he became highly skilled at, but was working as a traveling salesman when he met Rose in Nashville, Tennessee. They married in 1911, settling in Clarksville, Tennessee, near Rose's parent's home. Rose's father was in the clothing manufacturing business and Abraham picked up the trade as well, running a women's clothing business in Clarksville. Aaron Green's older brother, and only sibling, Sol, was born on May 8, 1914 while their father was

Green family home at 427 East Mobile Street, Florence, Alabama.

expanding his women's clothing business by selling furs. The family soon moved to Corinth, Mississippi, where they had the finest women's fur business in the area.

After Aaron was born, the family moved 60 miles southeast to Sheffield, Alabama, where Abraham continued to sell furs. When the Greens moved from Sheffield across the Tennessee River to Florence, Alabama, Abraham began investing in real estate, buying the family a home at 427 East Mobile Street. He rented this out in 1922 when the Greens moved almost 300 miles south to an 8,700-acre cattle ranch near Apple, Alabama where Abraham was going to set up a plant to manufacture turpentine from the pine trees on the property. Unfortunately, the plan never came to fruition due to difficulty in finding workers.

He developed serious health problems and, at St. Thomas Hospital in Nashville, had a kidney removed, a risky procedure for that time. It was a failure, leaving Green only one damaged kidney and in poor health for the remainder of his life. On advice from his doctor, Abraham moved his family to Miami, Florida, in 1925, spending several years in the automotive paint removal business and living through the devastating hurricanes of 1926 and 1928. After the stock market crash in October 1929 and the onset of the Great Depression the Green family returned to Alabama, moving back into their home in Florence.

Aaron's earliest interest, when he was seven or eight, was art and he became proficient in drawing. When he entered his teen years, his parents sent him to Chicago, where he lived with his Aunt Helen and Uncle Ben, so that he could get better training in art, as Florence had little to offer. He first attended Marshall High School on the west side of Chicago in the West Garfield Park neighborhood,[1] before transitioning to the newer Roosevelt High School in the Albany Park neighborhood, almost twenty miles north. To supplement his art training, on weekends Aaron also attended the Chicago Academy of Fine Arts at 18 South Michigan Avenue, which was founded in 1902 by Carl Werntz to give students practical career training, offering courses in commercial and applied arts, the fine arts, cartooning and illustration, and fashion design and illustration.[2] Aaron's interest in the art world grew as he became more and more comfortable with life in Chicago, and he recalled, "That was my first culture shock,

Aaron's parents, Rose and Abraham Green.

Aaron with his uncle Ben Drew in Chicago, c. 1932.

Aaron's senior picture, Coffee High School class of 1934.

being in Chicago. I remember it with fond memories, and I remember Chicago being a beautiful area. My activities were downtown, and Michigan Boulevard, where I went on the weekend, has always been a favorite spot of mine. I had no idea that Frank Lloyd Wright existed at the time and had no interest in architecture."[3]

Aaron returned to Florence to help care for his father while finishing his schooling at Coffee High School, which was three miles northeast of the Green family home. He grew to consider Florence his hometown: "Florence was somewhat contaminated by Northerners. In the New Deal era when the Tennessee Valley Authority started, Florence was at its center. We lived close to the Wilson Dam. It was a good place to grow up; I think the schools were very good. It was a very friendly community."[4] Despite having to leave Chicago, he continued with his art and was featured in the 1933 and 1934 *Coffee Pot*, the high school yearbook. After he graduated in 1934, Aaron, thinking that he'd obtain two years of general education before going somewhere else where he could focus on art, attended Florence State Teacher's College (now known as the University of North Alabama), located less than a mile north of his parent's home. He attended Florence State from 1934 to 1936 and worked throughout his college years for Louis Rosenbaum (1887–1962), a Polish immigrant who owned numerous movie theaters in the Florence area. Starting as an

usher, he soon became Rosenbaum's graphic artist, making signs and displays at Rosenbaum's theaters – including the Princess Theater in Florence. This continued to develop his artistic interests while broadening his perspective and technique in creating advertising art and illustrations.

With a more committed focus towards the arts, in the fall of 1936 Aaron was admitted to Cooper Union in New York City – a prestigious college offering degrees in art, engineering, and architecture. He lived in an apartment in Greenwich Village within walking distance of Cooper Union. He soaked up the culture of the city while attending classes, and worked as a shoe salesman on Saturdays. He also painted signs for a drugstore chain, did cartooning for a trade newspaper association and a variety of free-lance advertising jobs. Green recalled, "It was during the depression. It wasn't easy. I did anything."[5]

A year into his studies in art at Cooper Union, on one of his trips between New York and Florence, Green first became aware of the American architectural icon Frank Lloyd Wright (1867–1959). He was reading the September 1937 *Reader's Digest* article "Building Against Doomsday," an excerpt from Wright's own *An Autobiography* (published 1932), on the train. He was spellbound and bought the full autobiography, and after viewing the January 1938 *Architectural Forum* issue that was entirely dedicated to the work of Wright, he took a trip to view Wright's recently completed Rebhuhn residence in Great Neck Estates on Long Island, New York, an unusual cruciform Usonian.[6] That was Green's "dramatic determining factor. It had just been finished and it was really an emotional experience. From then on, I decided on architecture. I would never have been interested in architecture had it not been for Frank Lloyd Wright."[7] Aaron became one of Cooper Union's two architectural students at that time and, "I had only one aim, and that was to get close to Frank Lloyd Wright."[8] Before returning to Florence in 1939, Aaron established himself as an exceptional architecture student, winning the J.P. Morgan Presentation First Honor Award for Architecture in 1938 and the annual student award, the First Award in Design Excellence for Architecture, the following year.

Aaron had already received his first architectural commission, from the son of his old employer Louis Rosenbaum, before graduating from Cooper Union. Stanley Rosenbaum (1910–1983)

Large scale movie posters done by Aaron during high school and college for the Rosenbaums' theaters.

C14 Chanties OF THE SEA

O the anchor is weighed
and the sails they are set
‡ The maids that we're leaving
will never forget
‡ Away Rio
‡ Sing fare ye well my
bonny young gel

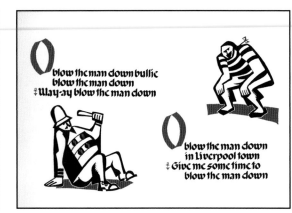

O blow the man down bullie
blow the man down
‡ Way-ay blow the man down

O blow the man down
in Liverpool town
‡ Give me some time to
blow the man down

My name is
Captain Kidd
‡ As I sailed,
as I sailed,
My name is
Captain Kidd
‡ As I sailed.

Oh whisky is the life of man
‡ Whisky, Johnny!
I drink whisky when I can,
‡ Oh whisky for my Johnny!

Tommy's gone, what
shall I do?
‡ Hey-yay to Hilo!
Tom is gone and I'll go too
‡ Tommy's gone to Hilo!

Oh way round to Callao
‡ Hey-yay to Hilo!
The Spanish gels he'll see
I know
‡ Tommy's gone to Hilo!

Oh Shenandoah, I long to
hear you,
‡ Away you rolling river!
Oh Shenandoah,
I long to hear you,
‡ Away! We're bound
to go
‡ Cross the wide
Missouri.

Oh Shenandoah,
I love your daughter
‡ Away, you
rolling river!

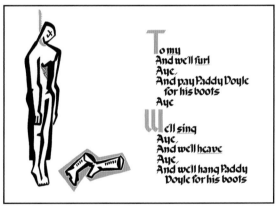

Aaron's innate artistic talent was clear in this calligraphy and illustration project from his days at Cooper Union.

was living in New York and the two would get together for dinner along with Stanley's fiancée, Mildred Bookholtz (1917–2006). Knowing Aaron's newly discovered obsession with architecture, they asked him to design a house for them that Stanley's father was going give them as a wedding present. The budget for the home was $7,500 and it was to be built across the street from the elder Rosenbaum's house on Riverview Drive in Florence. Green recalled, "I was amazed and astounded and pleased, and I managed to get that [as] my class project, the design of the Rosenbaum house. So I did it when I was still in school."[9]

Aaron returned to Florence after his three years at Cooper Union, and took a job from May 1939 through October 1940 with a local architect, Ben Frank Riley III, who assigned him design and drafting tasks in the office, and used him as a superintendent on construction projects. Aaron also completed the Rosenbaum project for bidding and construction. The project came in over budget at $8,000, so, faced with the task of redesigning the project, Green thought that perhaps they could talk Frank Lloyd Wright into taking on the project, "get these clients sold on Mr. Wright rather than my own design, to get close to him, which I did."[10] He wrote Wright a letter on April 20, 1939:

> Bids for a house which I have designed were excessive. Rather than begin again or destroy the unity of the house by the usual methods of cutting, I suggested to the client, optimistically, that you be asked to design the house.

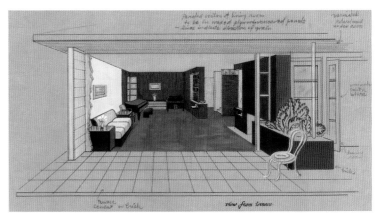

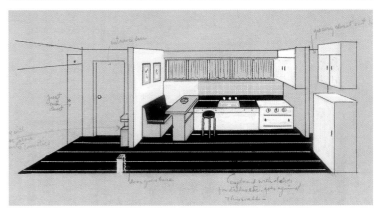

Aaron abandoned this design he did for a house for the Rosenbaums in favor of asking Frank Lloyd Wright to design the house.

Because, as well as clients, the people are my friends, and because your solution would be far superior to another's attempt in applying your ideas and philosophy, I would very much prefer your personal solution.[11]

Wright responded on July 26 in a letter to Green agreeing to do the project and hoping Green would follow through with assistance on the execution of the project. Wright often recalled that he immediately recognized the uniqueness of Green's gesture, knowing that most architects sought to take projects away from him, not give them their projects. The design arrived by mid-September 1939 and was followed by the working drawings in late October. Wright's on-site supervising apprentice, Burton Goodrich (1911–2007), arrived in early December to get the construction underway with Green's assistance.

At the end of August 1940, with the construction of the Rosenbaum house substantially complete, Aaron left with Goodrich to meet Frank Lloyd Wright at Taliesin, Wright's remote home and studio on ancestral family land near Spring Green, Wisconsin. Upon his return, Green quickly sent a thank you letter to the Wrights saying, "Your hospitality equals the beauty of the whole of Taliesin. After having experienced it, Alabama holds little interest and I am eagerly hastening my return to take advantage of the honor of being a part."[12] Two weeks later he left Florence, returned to Taliesin, and entered the Taliesin Fellowship as an apprentice to Frank Lloyd Wright. The Taliesin Fellowship, started in 1932 by Wright and his wife Olgivanna (1898–1985), was a group of tuition-paying young apprentices who "learned by doing" under the tutelage of the patriarch and matriarch of Taliesin.

The Fellowship at that time was busily preparing models and drawings for the upcoming exhibition of Wright's work at the Museum of Modern Art in New York City. Green's initial task was to complete the model of Usonia I, a project Wright designed that con-

sisted of seven Usonian-type dwellings for seven teachers from Michigan State College on forty acres in Okemos, near Lansing, Michigan. After completing the model earlier than expected, and being intrigued with the Ralph Jester design (Wright's first residential design based entirely on a circular geometry), he asked and received permission to build the Jester house model.

Once the exhibition materials left for New York, winter had set in and Green caravanned with the Fellowship across the country to Taliesin West, Wright's remote desert camp outside of Scottsdale, Arizona. Green recalled, "My impression was absolute astonishment at the beauty of the desert and the relationships. I thought it would be very similar to what I would expect of a trip to the moon!"[13]

Green was assigned various tasks, including working on the large fireplace in the drafting studio (an ill-fated attempt to create a ceramic surface to the back of the firebox) and working on the plumbing, of which Green remembered, "I didn't know anything about plumbing. It was on the job training, I'll tell you. God knows how many things are wrong as a result. I spent my whole winter in terribly dirty, greasy clothes."[14] While at Taliesin West, Wright gave Green the responsibility to do the construction drawings and some of the presentation drawings for the library building for Florida Southern College in Lakeland, Florida.

It was during Green's first season at Taliesin West that he met his first wife, Jean Carol Haber (1919–2013). Haber was the niece of Rose and Gertrude Pauson. The Pauson sisters, from San Francisco, were building a winter home, designed by Wright in 1939, near the Arizona Biltmore in Phoenix. The Fellowship was assisting with landscaping around the newly constructed home when Haber and Green met. Haber had recently graduated from Stanford University and was to begin her internship in Los Angeles in anesthesiology.

Sometime early during his tenure within the Fellowship, Green took a three month sabbatical to travel with Morris R. Mitchell (1895–1976), a man he had previously met in Alabama. Mitchell

Jean Haber and her mother Jeannette observe Taliesin West apprentices, one of whom was Aaron, working at the Pauson house, 1941.

was the Dean of Education at Florence Teacher's College and had taken quite an interest in the construction of the Rosenbaum house. He had contacted Green and asked if he would accompany him on a trip to visit cooperative communities that existed from Canada to Georgia, including a visit to the community Mitchell had started outside of Clarksville, Georgia. Mitchell made a lasting impression upon Green, "next to Frank Lloyd Wright as an influence on my life, he might have been the next most important one."[15] When Green returned, he brought to Wright two new projects—the Cooperative Homestead project outside of Detroit, Michigan (in Royal Oak) for Ford workers and the Circle Pines Camp in Cloverdale, Michigan— as well as one for himself, a house and dormitory for Mitchell, to be built at his Macedonia Cooperative Community in Clarksville.

Green worked on the drawings for the Cooperative Homestead project and the early drawings of the Circle Pines project. By mid-July of 1941 he was in Royal Oak as Wright's on-site representative for the former project, located at the northeast corner of the intersection of 13 Mile and John R. Roads. Green had suggested to Wright the idea of using rammed earth, after conducting tests to de-

termine that the soil was ideal. Green recalled, "It seemed ideal here. It didn't cost anything because they had the soil, and their labor wasn't going to cost anything either. They didn't have any money because they had spent all they could possibly scrape together to buy that farm. All their efforts would go into one house."[16] The idea obviously appealed to Wright as both practical and economical for this cooperative effort as he implemented rammed earth berms as a primary component in the design of the homes. The cost of each home was estimated at $1,700. Green and the members of the co-operative proceeded in the construction of a prototype with enthusiasm but soon ran into unforeseen obstacles, not the least of which was the war effort taking capable workers from the project and restricting the availability of materials and gasoline. The rammed earth work also proved difficult under the extreme winter weather conditions. Eventually the construction of the partially completed home was abandoned and literally washed away over time.

Frank Lloyd Wright opposed war, including the government's right to conscription, which had just been renewed in 1940 with the passage of the Selective Training and Service Act (the coun-

Green at pilot training, United States Air Force, 1943.

Above: *Lieutenant Aaron Green, U.S.A.F., and with his mother Rose, Miami, Florida, December 1945.*

Right: *Aaron with his "Jolly Rogers" crew, Netherlands East Indies, January 1945 (top row, second from right).*

try's first peacetime draft). Many of the members of the Fellowship became Conscientious Objectors, Green included. "I was the first number in Dodgeville to be drafted. So I became the first Conscientious Objector at Taliesin ... on pure moral grounds ... I was much more important to the country helping Frank Lloyd Wright's work than going to learn how to carry a gun when we weren't at war ... All the time I was at Taliesin, I was fighting the Dodgeville draft board."[17]

However, after the bombing of Pearl Harbor and the United State's subsequent and immediate entry into World War II, Green decided, "We were in a war, and I was patriotic, so I decided that was a different situation. I'd be damned if I let that draft board have me if I could help it. I was also anxious to join something that was dangerous, to be sure that I hadn't appeared as a coward. I decided to join the Air Force."[18] Weeks after receiving his induction notice, on May 13, 1942, Green enlisted in the Air Force. As his enlistment was unknown to the Dodgeville draft board back in Wisconsin, a grand jury indicted Green as a draft evader and issued a warrant for his arrest. The FBI appeared on site at Royal Oak in mid-August 1942, providing Green, as he called it, "an involuntary two day vacation."

On his California architecture license application several years later, Green noted that he left the Fellowship on February 27, 1943. This was when he began his basic training in the United States Air Force, stationed in Cleveland, Ohio. In a letter to Olgivanna Lloyd Wright, Green offered:

In spite of the above words which might seem to indicate otherwise, I am not at all in an agonized state of self-pity

or lack of assurance in the route I chose. Under the same circumstances, I have no doubt but that my feelings would allow no other step. I felt and still do that it was the harder of the choices to make, but that it could not, after much thought and weighing of the choices, be otherwise. If war can be justified under any condition it would be for that privilege of being allowed to make up one's own mind about one's own duty and destiny. Having experienced the Taliesin way has left an indelible print and precious recollections which makes life more complex but, yet, easier. Frankly, and you may not like the statement, more to fight for.[19]

Green began active duty as a Lieutenant in the United States Air Force in July 1944, with duties as a bombardier and gunner with the "Jolly Rogers," a heavy bombing unit in the 319th Bombardier Squadron of the 90th Bombardment Group. Their principle involvement in the war was in the Southwest Pacific theater. After the war Green returned to the United States, boarding a ship in Manila on October 26, 1945, for the 21-day trip across the Pacific Ocean destined for Vancouver, Washington. Upon arriving, he initially had difficulty locating his family.

I came back to the States on a troop ship, just before Thanksgiving. I phoned my family in Florence, Alabama and got no answer ... My family wasn't there! I didn't know what had happened. It took me a few more phone calls, to relatives and so on, and I found out that my father and mother had left Alabama in a hurry because my father had been given six months to live … the doctor had said, 'Well, maybe you can take him to a benign climate.' So they went to Florida where they had relatives.[20]

Before leaving for Florida Green took the time to travel down to San Francisco to see Jean Haber, whom he had been corresponding with while overseas. Green eventually arrived by train in Miami in early December 1945 and wrote Wright on December 2, "My being in Miami is necessitated by the fact that my parents are here for my father's health, having been very seriously ill … my plans for the future are most indefinite."[21] While awaiting his formal discharge, Green designed a home for an unnamed Russian "doctor friend" of Haber's in Los Angeles, "I have designed the house and believe it fulfills all the requirements you wrote me—in fact I believe it's one of the best things I've done in quite a while and although perhaps too much in the style of our dear friend Mr. Wright to satisfy my personal aims for individualism … is he prepared to accept unconventional design?"[22]

Green's college roommate was living in Los Angeles and urged Green to join him, even finding Green a job in set design at Metro-Goldwyn-Mayer in Hollywood, California. Green had experienced California life when training before the war and had become enamored with the climate (not to mention his budding romance with Jean Haber). A move to California would also bring him closer to a few house-clients that he had been working with, one of whom was undoubtedly Haber's friend. However, as his father's health continued to be a serious concern, Green continued to delay his departure. After his formal discharge from the Air Force on January 8, 1946, given at the Separation Center at Camp Blanding, he promptly found work as a designer/drafter with Joseph Bailey, a Miami architect. He remained in Miami for less than five months as his father passed away on April 6.

After the funeral in Nashville, Tennessee, and returning to Miami to take care of personal and business details, Green left for California. Along the way he made stops in Lakeland, Florida to see Wright's Florida Southern College (especially the just completed library for which he had done the drawings); Georgia, where he spent time with Morris Mitchell; Florence, to see family and friends; and Nashville, to visit his mother who had decided to remain in the city after her husband's funeral.

Arriving in Los Angeles in May 1946, Green was faced with a choice: to work for MGM creating "modern set designs"; working for ex-Wright apprentice John Lautner (1911–1994); or with the Los Angeles office of Raymond Loewy (1983–1986), an industrial designer with offices throughout the United States. After hearing more about the motion picture business he declined Metro-Goldwyn-Mayer's offer, and after working with Frank Lloyd Wright he couldn't see himself working for any other architect. So, in June, he accepted a position in Loewy's office, working as a draftsman, designer, and store planner – eventually becoming the office's chief draftsman. It wasn't long before Green decided that he wanted to open

Miami, Florida, 1946.   *Los Angeles, California, 1946.*

his own architectural practice in Los Angeles and began that process while working for Loewy, applying for his license with the California Board on October 4, 1946. It was also at this time that Green's long time courtship with Jean Haber finally formalized as they became engaged and then married on March 15, 1947.

Green left Loewy's office in October 1947 to prepare for the written and oral exams that were required by the California State Board of Architectural Examiners. Green took the written portions in December 1947 and June 1948. Passing his oral exam on October 15, 1948, Green immediately received his license and opened his office in the building where he and Jean lived on Pacific Coast Highway, overlooking the ocean.[23]

While receiving a steady stream of mostly small architectural commissions, Green's tenure in Los Angeles was nevertheless short, less than three years. He realized that he was getting work from clients in San Francisco and the Bay Area and the potential was perhaps greater in that area because of his wife and her family's contacts. So they decided, in 1950, that they would move to San Francisco the next year. While on a layover in Phoenix on his way to Gallup, New Mexico to pick up his newly purchased Buick convertible, he stopped in to visit Frank Lloyd Wright, with whom he had continued to stay in contact while in the service and in Los Angeles.[24] After Wright heard Green's plan to relocate his office to San Francisco Wright mentioned that he had a considerable amount of work in California and he suggested that they open an office together, with both of their names on the door. Green would take care of Wright's west coast work as well as his own. Green recalled, "I was certainly much more than surprised, and I thought surely he was joking. But I found out he was very serious about it."[25]

Obviously, Wright had a tremendous amount of trust in his young protégé. So, at the end of June 1951 Green moved to San Francisco and opened an office that doubled as his own architectural practice and Wright's west coast headquarters with Green being

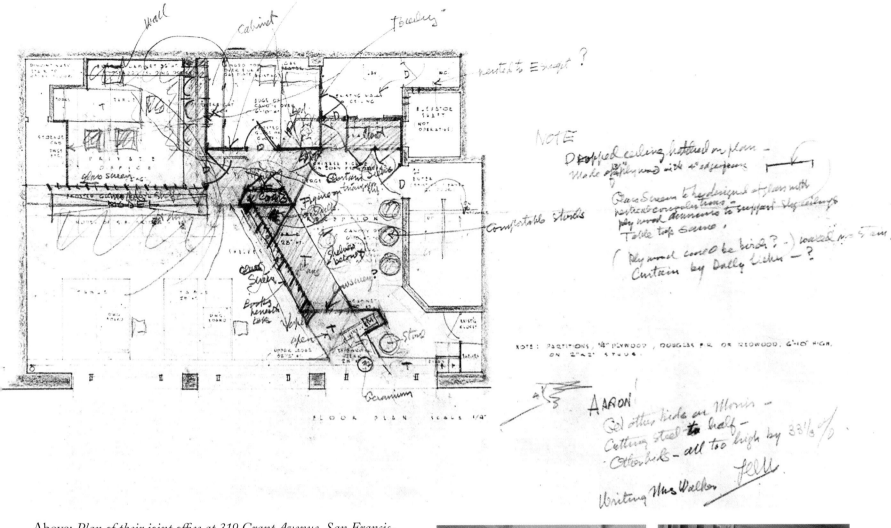

Above: *Plan of their joint office at 319 Grant Avenue, San Francisco, drawn by Green with comments by Frank Lloyd Wright, 1951.*

Right: *Reception area of the office, with and without Frank Lloyd Wright, 1951.*

Wright's west coast representative. The office space was on the second floor of a building that Wright liked because, to him, its exterior resembled a Chicago office building, with nine large square "Chicago-style" windows in an overall square grid. Wright was familiar with it as it had recently housed the office of ex-Taliesin apprentice Frederick Langhorst (1905–1979). After Wright described his thoughts on the layout and design of the space to Aaron, Green drew the plan. Wright modified Green's work after which Green and Paul Bradley, another ex-Taliesin apprentice, started the construction of the interiors in late July. "Dear Mr. Wright: We are going ahead with the office as per your improved design."[26]

Green's relationship with Frank Lloyd Wright was singularly unique. Wright obviously trusted his young protégé, and Green, in turn, earned that trust early on with the projects he brought to his mentor. He was a talented, dedicated, and committed apprentice and, after leaving the Taliesin Fellowship, continued to revere the master architect. Mary Summers, the Planning Director for Marin County recalled in a letter to Green, "I remember that the three of us were driving along U.S. 101, having just left the Marin County Civic Center site where he was to design us a civic and cultural center. I asked Mr. Wright what your professional position or relationship with him was. Mr. Wright's reply was, 'Why, Aaron is my son.'"[27]

Green's first thirty-four years of life, from birth to his move to San Francisco in 1951, were filled with constant change – growing up in the deep south; with stints in Chicago, Miami, New York, Taliesin in Wisconsin and Taliesin West in Arizona, and Detroit;

followed by life in the Asia-Pacific region during the war; and then ending up in California, first in Los Angeles and then San Francisco. Interestingly, his final 50 years were fairly stable. Green lived out the rest of his life in San Francisco.

During Wright's final years, from 1951 until Wright's death in 1959, Green participated in more than 30 west coast projects of Wright's (starting with the Walker house in Carmel, California in 1950 prior to his leaving Los Angeles). Many of those projects came to Wright through Green's involvement, including two unbuilt projects – the striking industrial plant building for Lenkurt Electric in San Mateo (1955) and the visionary reinforced concrete Butterfly Wing Bridge that was originally designed in 1947 for Spring Green, Wisconsin, but was resurrected at Green's urging to span the San Francisco Bay south of the current Bay Bridge connecting San Francisco with Oakland. A third, and most well known, is the Marin County Civic Center, unquestionably one of Wright's masterstrokes.

Green personally and professionally struggled with his feelings toward the pursuit of his own work while acting as Wright's representative. In a letter to Elizabeth Gordon (1906–2000), Editor of *House Beautiful* magazine, Green wrote,

In this matter of publicity regarding my own work, my attitude has changed somewhat in the last year or so. While for several years I avoided and would not allow publication of my own work thinking that it might not be the proper thing to do while acting as his representative, and being more interested in furthering his work than my own—and incidentally this is still true—it finally became apparent to me that making my own name better known, with whatever reputation for professional ability my work could develop, actually helps me locally to pursue Mr. Wright's interests, as it lends to my service as his local liaison that much extra prestige.[28]

After working with Marin County on Marin City, a federally funded public housing project, Green recognized that, "this allowed an entrée into the official family of the county and an opportunity to develop confidence in both Mr. Wright and myself within said officialdom. As a result, Mr. Wright and I simultaneously have the two most important architectural commissions the county has ever had."[29] Green certainly played no small role being the matchmaker and liaison between his mentor and the Marin County Board of Supervisors. Wright designed the project starting in 1957. The construction of the initial phase of the Marin County Civic Center—the Administration Building—began in 1960, shortly after Wright's death, and was completed and dedicated in 1962. Green was instrumental in seeing that the project was completed in accordance with Wright's design. The following year, when the county decided to complete Wright's full vision with the addition of the Hall of Justice wing, Green again partnered with Wright's successor firm Taliesin Associated Architects to bring its design, detailing, and construction to a successful conclusion.

While Wright was alive, that work had always taken precedence over Green's own architectural commissions. Because of his unconditional respect for his mentor, Green was selective and sometimes exclusionary with regards to projects that he undertook. With the death of Frank Lloyd Wright, April 9, 1959, he transitioned towards focusing more on his own projects, all the while remaining cautious and selective of the clients he took on and choices he made.

Like Wright, commissions that came to Green were widely varied in type and scope although the preponderance was the single-family home. But because of the attention and exposure he received from his unconcealed association with the Marin County Civic Center project, Green received much more substantial projects, like the large Hunter's Point housing project in San Francisco. He maintained a professional relationship with Wright's successor firm, Taliesin Associated Architects and its President William Wesley Peters (1912–1991), Wright's son-in-law. Green continued to bring the ongoing Wright-designed projects he was overseeing to their respective conclusions and Green and Peters often partnered for potential projects, like the Marin County Civic Center's Hall of Justice, the Marin County Veteran's Memorial Auditorium, a remodeling of the Bazett residence in Hillsborough, renovations to the Hanna house at Stanford, and the San Jose Community Theater.

While his architectural practice was developing, Green also was a visiting lecturer and instructor at Stanford University. In fact, many of his employees came from Stanford University, if not from the Taliesin Fellowship. He also wrote numerous articles, and, in 1990, with client Donald DeNevi, wrote the book *Frank Lloyd Wright: An Architecture for Democracy, The Marin County Civic Center.*

Green received many design awards throughout his career and is arguably one of California's most creative architects. In 1968, Green was recognized for his design excellence and inducted as a member of the American Institute of Architect's College of Fellows,

The Aaron Green/Frank Lloyd Wright joint office as installed at the Carnegie Museum of Art in Pittsburgh, Pennsylvania.

one of the institution's highest recognitions for members. While Green's professional life in California continued smoothly, his personal life was otherwise. After 26 years of marriage and having two sons (Allan Wright Green, born in 1949, and Frank Haber Green, born in 1952), Green and his wife Jean divorced in 1973. In 1975 he married Mary Davey Wagner, a past client, in a ceremony at Taliesin in Wisconsin. They divorced in 1983. Late in life, in 1998, Green married Nancy Klein, who remained his wife until his death in 2001.

As Green's architectural practice grew so did the need for additional staff and space. Over the years the offices at 319 Grant Avenue expanded from the original second floor space to the building's third floor, and, at the peak of the Hunter's Point project in the late 1960s and early 1970s, onto the fourth floor with 25 employees. However, Green preferred a smaller office, typically maintaining a more manageable staff that averaged six. Employee James Dixon

recalled that, "Aaron was promulgating an idea, a philosophy of architecture. Other firms are just promulgating other firms. At Aaron's you felt you were part of something larger."[30]

In 1988, Green sold the entire second floor office interior of 319 Grant Avenue—including the reception area, drafting room, and Wright's private office—along with the original Wright designed furniture, and the original drawings associated with the collaboration of the design by both Wright and Green to Thomas Monaghan (1937-), the then-owner of Domino's Pizza and the Detroit Tigers. Monaghan also was, at the time, a fervent collector of Wright artifacts and ephemera and he willingly paid $250,000 for the lot. Monaghan had built a museum for his National Center for the Study of Frank Lloyd Wright in Ann Arbor, Michigan and most likely saw the opportunity to incorporate it as an exhibit piece.

The office interior was expertly field-measured prior to being carefully dismantled, vigilantly packaged and shipped to Michigan for later installation. For unknown reasons, the reconstruction never came to fruition, and, in the early 1990s, when Monaghan refocused his energies and vast financial wealth towards his philanthropic missions with the Catholic Church he grew disinterested in Frank Lloyd Wright and divested himself of his vast holdings. In 1993, the Carnegie Museum of Art in Pittsburgh, Pennsylvania purchased it and installed the approximately 900 square foot "period room" in their newly created Heinz Architectural Center. The interior remained in place until 2004 when, after a failed attempt to sell it through Sotheby's auction house, it was dismantled, stored in Baltimore and eventually sold privately by the Carnegie Museum of Art to a buyer in Buffalo, New York.

The 1988 sale of the office to Monaghan was precipitated by the economical circumstances of the time. In the 1980s, with for-

eign investment rampant in the Bay Area, and office rents increasing exponentially, Green relocated his architectural practice several blocks south into the Hearst Building, at the corner of Market and Third Street. Here Green saw his architectural practice continue, but at a more comfortable and manageable pace. Much of his work during this period of his career was interment projects from repeat clients.

However that all changed in 1998 when he was invited to participate in a national competition for the design of a new school to be built on one hundred acres in Greensboro, North Carolina. The vision of the school's benefactor coincided with Green's philosophy and the design that he proposed. He was awarded the contract for the American Hebrew Academy, a private pluralistic college preparatory boarding school for Jewish students. Initially concerned about the commitment, size, and complexity of the project when he had just entered his eighties, Green nevertheless proceeded to design the master plan and each of the almost forty buildings with zeal and youthful creative energy. He completed the design sketches for all the building units in 1999 and they broke ground on the project in March 2000. The work began with the dining pavilion, the first classroom building, and the initial ten residence halls.

Tragically, Green would never see his final project come to fruition as he died on June 5, 2001 after suffering a severe heart attack. His final honor, a Gold Medal from the Frank Lloyd Wright Foundation, was bestowed on Green only days before.

AARON GREEN: HIS WORK

Green's position as a leading and proven proponent of the principles of Frank Lloyd Wright and Wright's philosophy of organic architecture is unquestioned. One of Wright's more prolific disciples, Green was also undeniably one of Wright's most creative. Green never shied away from giving his mentor his due, "Everything I know about architecture, I know from Frank Lloyd Wright. There is no question about it. That is my whole direction."[31] While he referred to some of his peers from the Taliesin Fellowship as revolutionaries, he saw himself as more of an evolutionist. The quality of his work was founded and built upon the principles he learned from Wright, from stem to stern, beginning to end. Like that of Wright's, Alan Hess said of Green's architecture, "Aaron Green conceived his buildings as a unified whole made up of articulated parts, just as a tree is a unified whole, with trunk, branches, leaves, and roots taking different forms to serve their specific purposes."[32]

Green's work, spanning more than sixty years, differed in use and purpose but was characteristically similar in an aesthetic to, but subtly independent of, Wright's aesthetic. While he respected his mentor, believed in Wright's organic philosophy, and was certainly inspired by Wright's architecture, Green worked towards not imitating but transcending Wright's influence. Throughout his work, he used natural and direct materials and an architectural grammar that he learned from Wright: masonry and wood structures, sheltered by low roofs with overhanging, protective eaves, solid walls contrasted by walls of glass, and the placement of clerestory windows; the presence of natural light, varying but valid geometries, and cantilevered shapes and forms. He combined them to create familiar but stimulating solutions for each creative opportunity.

Like Wright, Green provided his clients *Gesamtkunstwerk* in architecture—complete creative design—from the site, the architecture, the materials, the building systems, the furnishing and fixtures, to the colors. He recognized that "Organic Architecture has to do with relating to the immediate site, the client's program of needs, the climate in which the building exists, a natural and logical use of materials, whether structural or aesthetic. It is a very direct, simple philosophy that I can't see how anyone would deny."[33] By weaving the built environment into the natural environment, Green made buildings that responded to and complemented the sites they were built on using honest materials, textures, and colors found in nature. Like nature, through the use of two-dimensional organic unit systems and the three-dimensional manipulation of the floor, ceiling, and wall planes, he effortlessly created both interior and exterior spaces that interconnected seamlessly, often eliminating all cognizant lines between them. The result was simple, clear, direct, and subliminally complex built space that, given a purpose, could be contemplative, protective, comfortable, inspiring, or exhilarating.

Not only was Green an extremely creative architect, but also a talented landscape designer. Beyond his sophisticated ability to marry building to land—the built environment with the natural environment—he often carefully manipulated and subtly augmented the natural environment with additional landscaping. He typically included landscape design as an integral part of the scope of services that he provided his clients. It wasn't an additive to him, but an essential part of the overall creative composition. The Aaron Green Archives contain hundreds of drawings of landscapes designed for private and public sector clients from the early residential projects of the late 1940s to the work he did at the 100-acre site of the American Hebrew Academy in the late 1990s. Daniel Ruark, an employee who worked closely with Green during the office's final years, recalled Green sharing with him his affection for landscape design: "He enjoyed this creative task. It was very relaxing for him. He went so far as to say that, if he could start all over again, he would rather have chosen instead a career as a landscape architect."[34]

Like Wright, Green wasn't afraid to mix structure and nature by incorporating small garden features into the interiors, often sky-lit and sometimes open-air. This obliterated any sense of enclosure while eliminating any demarcation between the interior and exterior. Examples abound throughout Green's work from his early Reif residence (1950) to the administration building at the American Hebrew Academy (1998).

Green's work also included the design of integrated built-in furniture, casework, cabinetry and shelving, lighting fixtures, wood trim, and occasional furniture that all worked in concert with the architecture and its purpose. In addition, he would work with his clients in the selection of furniture, carpets, window coverings, and colors for their projects.

In 2005 Dave Weinstein, a Bay Area journalist, wrote an illuminating retrospective article in the *San Francisco Chronicle* titled "Signature Style: Aaron Green." In that article Weinstein observed that "Green was elegant, well-dressed, a Southern gentleman who regarded architecture as the noblest of professions."[35] He quoted Daniel Liebermann, who worked with both Wright and Green, noting that "His work is quiet and fine and modest ... in some respects I think Aaron's earlier smaller buildings were better than a Wright building. They were a little more open and a little quieter and a little smoother."[36] But the most telling quote in the provocative piece came from Green's son Allan, who said of his father: "He had to build things. For him, it was like breathing."[37]

Aaron Green produced more than 300 works of architecture during his fifty-plus-year career, with a majority of his projects in California. The quality of his creative works is extraordinary. He took to architecture very quickly, almost immediately exhibiting a highly refined and rare ability in creative architectural design founded upon the organic philosophy espoused by his mentor, Frank Lloyd Wright. Perhaps this was due to his artistic background, or his tenure with Wright; most likely it was a combination of both. The following thirty-nine projects span his entire career in chronological order and provide a tip-of-the-iceberg glimpse of Green's creative genius.

■ MORRIS MITCHELL RESIDENCE
■

■ Morris R. Mitchell (1895-1976) was considered a social and educational visionary. He was also an early mentor of Green.[38] Their paths crossed when Mitchell took an interest in the construction of the Rosenbaum house in Florence, where he was teaching at Florence State Teacher's College. Mitchell had just started the Macedonia Cooperative Community outside of Clarksville, Georgia, on 1,000 acres of property. He founded the community as an experiment to improve life in rural America through the cooperative and collective means of vested individuals and families. Green would eventually take a three-week leave, early in his tenure in Frank Lloyd Wright's Taliesin Fellowship, to travel with Mitchell to experience other cooperative communities in the U.S. and Canada. Again, as he did with the Rosenbaums, Green brought back to Frank Lloyd Wright two projects – the Cooperative Homesteads project located outside of Detroit, Michigan and the Circle Pines Center in Cloverdale, Michigan. Green kept a third one for himself, a home for Morris Mitchell and his second wife, Barbara.

The preliminary drawings, completed in the spring and summer of 1942, state, "House for Dr. Morris R. Mitchell, Macedonia Cooperative Community, Aaron G. Green, Design, Taliesin Fellowship, 1942." The design consisted of a primary main house for Mitchell and his wife with a secondary building linked by a roofed carport that served as a guest house or dormitory for college students.

The original preliminary plans and rendering presented the main house at the highest level, allowing a view from the living space over two nearby lakes, with the lesser guest house pushed back and lowered four feet. The whole plan was based on a four-foot-square unit system. After reviewing the initial sketches the Mitchells were basically happy but requested a few changes, one of which was a single room that Green had designed to contain the living, dining, and cooking functions. The Mitchells were uncomfortable with this radical informality of the kitchen being combined with the living room and asked that some privacy be provided between functional spaces. They also requested modification of the exterior terraces and the possible addition of a small screened porch. One other stylistic request they asked for was that the windows in the living room be changed to French doors, similar to the well-known Jacobs house designed by Frank Lloyd Wright.

They hoped to begin construction by June 5, 1942 on a budget of approximately $1,500. Green's revised construction plans were completed by mid-June 1942 and adequately addressed the majority of the requested changes. The design used the abundant materials at hand—stone and wood—"in a 'rough' but orderly and natural way, and representative, I hope, of the way of life of Macedonia."[39] Stone was used predominantly for the exteriors, and was to be laid up in the manner of the stone at Wright's Wisconsin home, Taliesin. Green initially oriented the exterior board and batten walls horizontally. However, in the revised design he changed this to incorporate a four-inch-thick wall of vertical boards and battens (with the cavity filled with sawdust for insulation), "The building mass itself is to such a great extent horizontal that the vertical boards will add interesting contrast."[40]

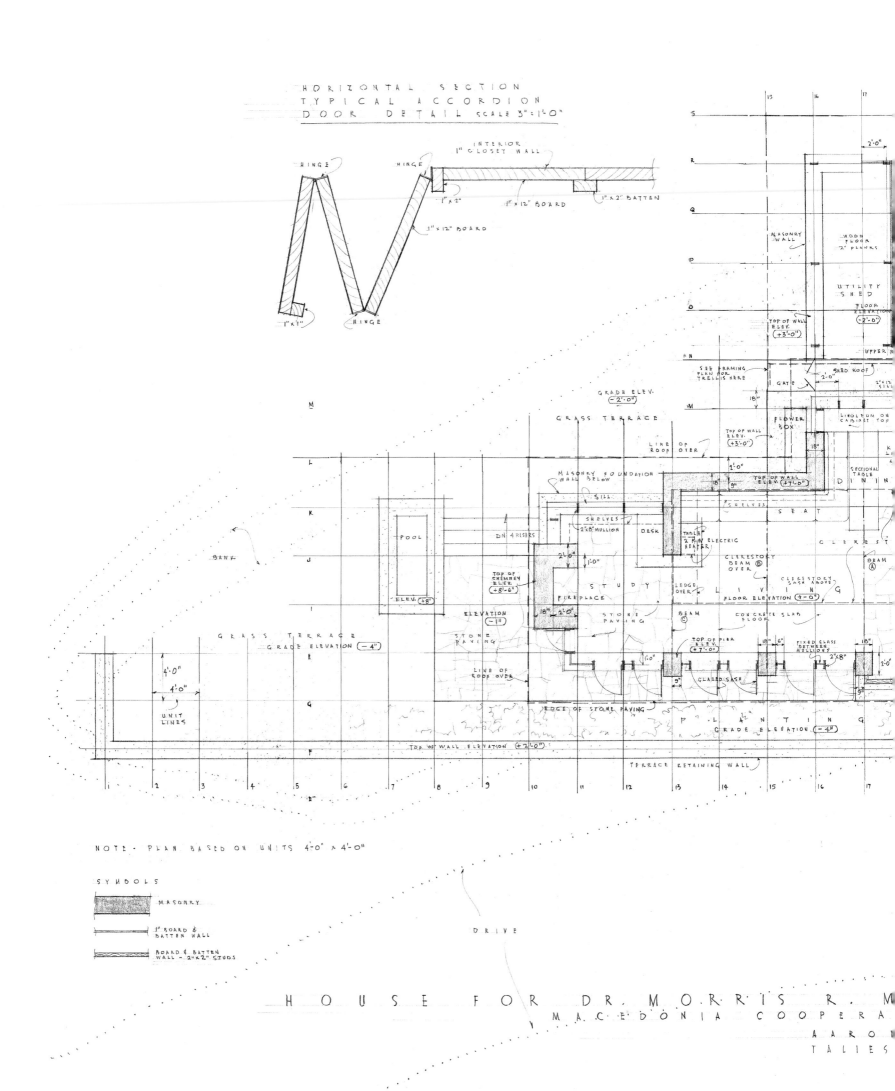

HORIZONTAL SECTION
TYPICAL ACCORDION
DOOR DETAIL SCALE 3"=1'-0"

HINGE   HINGE

INTERIOR
1" CLOSET WALL

1" x 2"   1" x 12" BOARD   1" x 2" BATTEN

1" x 12" BOARD

1" x 1"

HINGE

NOTE - PLAN BASED ON UNITS 4'-0" x 4'-0"

SYMBOLS

MASONRY

1" BOARD &
BATTEN WALL

BOARD & BATTEN
WALL - 2"x2" STUDS

HOUSE FOR DR. MORRIS R. M

MACEDONIA COOPERA

AARO

TALIES

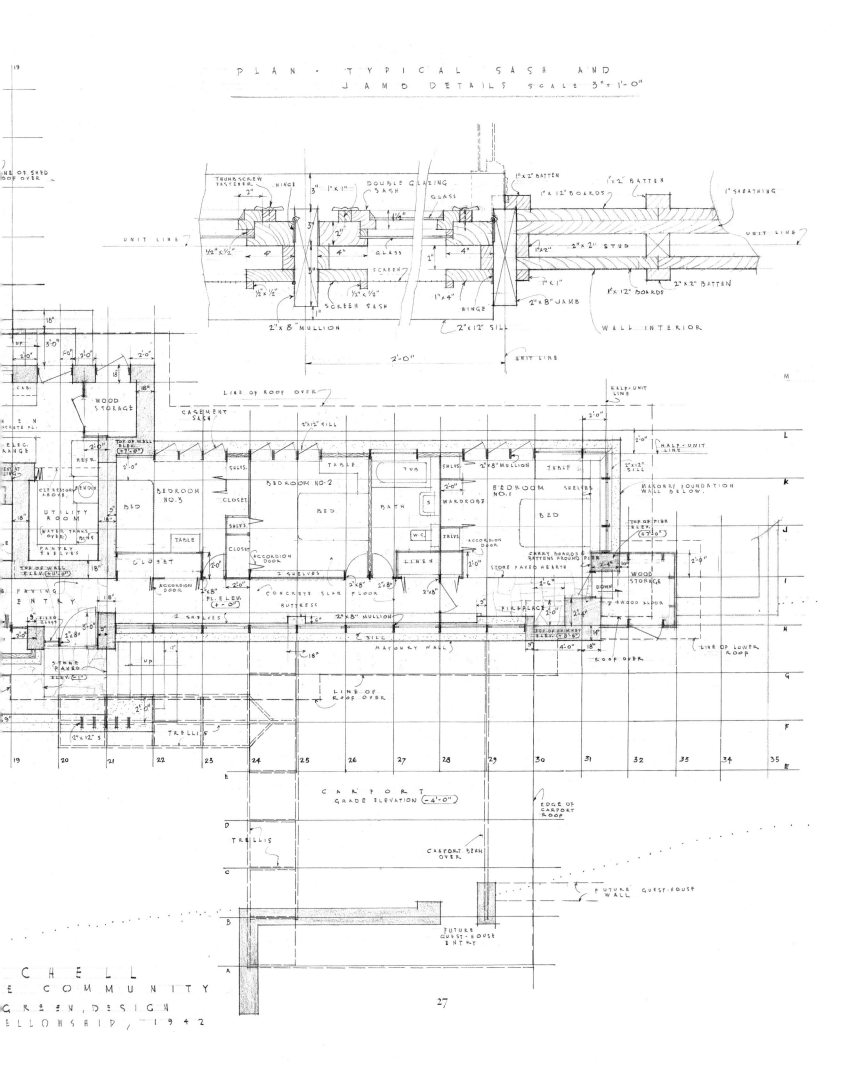

PLAN · TYPICAL SASH AND
JAMB DETAILS SCALE 3" = 1'-0"

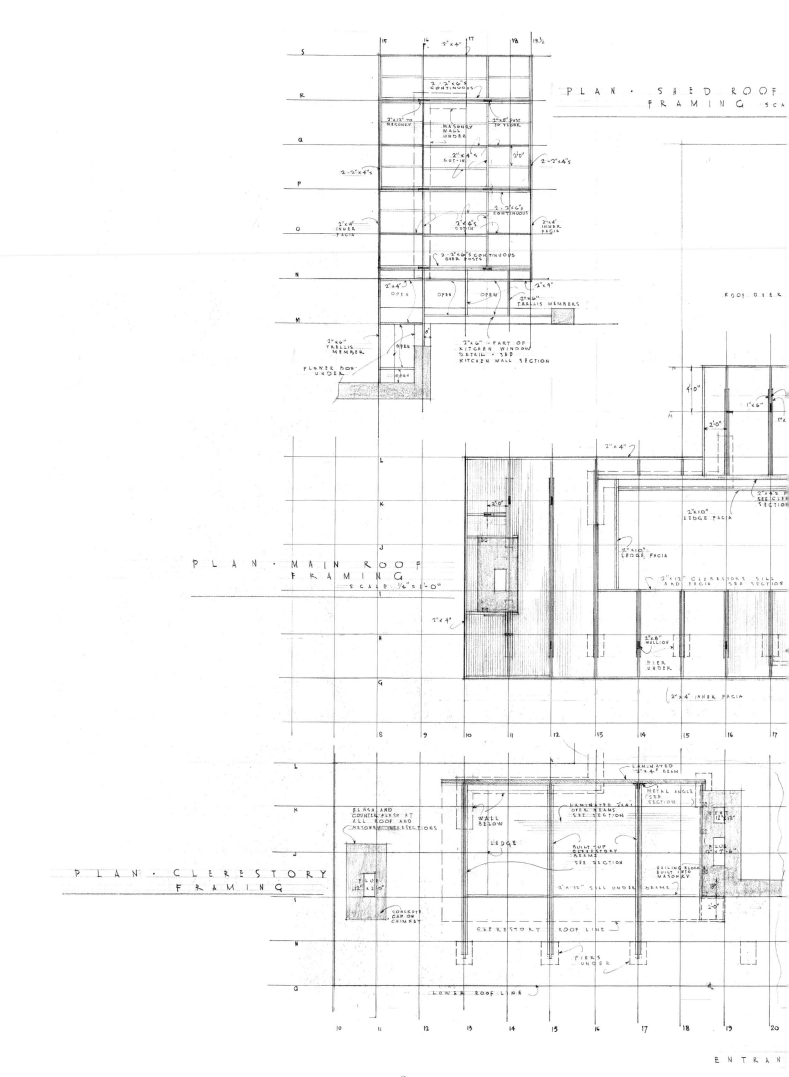

PLAN · SHED ROOF
FRAMING SCA

2 - 2"x6's
CONTINUOUS

2"x12" TO
MASONRY

MASONRY
WALL
UNDER

2"x8" POST
TO FLOOR

2"x4"'s
CUT-IN

2'-0"

2 - 2"x4's

2 - 2"x4's

2"x4"
INNER
FACIA

2"x4"'s
CUT-IN

2 - 2"x6's
CONTINUOUS

2"x4"
INNER
FACIA

2 · 2"x6's CONTINUOUS
OVER POSTS

2"x4"
OPEN

OPEN

OPEN

2"x4"

2"x6"
TRELLIS MEMBERS

2"x6"
TRELLIS
MEMBER

OPEN

8"

2"x6" - PART OF
KITCHEN WINDOW
DETAIL · SEE
KITCHEN WALL SECTION

FLOWER BOX
UNDER

OPEN

ROOF OVER

4'-0"

1"x6"

M

2'-0"

1"x

2"x4"

2"x4 's
SEE CLER
SECTION

2"x10"
LEDGE FACIA

2"x10"
LEDGE FACIA

2"x12" CLERESTORY SILL
AND FACIA   SEE SECTION

2"x4"

PLAN · MAIN ROOF
FRAMING
SCALE 1/4" = 1'-0"

2"x8"
MULLION

PIER
UNDER

2"x4" INNER FACIA

8   9   10   11   12   13   14   15   16   17

LAMINATED
2"x4"'s BEAM

METAL ANGLE
SEE SECTION

FLASH AND
COUNTER-FLASH AT
ALL ROOF AND
MASONRY INTERSECTIONS

WALL
BELOW

LEDGE

LAMINATED 2"x4"'s
OVER BEAMS
SEE SECTION

BUILT-UP
CLERESTORY
BEAMS
SEE SECTION

VENT
12"x12"

FLUE
12"x2'

PLAN · CLERESTORY
FRAMING

FLUE
12" x 2'-0"

NAILING BLOCK
BUILT INTO
MASONRY

18"

2"x12" SILL UNDER BEAMS

2'-0"

CONCRETE
CAP ON
CHIMNEY

CLERESTORY   ROOF   LINE

PIERS
UNDER

LOWER   ROOF   LINE

10   11   12   13   14   15   16   17   18   19   20

ENTRAN

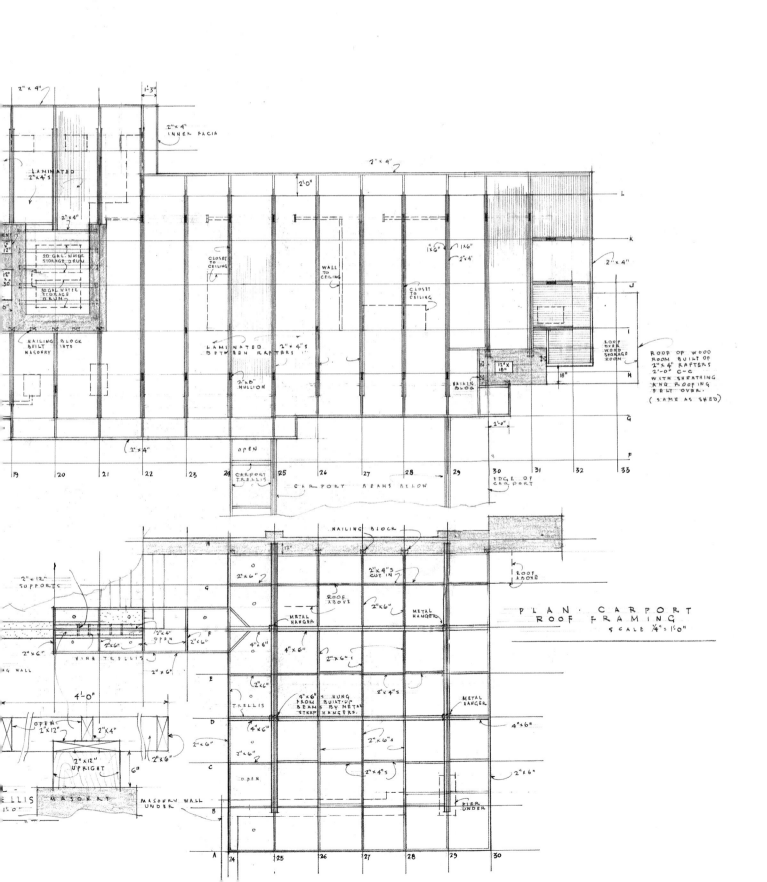

P L A N · C A R P O R T
R O O F   F R A M I N G
SCALE ¼" = 1'-0"

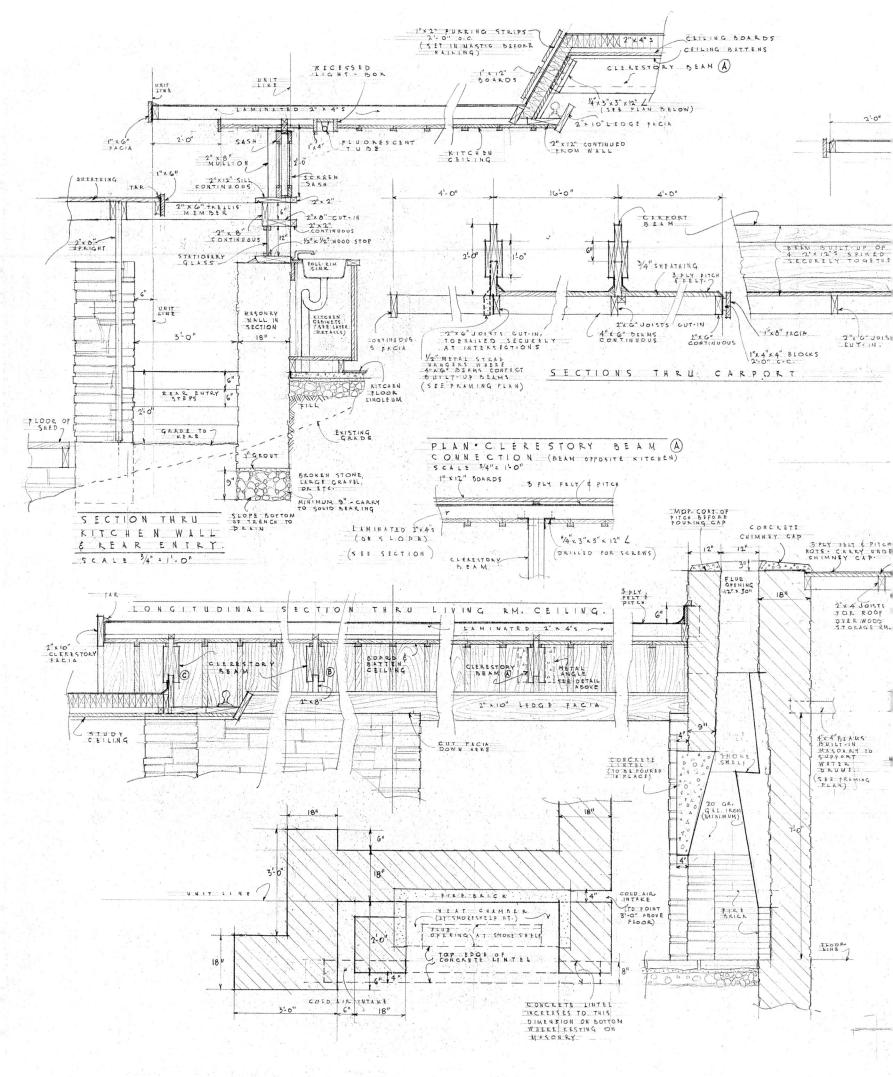

SECTION THRU
KITCHEN WALL
& REAR ENTRY.
SCALE 3/4"=1'-0"

SECTIONS THRU CARPORT

PLAN·CLERESTORY BEAM Ⓐ
CONNECTION (BEAM OPPOSITE KITCHEN)
SCALE 3/4"=1'-0"

LONGITUDINAL SECTION THRU LIVING RM. CEILING.

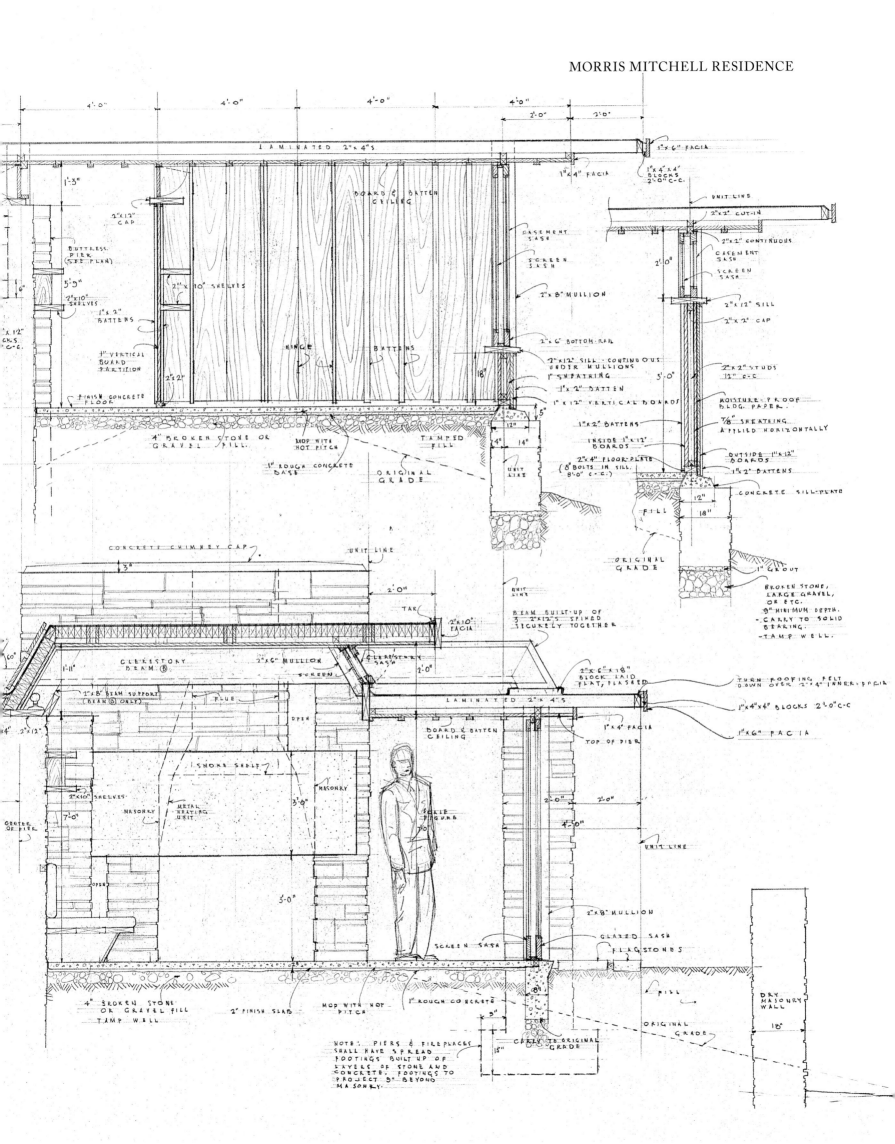

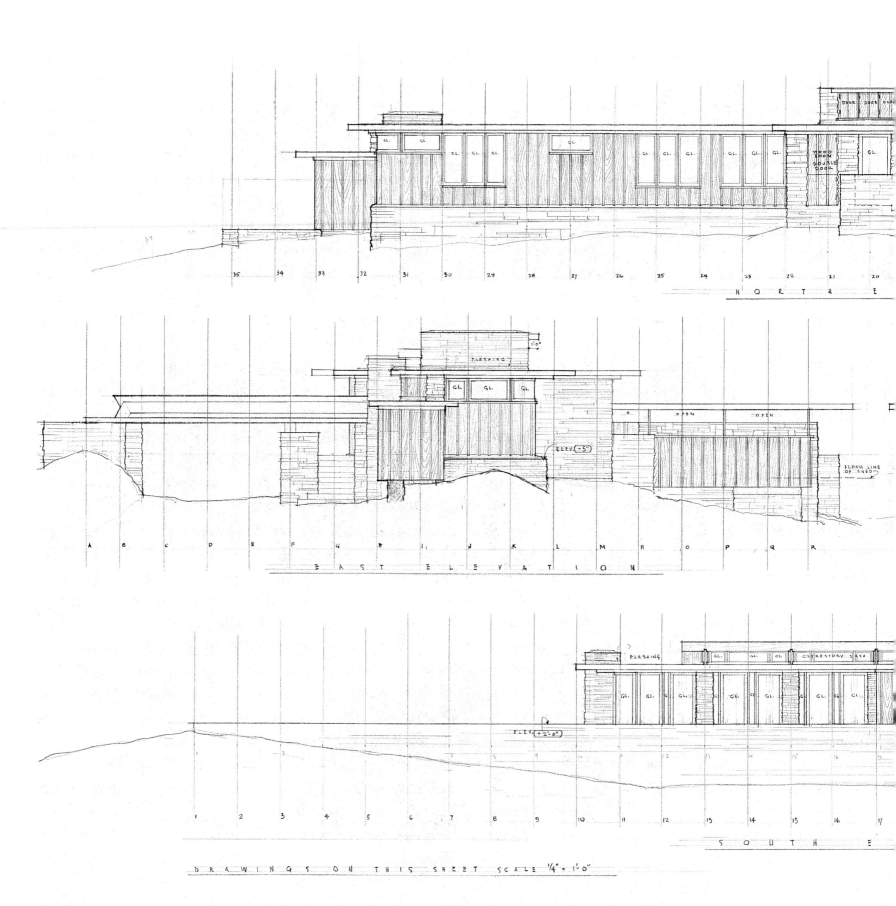

NORTH E

EAST ELEVATION

SOUTH E

DRAWINGS ON THIS SHEET SCALE ¼" = 1'-0"

32

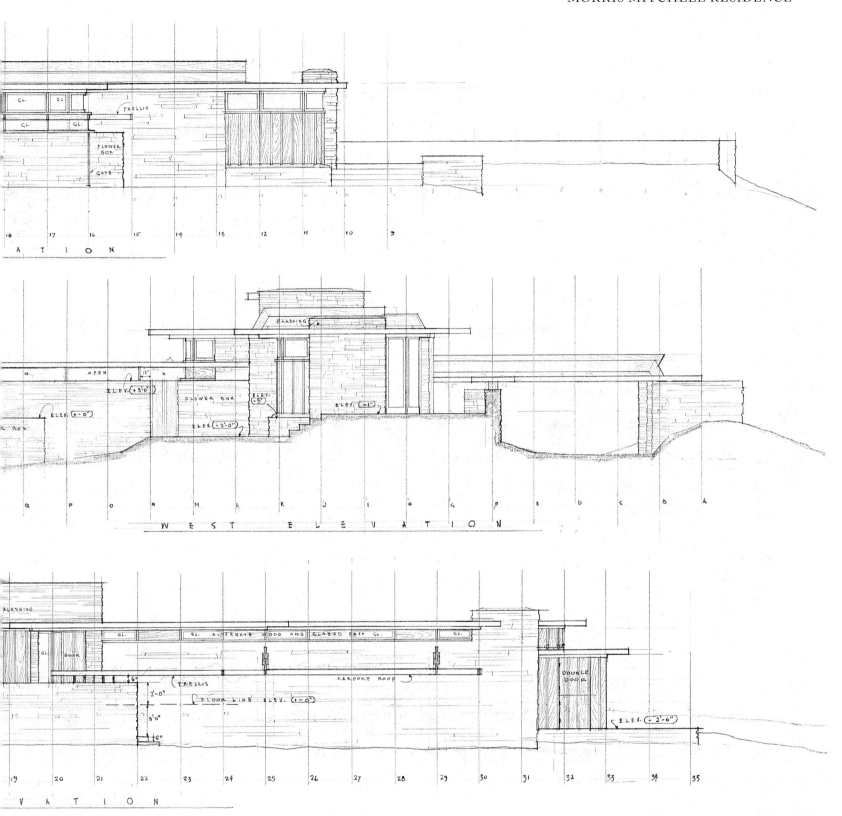

The design never moved forward though, as Mitchell was unable to obtain a loan for the project and Green soon became unavailable, working at the Cooperative Homestead project outside of Detroit, Michigan as Frank Lloyd Wright's representative on site, which was followed by his service in the Air Force during World War II. After the war, Green reestablished contact with Mitchell in late 1945, but, unfortunately, the design was still not to be built. He was obviously proud of the early design as later, sometime after he became a licensed architect and member of the American Institute of Archi-

tects in early 1950, Green redrew the rendered perspective and labeled it, "Residence and Student Dormitory, Macedonia Cooperative Community, Clarksville, Georgia, Aaron G. Green, AIA, Architect."

CHAPEL OF THE LIGHT GARDEN MAUSOLEUM

Aaron Green, like his mentor Frank Lloyd Wright, designed a wide variety of projects without specializing in any single type. However, Green did gain recognition over the years as an innovative designer of interment projects – mausoleum and columbaria structures, cemeteries, chapels, mortuaries, and funeral homes. He often expressed that these projects were not so much for the dead but for the living, and he felt it was important to make the architecture dignified, respectful, and beautiful, and the experience comfortable and uplifting for the living to memorialize and honor the dead. While he always planned for low maintenance, function,

and efficiency, he wanted to provide visiting families with a celebration of the senses through scale, light, sound, intimacy of space, and spiritual detailing.

The Chapel of the Light was Green's first venture into the interment niche. He was commissioned to design a garden mausoleum addition for an operating facility on West Belmont Avenue, several miles northwest of downtown Fresno, California. The project was located adjacent to an existing California Mission Revival style chapel and cemetery offices. How the project came to Green is lost to history, but he certainly took advantage of the opportunity to create in-

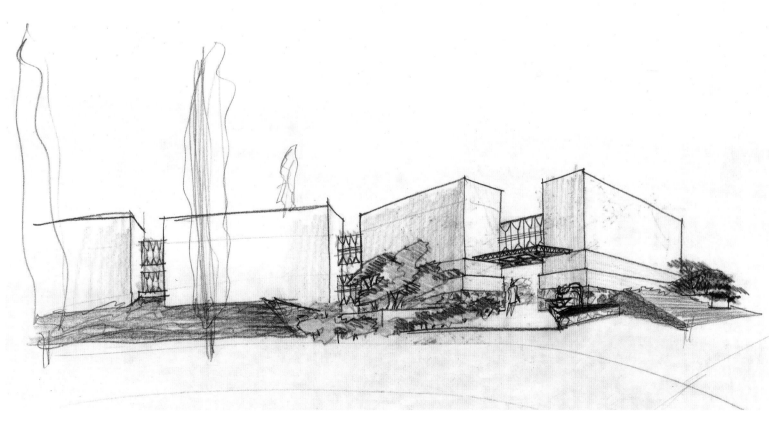

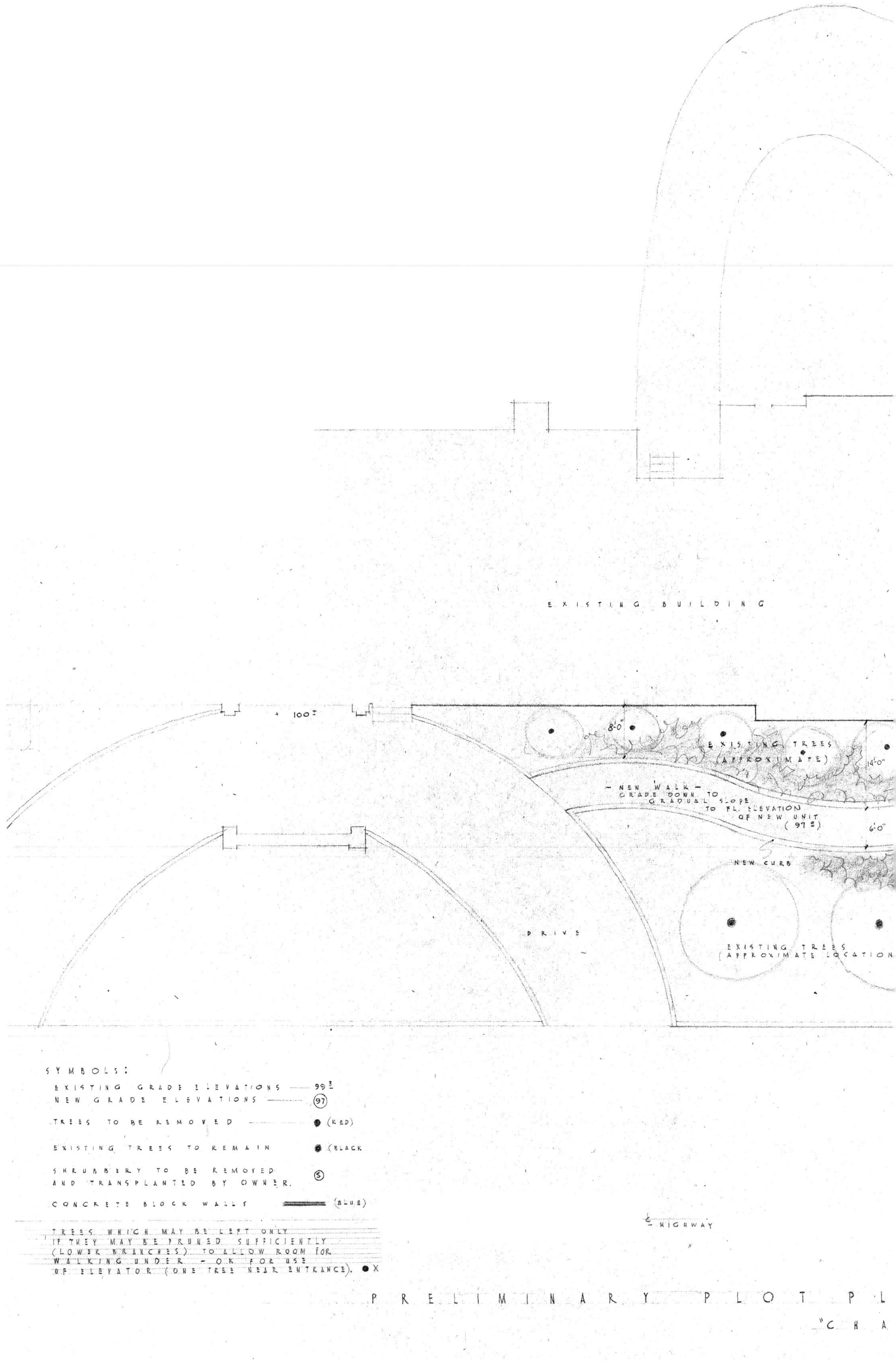

EXISTING BUILDING

EXISTING TREES
(APPROXIMATE)

8'-0"

14'-0"

— NEW WALK —
GRADE DOWN TO
GRADUAL SLOPE
TO FL. ELEVATION
OF NEW UNIT
(97±)

6'-0"

NEW CURB

100±

DRIVE

EXISTING TREES
(APPROXIMATE LOCATION)

SYMBOLS:

EXISTING GRADE ELEVATIONS ——— 99¾
NEW GRADE ELEVATIONS ——————— (97)

TREES TO BE REMOVED ——————— ● (RED)

EXISTING TREES TO REMAIN ● (BLACK)

SHRUBBERY TO BE REMOVED (S)
AND TRANSPLANTED BY OWNER.

CONCRETE BLOCK WALLS ▬▬▬▬ (BLUE)

TREES WHICH MAY BE LEFT ONLY
IF THEY MAY BE PRUNED SUFFICIENTLY
(LOWER BRANCHES) TO ALLOW ROOM FOR
WALKING UNDER — OK FOR USE
OF ELEVATOR (ONE TREE NEAR ENTRANCE). ● X

℄ HIGHWAY

PRELIMINARY PLOT PL

"C H A

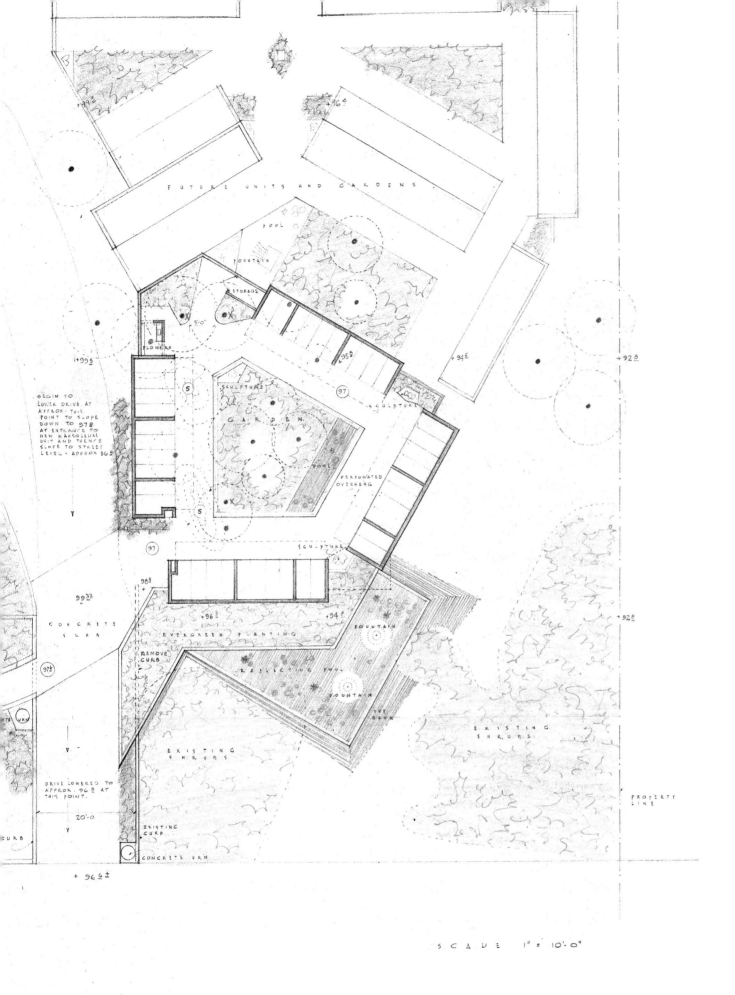

FUTURE UNITS AND GARDENS.

POOL

FOUNTAIN

STORAGE

5'-0"

FLOWERS

SCULPTURE

GARDEN

SCULPTURE

POOL

PERFORATED
OVERHANG

SCULPTURE

BEGIN TO
LOWER DRIVE AT
APPROX· THIS
POINT TO SLOPE
DOWN TO 97⁸
AT ENTRANCE TO
NEW MAUSOLEUM
UNIT AND THENCE
SLOPE TO STREET
LEVEL · APPROX 965

CONCRETE
SLAB

REMOVE
CURB

EVERGREEN PLANTING

FOUNTAIN

REFLECTING POOL

FOUNTAIN

IVY
BANK

EXISTING
SHRUBS

EXISTING
SHRUBS

DRIVE LOWERED TO
APPROX· 96⁸ AT
THIS POINT.

20'-0

EXISTING
CURB

CONCRETE URN

+96⁵

PROPERTY
LINE

+96¹⁰

SCALE 1" = 10'·0"

· G A R D E N   M A U S O L E U M ·
" O F   T H E   L I G H T " · F R E S N O   C A L I F O R N I A
A R O N G. G R E E N , A R C H I T E C T .   F E B. 2 , 1 9 5 0

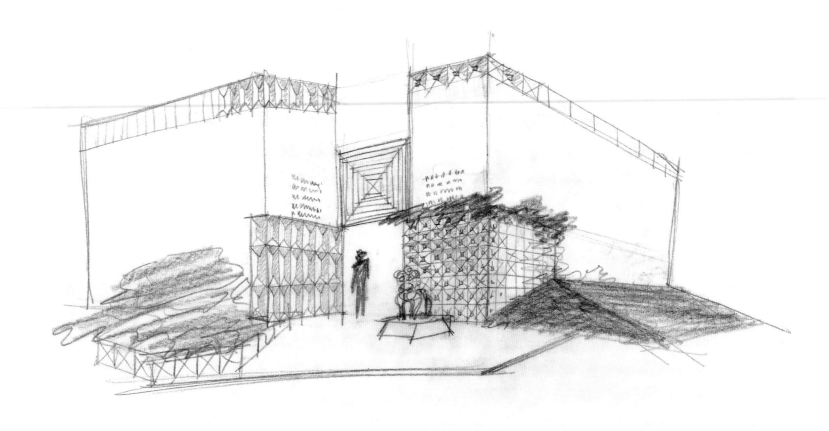

GARDEN MAUSOLEUM · CHAPEL OF THE LIGHT
FRESNO, CALIFORNIA
AARON G. GREEN · ARCHITECT

AARON G. GREEN,
A.I.A., ARCHITECT.

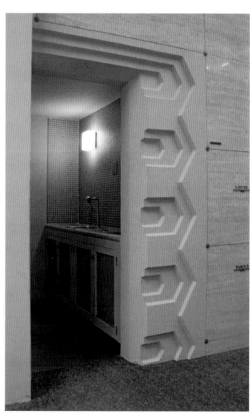

timate spaces within open areas by manipulating the crypt structures geometrically. His plan showed rectangular blocks containing the multiple crypts arranged asymmetrically to loosely enclose an open space with a garden planter. Green incorporated multiple devices for this project that he continued to use and refine in his subsequent interment projects, including landscaping, planters, seating, pools, fountains and places for art, icons, and sculpture. Green incorporated poured-in-place concrete construction as the primary material, which contrasted with desert masonry used for other elements of the design. The latter was a system that he was familiar with, as it was used by Frank Lloyd Wright to create Taliesin West outside Scottsdale, Arizona. At the face of the mausoleum crypts Green provided what he referred to as "perforated overhangs" – flat roofs that projected beyond

the crypt face that he then pierced and fitted with amber glass in the voids to add light and color. These overhangs would also help to bring a more human scale to these large solid blocks.

Evidenced by the copious design studies found in the archives for this project, Green was driven to provide an exceptional overall aesthetic for the project. And typical of all his interment projects, Green was commissioned to expand the Chapel of the Light with additions in 1963, 1969, and 1975.

■

■

■

REIF RESIDENCE

The Reif residence, one of Green's earliest built works, was designed in his Pacific Palisades office a year prior to relocating to San Francisco. The clients, Elias Herschel ("Harry") Reif (1907-1978) and his wife Cecelia Margaret Conn Reif (1903-1977), were long time family friends. Both Reif and Green attended Cooper Union, the former graduating in the early 1930s with a major in architecture. Coincidently, both shared an admiration for the work of Frank Lloyd Wright. The home was designed in 1950 and construction was finished the following year. It became Green's first published work, appearing in the April 1956 edition of *House Beautiful* magazine.

The title of the *House Beautiful* magazine article on the house, "Magnifying a Small City Lot Into a Private Paradise," describes the design well. The 1,650-square-foot home was located on a 50-foot wide by 150-foot deep suburban lot on Kings Road near Willoughby Avenue in Los Angeles (now West Hollywood). The house was built for less than $25,000, and only a short block away was the well-known Kings Road House designed by Rudolph M.

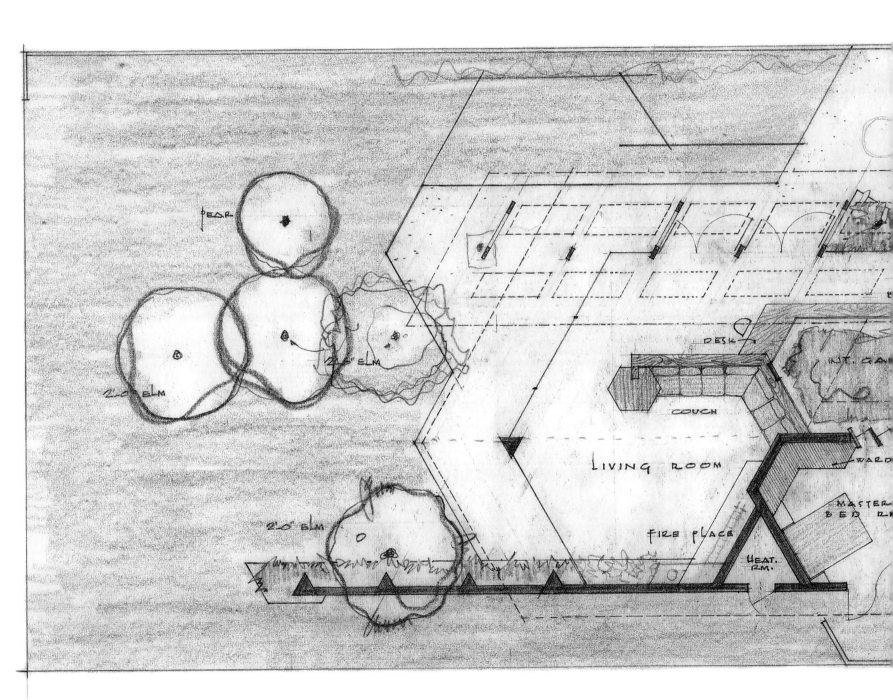

Schindler (1887-1953). Designed for four, the Reifs and their two daughters Harriett and Constance, the house had two bedrooms and one bath built around a central open court with private garden. Green's informal plan incorporated both rectilinear and angular walls, the latter used to open up the interior by increasing vistas through and across the various rooms helping to amplify the sense of continual flowing space. The living room, located at the rear of the plan, was roughly hexagonal in shape. It opened into the interior garden court as well as onto an exterior terrace with views of the fenced-in rear

yard, which enclosed three rare Copper Beech trees. Dominating the open beamed (stained green in color), spacious vaulted living room was a large masonry fireplace, with its hearth level with the exposed concrete floor and supporting a horizontal precast concrete "mantel" above. The home was furnished with built in seating, desks, wardrobes, shelving, and other casework and millwork designed throughout and for the home.

Green brought Frank Lloyd Wright to meet the Reifs and tour the home in the early 1950s. Reif's oldest daughter Harriet

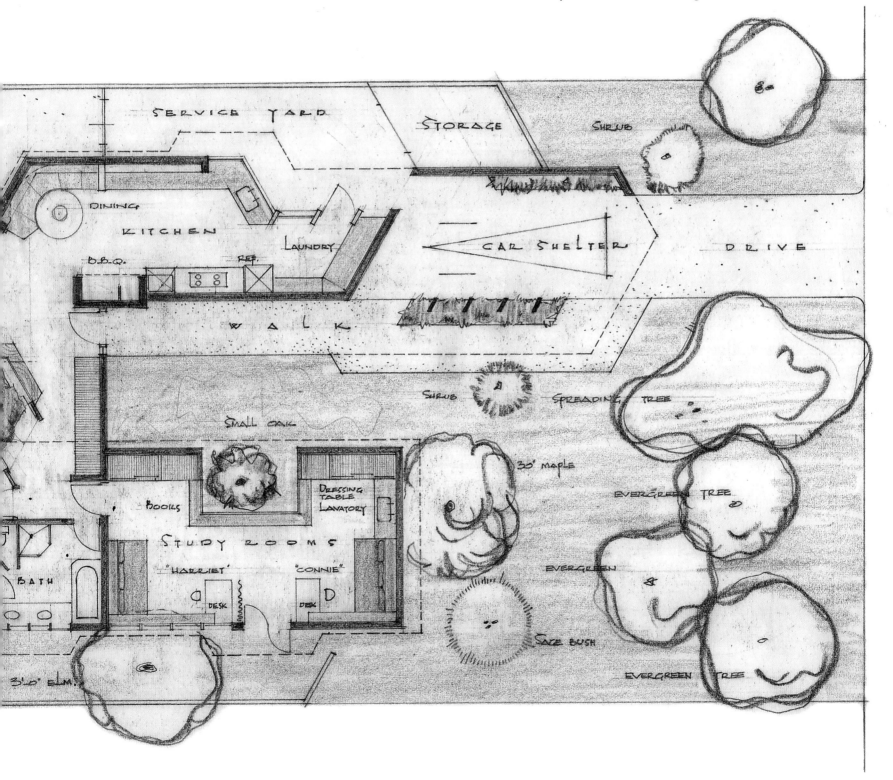

SOUTH ELEVATION

46

AARON G. GREER, A.I.A. ARCHITECT

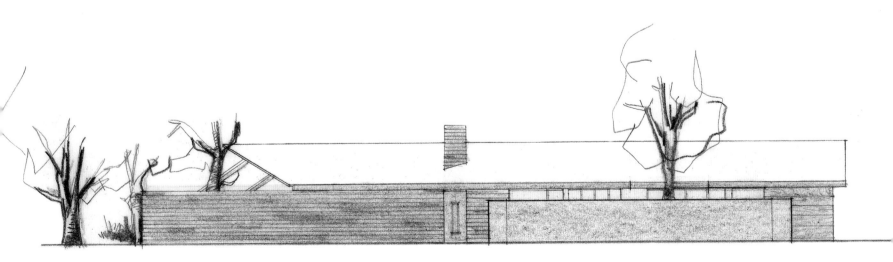

NORTH ELEVATION

recalled, "Before they left Mr. Wright turned to Gus (Green) and told him how pleased and proud he was of the design. He remarked that a lot of his students copied him but Gus had distilled the best."[41]

Their idyllic home became increasingly threatened over the years as the neighborhood changed from single-family homes to multi-family apartment buildings. In 2006, daughter Harriett Reif Greenwald reflected, "The house was totally destroyed by a fire of suspicious origin in October 1971. My parents were living in the house and had fought bitterly against any attempts to change the neighborhood by developers who wanted to tear down houses on Kings Road and build apartment houses. After the fire, the property legally had to be cleared and my father several years later, very reluctantly, sold the lot because it was such a painful reminder."[42]

PAUL RESIDENCE

Joseph Barry, writing for *House Beautiful* magazine in 1956, described the Paul residence as symbolizing, "the new spirituality of contemporary American life. It is a house with a quiet splendor of its own, available to all in our classless society. Standing among the trees on its own private plot of ground, it is independent, individual and in harmony with man and nature."[43] Designed by Green for two Stanford librarians, Allan Max Paul (1912-2007) and his wife Arline (1914-2012), the house was built for approximately $22,000. Paul had just graduated from the University of Michigan with his Master of Arts in Library Science and was beginning his new job at Stanford

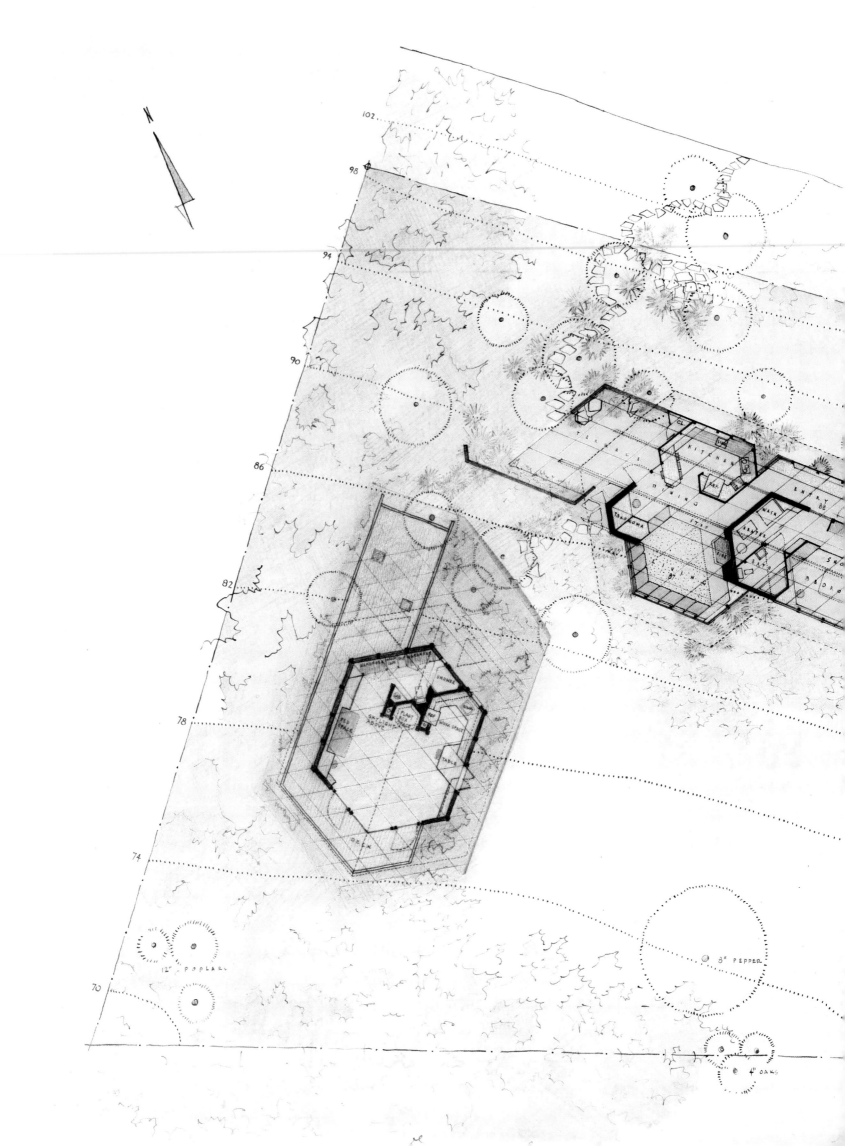

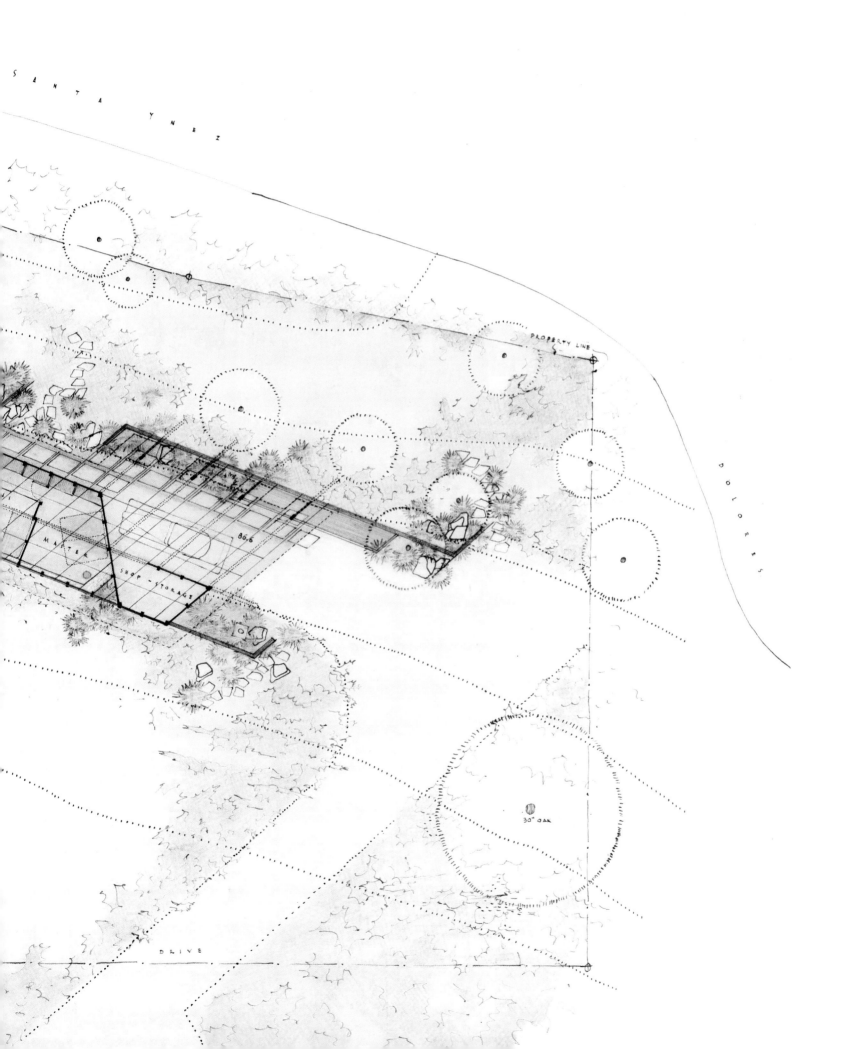

University. They chose a lot in the University City neighborhood near the Stanford campus, land owned by the university to be provided to faculty for housing. Nearby is the hexagonal Hanna house (also known as the Honeycomb House), designed by Frank Lloyd Wright in 1936.

Green designed the small two-bedroom one-bath home to fit snugly into its small suburban hillside site between Santa Ynez Street and Gerona Avenue. The plan, based on a diamond module, is a study in linearity, paralleling the slope with all the primary rooms overlooking the natural landscape through an abundance of windows.

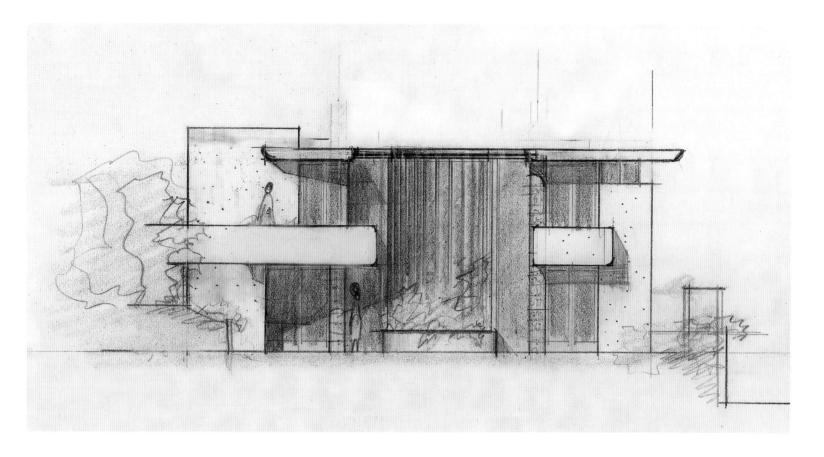

within the home. Green's floor plan interlocked a rectangle with a circle, with a second minor circle containing the stairs. Above the sub-level garage, he placed the living functions (living, dining, and cooking, plus a small hidden study) on the main level. On the upper level there are three bedrooms and two baths, with the hallway overlooking the living area below. In plan, Green's design could be interpreted as an urban version of Frank Lloyd Wright's solar hemicycle, designed in 1944 for Herbert and Katherine Jacobs on farmland outside of Madison, Wisconsin.

While evidence suggests that Green spent considerable time studying the possible exteriors, the project was soon shelved and eventually abandoned due to the expansion of "Nine Oaks" in 1955.

■

■

■

■ BARTHOLOMEW RESIDENCE

■

■   This 1,800-square-foot house on a hilltop site in Los Altos is without question one of Green's true gems in residential design, small in stature but huge in its creativity. Built by Len Marinello for M. W. Bartholomew, a druggist (pharmacist in modern day vernacular), and his wife, Green boldly combined the square unit system into what is primarily a triangular house.

House Beautiful magazine featured the Bartholomew house in its October 1959 issue dedicated to the heritage of Frank Lloyd Wright. They featured the home, as Curtis Besinger wrote, because it represented Wright's different quality – his contribution to architecture as "a true liberation of life and light within walls ... this liberation is not so much in the material form of the building as it is in the ef-

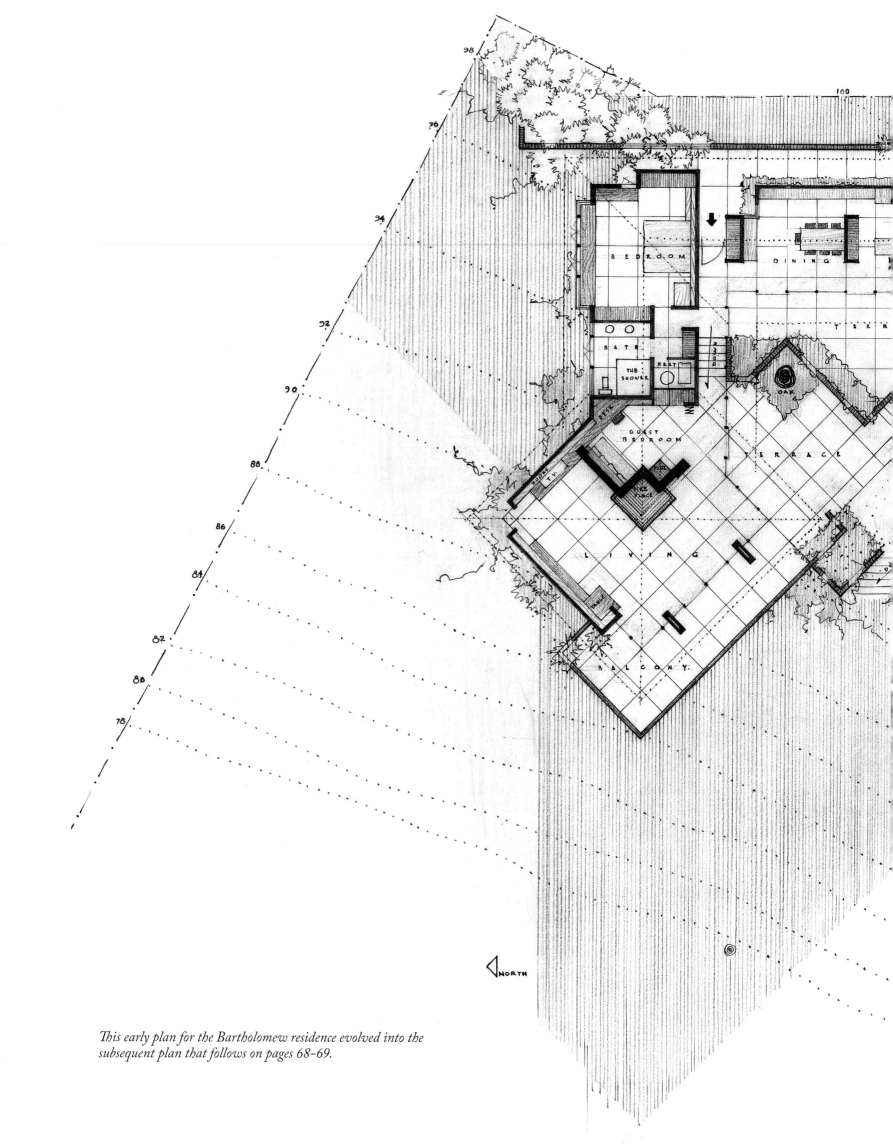

BEDROOM

DINING

TERR

BATH

TUB SHOWER HEAT DOWN

OAK

GUEST BEDROOM

TERRACE

ROOM T.V. FIRE FIRE PLACE

LIVING

BALCONY

NORTH

*This early plan for the Bartholomew residence evolved into the
subsequent plan that follows on pages 68-69.*

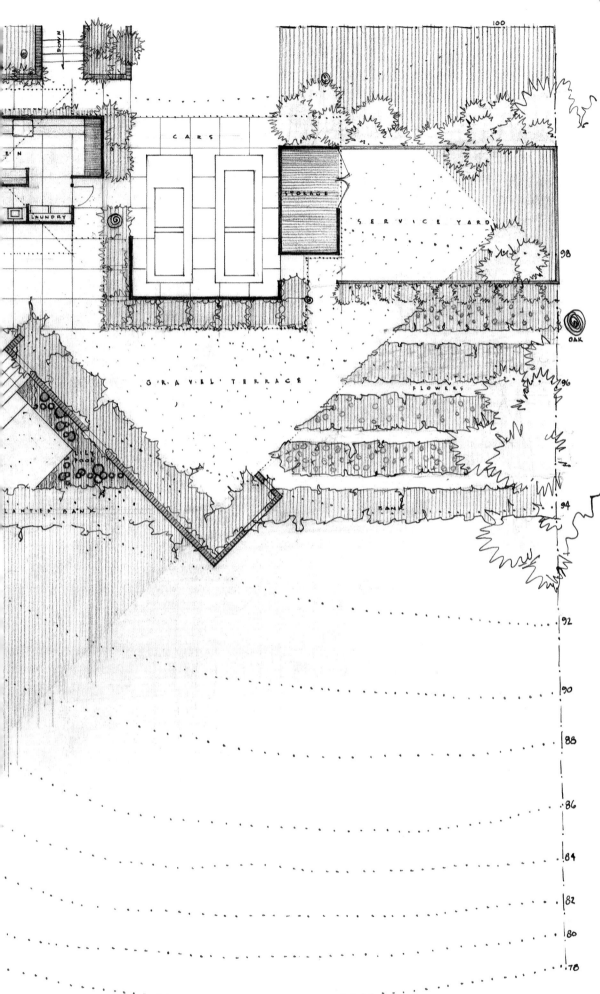

100

CARS

STORAGE

LAUNDRY

SERVICE YARD

98

OAK

GRAVEL TERRACE

FLOWERS

96

BANK

94

PLANTED BANK

92

90

88

86

84

82

80

78

FLOOR PLAN + PLOT PLAN
SCALE 1/8" = 1'-0"

67

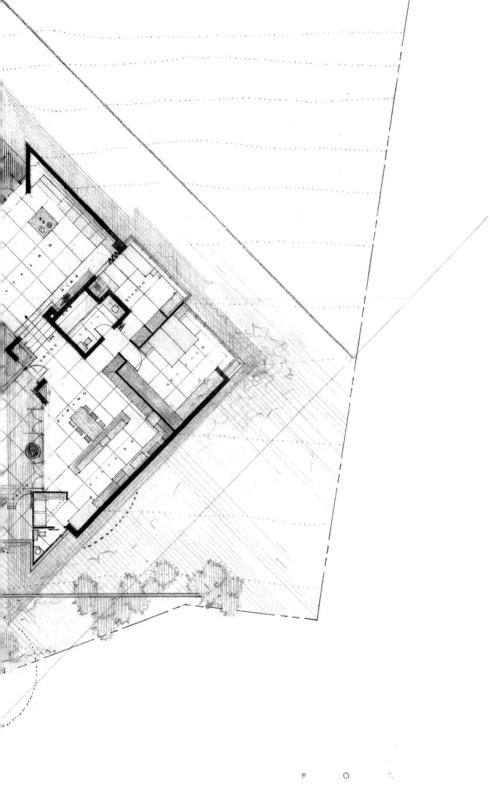

F O R

B A R T H O L O M E W

A R C H I T E C T

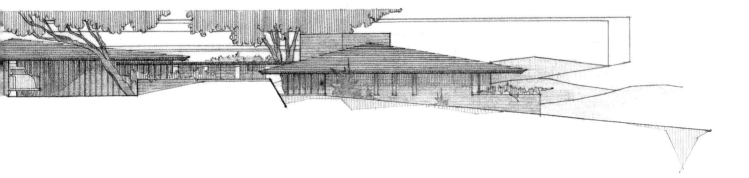

fect it has as an environment upon those living in it."[44] Using Green's Bartholomew opus as an example, Besinger went on to describe how,

> the interweaving of elements and establishing of inter-re-
> lationships between spaces, the environment, and the
> inhabitants help give a sense of liberation. In plan one can
> see numerous examples of the ways in which spaces, both
> inside and outside, are interwoven and interpenetrated
> to become one continuous space, how a space may have
> a sense of pushing or pulling in relation to an adjoining
> space setting up a dynamic interaction between them.[45]

Green deftly played the primary triangular residence off its secondary triangular carport, connecting the two with an effective screen element. The screen, with its repetitive masonry piers and wood pergola above, plays an additional role in physically separating while visually, albeit subtly, connecting the sunken outdoor entry plaza to the more private, protected, and expansive living terrace to the rear. Green's design created a clear and distinct sense of spatial transition, moving from the public through the semi-public and semi-private into the private interior and exterior areas. Approaching the home along Eloise Circle one looks out over the home's two low pyramidal roofs, as the home quietly nestles into its site naturally and unob-trusively. Transitioning through the various twists and turns, down the steps that coincide with the natural contours, one ends up in the

interior living room and the expansive exterior (but well protected) terrace. The living room is enclosed to the northwest for protection against the summer afternoon sun but fully open to the south to take full advantage of the vista across the valley and the view of the hills beyond.

The smaller triangular two-car carport (or, using Green's terminology, car shelter) also included storage space and an outdoor kitchen (oriented towards the rear terrace). The primary triangular house, with its vaulted interior, was anchored by its masonry core that doubled as the living area's fireplace while enclosing the home's single full bathroom. At the connection of the two legs of the triangle, Green placed the home's single bedroom along with a smaller study that doubled as a guest room. Both these spaces, like the bathroom, were rectangular in shape, while the remaining spaces—the dining and kitchen areas and the sunken living space—were triangular. Off the kitchen was another much smaller triangular form that enclosed a laundry area and half bath.

The living area violates the triangular form, protruding out towards the private exterior living terrace to the rear. Its simple shape and vaulted form belies the complexity of design and functions within the space. The fireplace and chimney along the northeast wall provide a focal point and the concealed television and stereo equipment behind built-in cabinets within the westernmost corner provide another. The built-in couch along the northwest wall across from a wall of windows to the south (protected by the sheltering deep roof

overhangs) responds to the prevailing views, while the solid masonry wall to the northwest provides protection from the relentless summer afternoon sun. The design provides unconfined openness as well as private seclusion. Perhaps the most private area in Green's entire design is the small private deck off the prow of the living room at the far west end of the home that dramatically cantilevers out and over the sloping ground below.

The Bartholomew opus featured a continuity of basic and natural materials, using exposed, scored, and colored concrete floors, terra cotta colored concrete masonry block exposed both inside and outside, and wood – with Philippine mahogany paneling on the interior walls and a shingled redwood roof. Green's use of wood trim was minimized in this project, including recessing the window glass into the masonry walls in lieu of using wood casing. Custom designed storage walls (including a five-foot-high island unit that physically, but not visually, separates the kitchen from the dining area) and built-in furniture give the house a unique feel.

HUGHES RESIDENCE

The site that Dr. Raymond Hughes brought Green was almost two acres of property on the east side of Camino Hermoso Drive in Los Altos Hills, less than three miles due south of Los Altos. Green designed an elegant single-story home sheltered below a low-sloped hipped roof. Eugene and Mary Van Tamelen (the previous owners of Wright's first pre-fabricated home built by Marshall Erdman in Madison, Wisconsin in 1956) purchased the home from Dr. Hughes in 1962 when Van Tamelen moved his family to Califor-

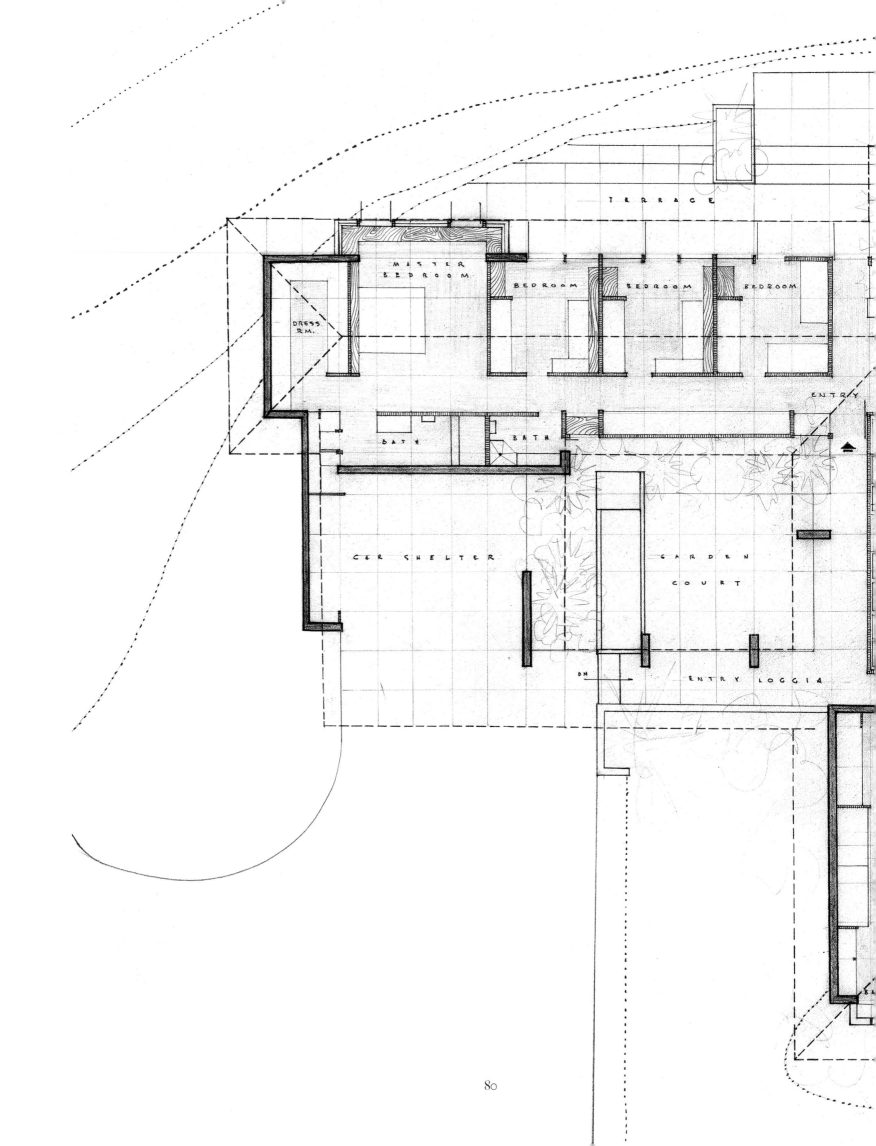

TERRACE

MASTER BEDROOM

BEDROOM   BEDROOM   BEDROOM

DRESS RM.

ENTRY

BATH   BATH

CER SHELTER   GARDEN COURT

DN   ENTRY LOGGIA

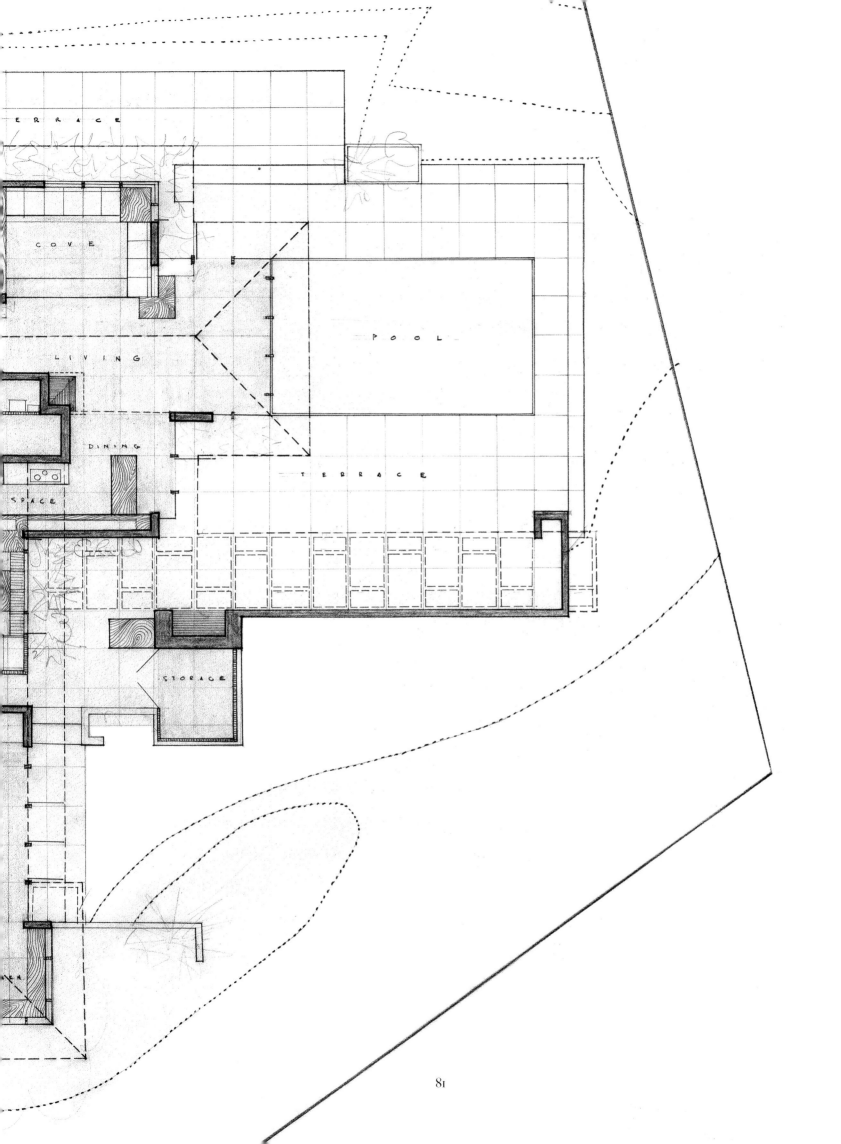

ERRACE

COVE

LIVING

DINING

SPACE

STORAGE

POOL

TERRACE

nia after accepting a position to chair the Chemistry Department at Stanford University.

The plan, based on a four-foot-square grid, is a modified cross shape with an eastern orientation towards the vistas, with its predominant axis just slightly off the north south line. Inspired by Wright's Usonian house formula, Green placed the primary rooms along the long axis, with three bedrooms sandwiched between the master suite at the north end and the living area at the south end. The minor axis of the cross contained the kitchen/laundry "work space" and terminated with a separate guest studio (connected only by the roof). The sunken "cove" area, just off the main living area and within sight of the fireplace, provides an intimate interlude from Green's flowing spaces below the vaulted ceilings. The symphony of natural

materials included brick masonry, wood, and plaster, all as backdrops to the built-in wood furniture, cabinetry, shelving, and trim. As always, Green accommodated exterior living, providing extensive terraces and a pool on the east and south sides.

■

■

■

DUKES RESIDENCE

Green's design for Charlton Arthur Dukes and his wife Effie was a single-level home on two acres northwest of Pasadena in Los Angeles County. It represents another successful, if not entirely natural, integration of house and land. Instead of man dominating the site with an unsympathetic intrusion, this is one of many examples of Green making a site better than it was with his creative abilities.

The property sits at the end of Pomander Place, presenting a large "auto court" behind a gated entry. Green sited the home almost directly on an east-west axis with the rear of the home primarily facing north. This is very unusual in Green's oeuvre, but, in this case, is most likely due to the glorious vistas afforded across the valley to the San Gabriel Mountains to the north. The plan of the home, based

89

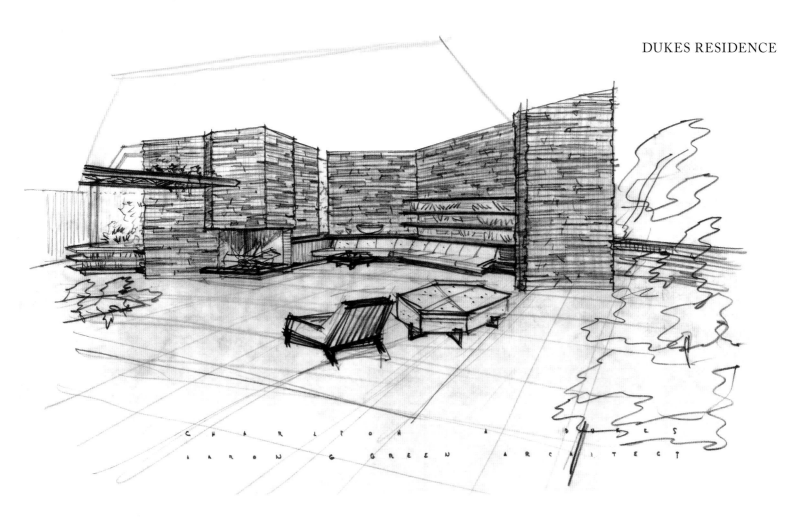

on a diamond module, extends out across the property in the east-west direction presenting a solid masonry face to the street (punctuated only by a single triangular window bringing light into the kitchen) as compared to its expansively open face to the north.

Green's master plan for the project shows the main house, an attached three-car "car shelter" (attached only by the roof) and a diamond-shaped separate studio detached from the building, which doubled as a guest house. A pool, small shop, greenhouse and extensive terraces were also planned as important parts of the built symphony. The layout of the main house incorporated an interior that was open to the sky in a truncated diamond-shaped garden atrium that allowed for the separation of the sleeping zone from the living zone in a most ingenious manner. The sleeping zone, directly off the entry foyer of the home, provided one guest bedroom and a bedroom for their son John (each with their associated bathrooms). The hallway accessing the bedrooms is bathed in natural light from the adjacent

94

garden atrium. At the end of the hallway was the Dukes' master suite, with separate bath and dressing areas. Effie's dressing area included a dramatic wall of two large mitered glass panels where the sunken tub was located. Just outside the glass Green placed a small private Japanese style fish pond. The composition of these elements created a surreal sense of bathing outdoors not to mention an intimate and very private view of the valley and mountains.

The dominant aspect of the home was its large living room, with its sloping ceiling from the stone fireplace ascending upwards and outwards as it opened up towards the exterior terrace, swimming pool, and views beyond. The dining area and a small but quaint breakfast nook were just off the living room, with the kitchen and utility room beyond. All these secondary spaces were also open to the north.

Green's preliminary renderings appeared to suggest that he was contemplating the use of desert masonry, the concrete and stone system that was used by Frank Lloyd Wright at Taliesin West. However, the built home's principal material was a buff colored Kaibab stone masonry, laid up as at Taliesin in Wisconsin. The floors were primarily terazzo with embedded brass strips demarcating the diamond unit system and the ceilings were plaster. The roof was clad with horizontal seamed copper that extended down and over the fascias of the broad, sheltering overhangs. Green, as always, incorporated an extensive amount of sophisticated built-in wood furniture, cabinetry, shelving and trim.

■

■

■

GRANGER AND MITCHELL RESIDENCE

Farley Earle Granger, Jr. (1925-2011) was an American actor whose most well known roles were in two of Alfred Hitchcock's psychological thrillers, *Rope* (1948) and *Strangers on a Train* (1951). James Mitchell (1920-2010) was both an actor and dancer. His best known role came late in his career, playing the self-made millionaire Palmer Cortlandt from 1979 to 2009 on the long running soap opera, *All My Children*. Both Granger and Mitchell later appeared on Broadway in 1955 in the production of *The Rainmaker* and in the musical *First Impressions* in 1959.

By 1954 they had become close friends. It is not known who first had the idea to approach Green to design a home they contemplated building together in Hollywood, although it was most likely Mitchell, as he had known Harriet Freeman, a client of Frank Lloyd Wright, and also was a fan of Green's Reif house.[46]

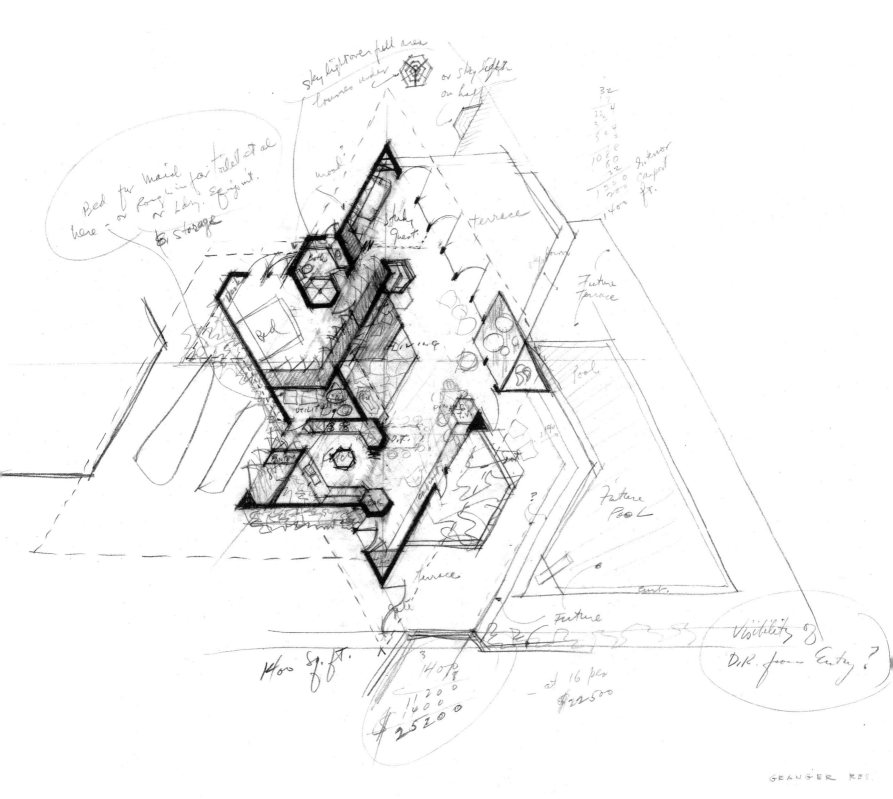

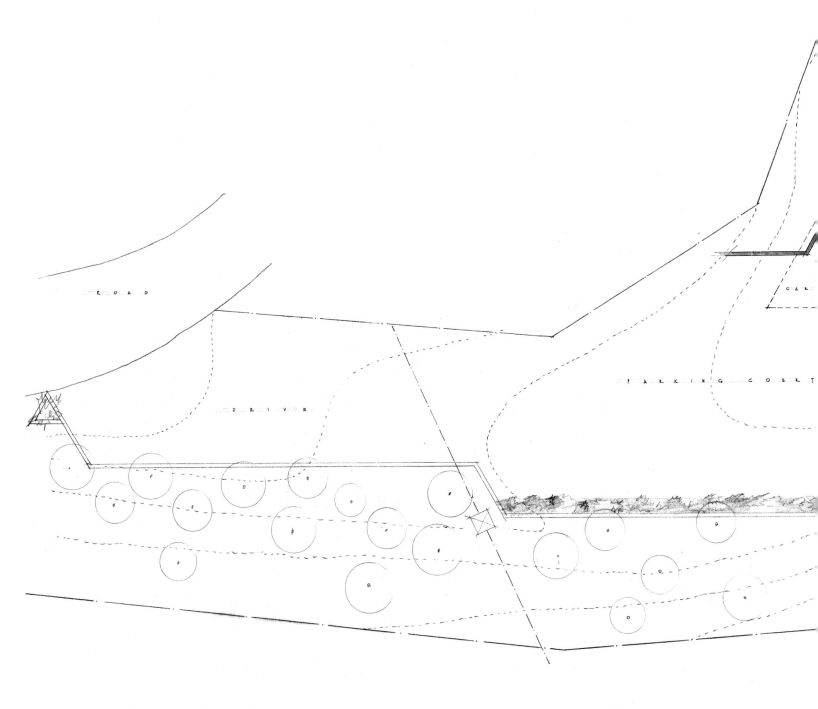

ROAD

GARAGE

PARKING COURT

DRIVE

RESIDENCE FOR FARLEY
JAMES

GRANGER AND MITCHELL RESIDENCE

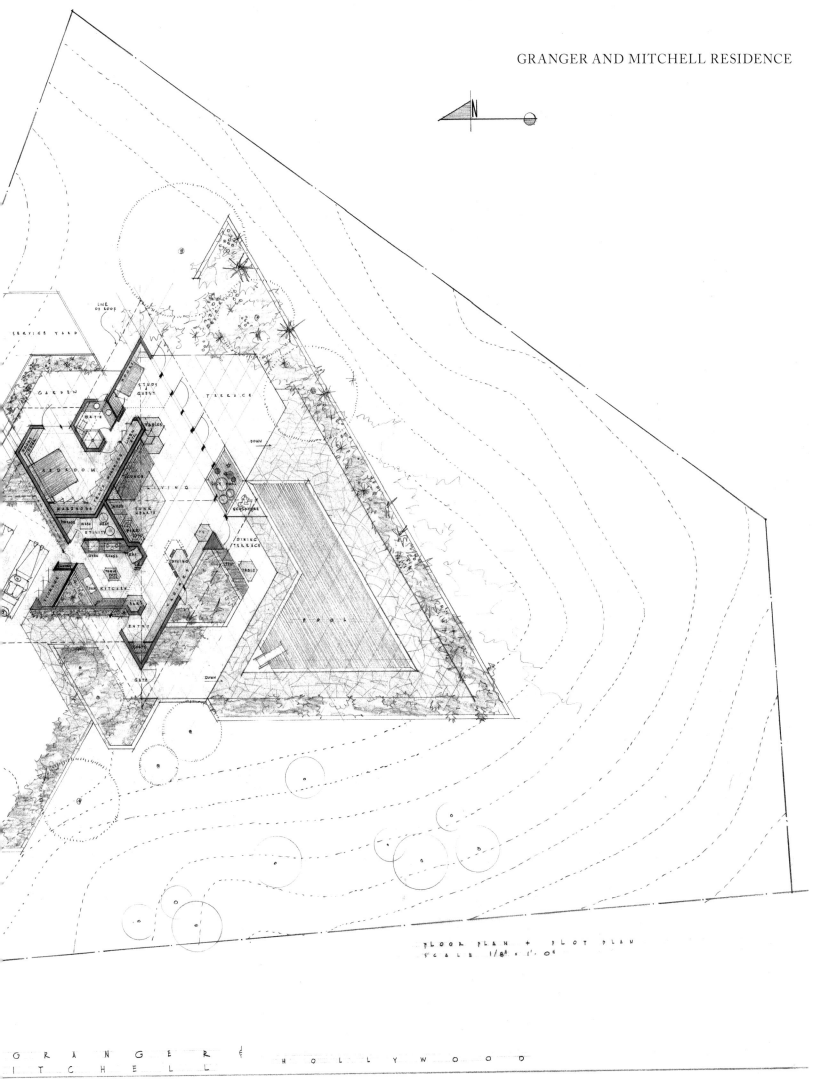

FLOOR PLAN + PLOT PLAN
SCALE 1/8" = 1'-0"

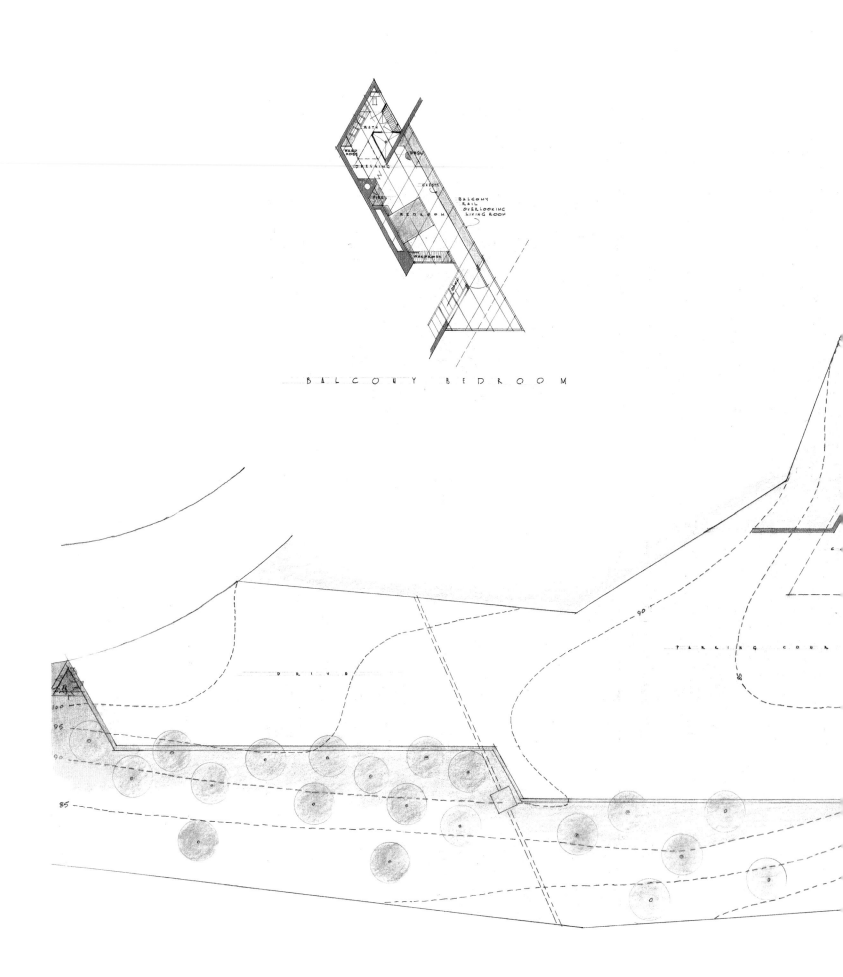

BALCONY BEDROOM

RESIDENCE FOR FARLE

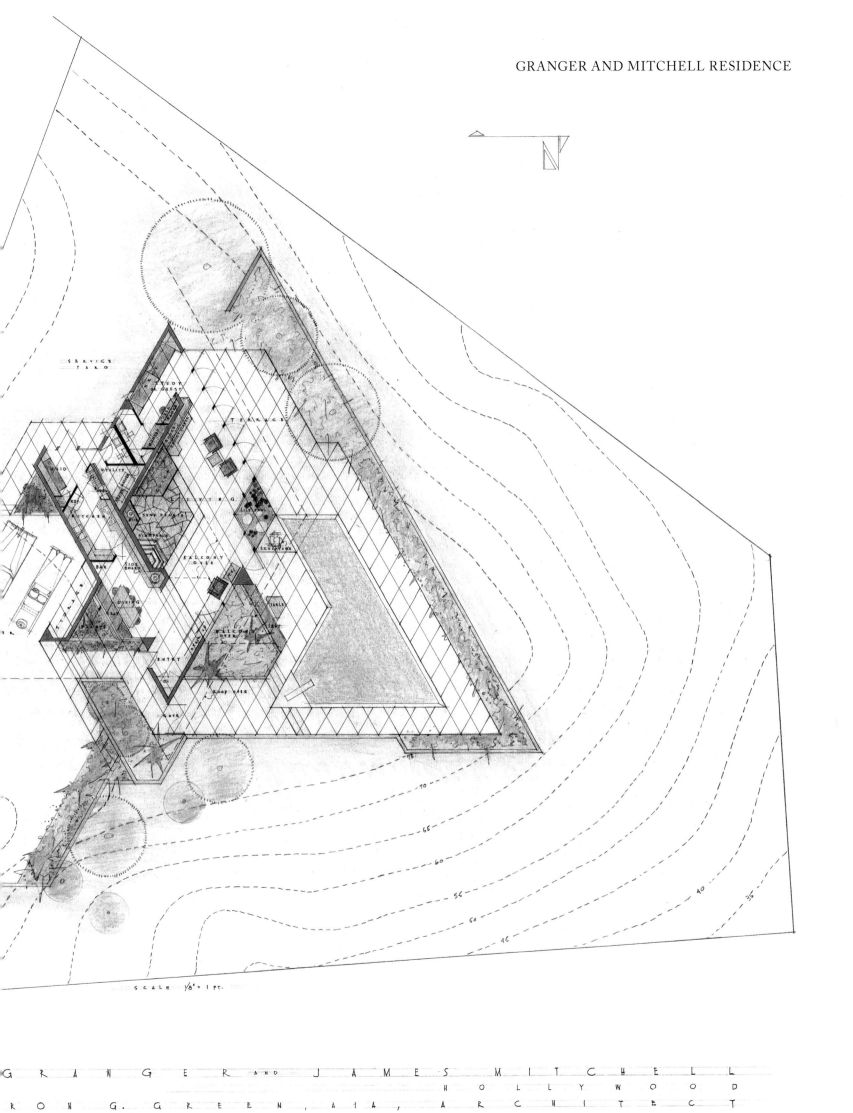

SCALE 1/8" = 1 FT.

GRANGER AND JAMES MITCHELL
HOLLYWOOD
RON G. GREEN, AIA, ARCHITECT

The preliminary drawings depict at least two schemes designed for his young bachelor clients and both were very similar in plan. Based on a triangular geometry and diamond unit system, Green produced one design that was entirely on one floor and another that included a second floor "balcony bedroom." The single-story scheme included plans for a future additional bedroom. With the location of their property long forgotten, clues can be found by studying the plans and perspective renderings. They show the house located in a hilly region, probably in the Hollywood Hills. The steep hillside site was irregular in shape, which most likely was the basis for both the geometry of the house and its overall compact layout. The approach from the street was from the north with only the open two-car shelter and entry perceptible off the parking court. The plan shows the living

and dining activities oriented to the south and west, opening out upon an expansive terrace and pool with distant views beyond. Both schemes had the same diamond shaped living and dining area with a sunken hearth in front of a masonry fireplace. Green also incorporated a small diamond shaped lily pool adjacent to a triangular pedestal for sculpture within the overall open composition. The clients obviously desired a casual home for both relaxation and entertaining. The two schemes differed mostly in the way Green resolved the third dimension. The single-story scheme was sheltered with a low-sloped, hipped roof; the two level scheme's roof was a simple gable that quietly folded over the plan.

The project never progressed beyond Green's preliminary studies and presentation drawings. Granger, after traveling to New

York to see friend Ethel Merman in the Broadway musical *Annie Get Your Gun,* moved to New York in 1955 to pursue opportunities in theater. Granger recalled in his published autobiography, *Include Me Out,*

> I had never seen a Broadway show, much less a Broadway musical. Even though I knew Ethel Merman was a big star, I had never seen any of her films, so I didn't know what to expect. She was extraordinary! She was magnificent! I was transported! I was blown away! ... Now I knew what my destiny was. I was going to up there on the stage someday. I had done three movies, all with good directors, but I had never experienced the feeling of electricity generated by the connection between audience and

actor at a live performance. It was something I had to be a part of. I was going to come to New York."[47]

Mitchell moved to New York around that time as well.

HICKS RESIDENCE

A gem from early in his career, the Hicks residence in Oakland, California was one of Green's most successful small house designs. Based on a diamond grid (four feet per side), the home was certainly influenced by Wright's Usonian home – small, efficiently designed, affordable homes for the American middle class. Like Wright's Usonians, the Hicks residence was a single-story home built with natural materials and a low-sloped sheltering roof, and was designed to almost entirely diminish the demarcation between inside

ELEVATION #1

ELEVATION #2

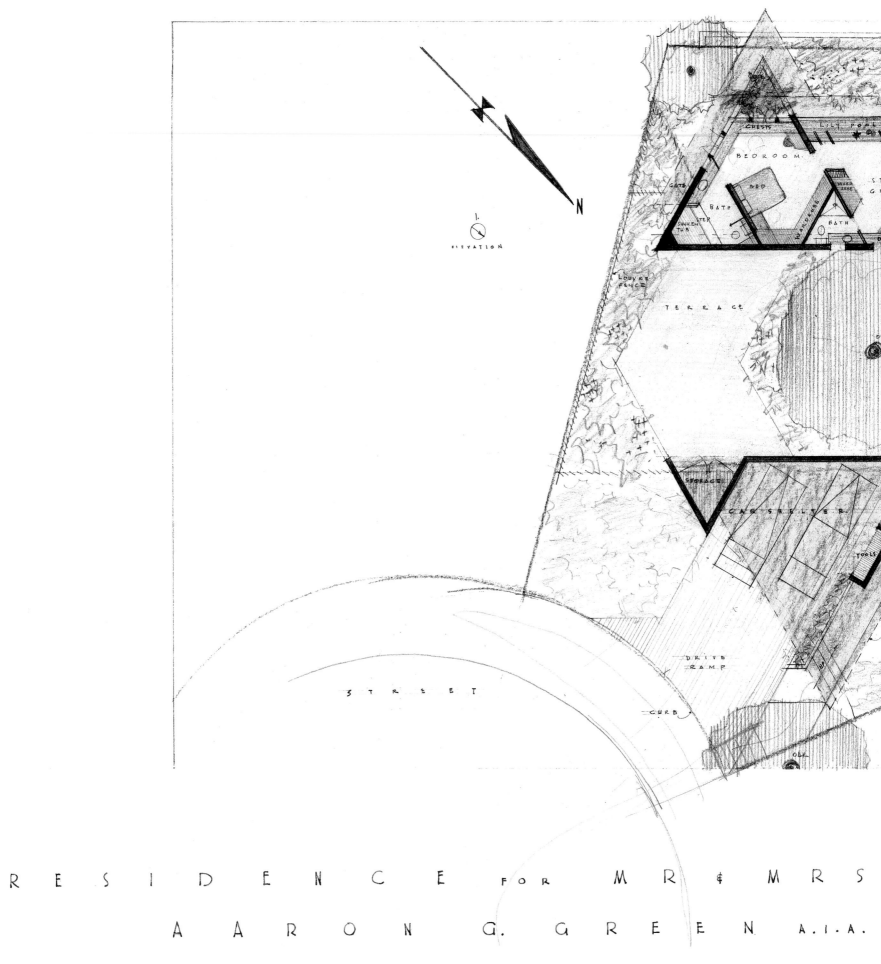

N

1.
ELEVATION

CHESTS   LILY POOL
BEDROOM
GATE   BED   WARD ESSE   ST GU
BATH   WARDROBE   BATH
SUNKEN TUB
LOUVRE FENCE
TERRACE
STORAGE
CAR SHELTER
TOOL
DRIVE RAMP
STREET
CURB
OAK

R E S I D E N C E   FOR   M R   &   M R S

A A R O N   G.   G R E E N   A.I.A.

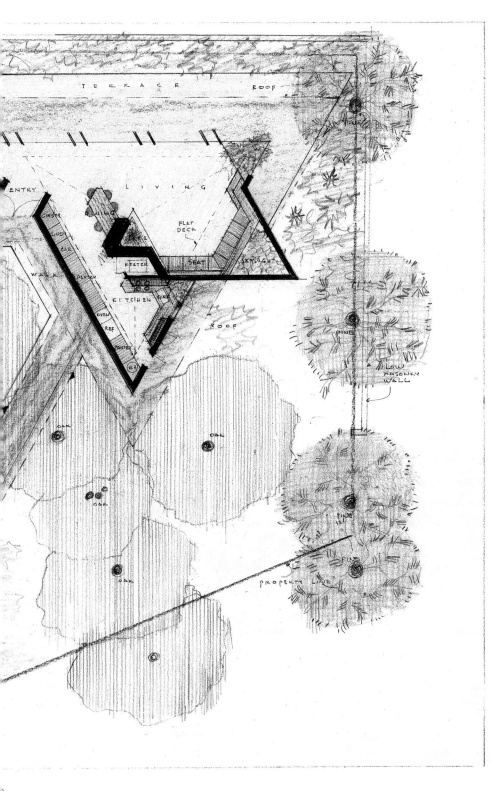

TERRACE ROOF

ENTRY

LIVING

DINING

FLAT DECK

CHESTS

LINEN

BAR

HEATER

SEAT

SKYLIGHT

WALK

PANTRY

KITCHEN

PINE

OVEN

REF

PANTRY

W.H.

ROOF

PINE

PINE

LOW MASONRY WALL

OAK

OAK

OAK

PINE

OAK

PINE

PROPERTY LINE

3.

ELEVATION

FLOOR PLAN - PLOT PLAN
SCALE 1/8" = 1'-0"

TION

HARRY HICKS OAKLAND CALIF.

RCHITECT SAN FRANCISCO

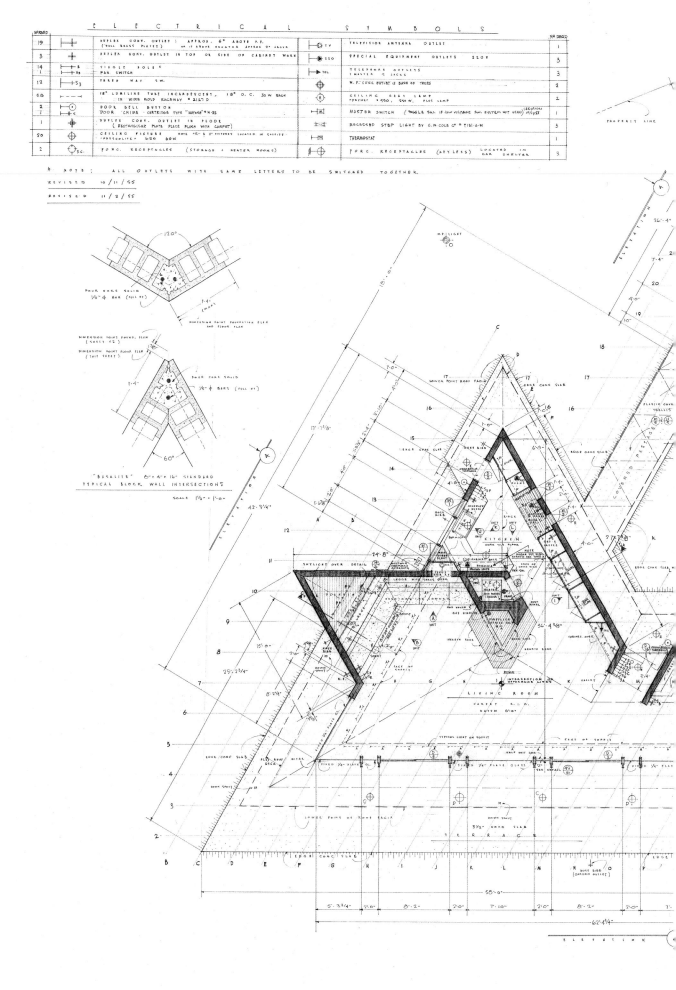

REVISED   10 / 11 / 55
REVISED   11 / 2 / 55

R E S I D E N C E   F O R   M R .   A N D   M R S .   H A R R Y

O A K L A N D ,   C A L I F O R N I A .

A A R O N   G .   G R E E N ,   A . I . A . ,   A R C H I T E C T ,

3 1 9   G R A N T   A V E N U E ,   S A N   F R A N C I S C O ,

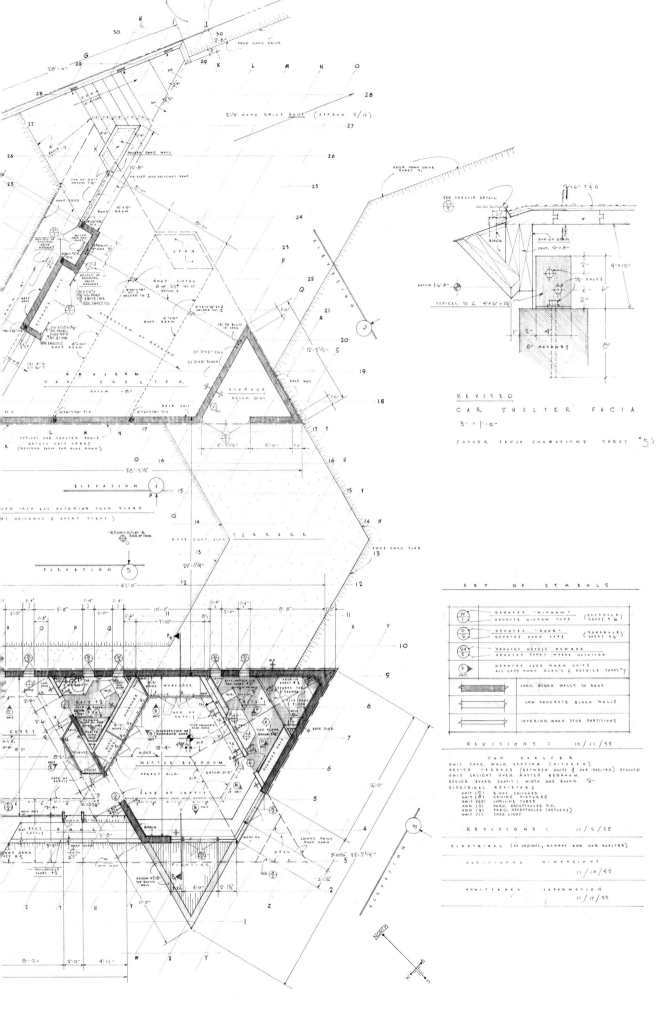

FLOOR PLAN

SHEET 3

and out. Highly refined and elaborately detailed in its design, the basically one-bedroom and one-bath residence was generally organized using simple geometry and common sense.

The property was located at the western end of Stark Knoll Place in Oakland. Green located a triangular shaped car shelter for two cars at the front and fenced off the remaining frontage to provide complete privacy. A private terrace is located between the fenced-in front and the home that is located to the rear of the irregularly shaped property. The rear of the home faces the southwest where the views and vistas are paramount, overlooking Green's Chapel of the Chimes, Oakland, San Francisco Bay, the Bay Bridge and San Francisco beyond. The home contains a space for living, dining, and cooking rotated around the fireplace core.

The working drawings for the project were dated September 1955. The Hicks returned to Green in 1962 for a guest house addition.

■ NINE OAKS
■

■

Green relocated from Los Angeles to the Bay Area in 1951 in part because of his wife's deep roots in San Francisco. They moved to Los Altos where they took the largest of the four cottages at "Nine Oaks," the five-acre family weekend and summer retreat that was frequented by the three Pauson sisters, Rose, Gertrude, and Jeannette. Built in 1919 amongst apricot orchards, the simple, symmetrical cottage was principally traditional in its design, but was well built with superb workmanship. Green clearly valued the existing asset when he decided to provide larger quarters for his family in 1955 (married eight years to Jean Haber Green, they had two sons: Allan Wright Green born in 1949 and Frank Haber Green born in 1952). The expansion was an extensive addition that left the original cottage intact. The January 1965 issue of *House Beautiful* magazine featured

a retrospective view of the 1955 project with the title, "This Modern House is Rooted in the Not-So-Distant Past," and stating, "Its nucleus was once the summer home of Mrs. Green's family, built circa 1919, when San Franciscans still regarded a trip to Los Altos and this land of live oaks as a trip to the country. They decided to keep the cottage intact, using it as a springboard for an ambitious extension that would suit their mid-century living habits."[48]

Green took considerable time in his work on this project and gave attention to every detail of this very personal expansion project. His son Allan recalled, "I remember my father spending several weekends tearing down the stonework the masons had done during the week and redoing it himself exactly the way he wanted it."[49] The two-story addition provided a new and larger living area on

SYMBOL	DESCRIPTION	N° REQ'D
	DUPLEX CONVENIENCE OUTLET	
	DUPLEX CONVENIENCE OUTLET IN CASEWORK — TOP, COUNTER OR SIDE	
	WATER PROOF CONV OUTLET – EXTERIOR PLANT LIGHTING	
	DUPLEX CONVENIENCE OUTLET IN FLOOR — FLUSH BRASS PLATE, ROUND BOX & R	
	SINGLE POLE SWITCH	
	3-WAY SWITCH	
	LUMLINE TUBE (18") INCANDESCENT 60 W EA. IN WIREMOLD STRIP. OR FLUORESCENT FIXTURE.	
	OUTLET FOR LUMLINE TUBE FIXTURE	
	RECESSED FIXTURE – NIGHT LIGHT 25 W	
	PINPOINT SPOT FIXTURE "MARCO" 100 W	
	OUTLET FOR FIXTURE WITH AUTOMATIC DOOR SWITCH IN CLOSET 25 W	
	PORCELAIN RECEPTACLE IN WOOD BOX CEILING RECESS 40 W	
	220 V OUTLET	
	TELEPHONE OUTLET	
	TELEVISION ANTENNA OUTLET	
	OUTLET FOR CEILING FIXTURE 75 W. SWITCH AS INDICATED	
	PORCELAIN RECEPTACLE — PULL CORD	

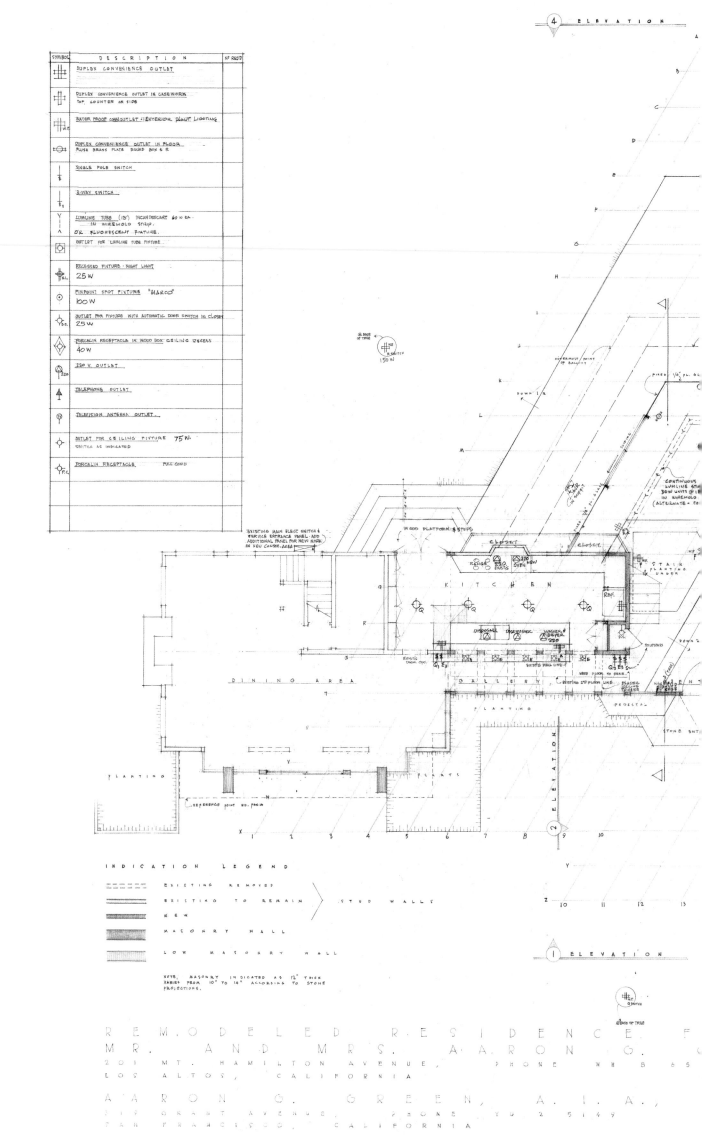

INDICATION LEGEND

EXISTING REMOVED

EXISTING TO REMAIN — STUD WALLS

NEW

MASONRY WALL

LOW MASONRY WALL

NOTE: MASONRY INDICATED AS 12" THICK VARIES FROM 10" TO 14" ACCORDING TO STONE PROJECTIONS.

REMODELED RESIDENCE F
MR. AND MRS. AARON G.
201 MT. HAMILTON AVENUE, PHONE WH 8 65
LOS ALTOS, CALIFORNIA

AARON G. GREEN, A.I.A.,
GRANT AVENUE, PHONE YU 2 5149
SAN FRANCISCO, CALIFORNIA

1 ELEVATION
2 ELEVATION

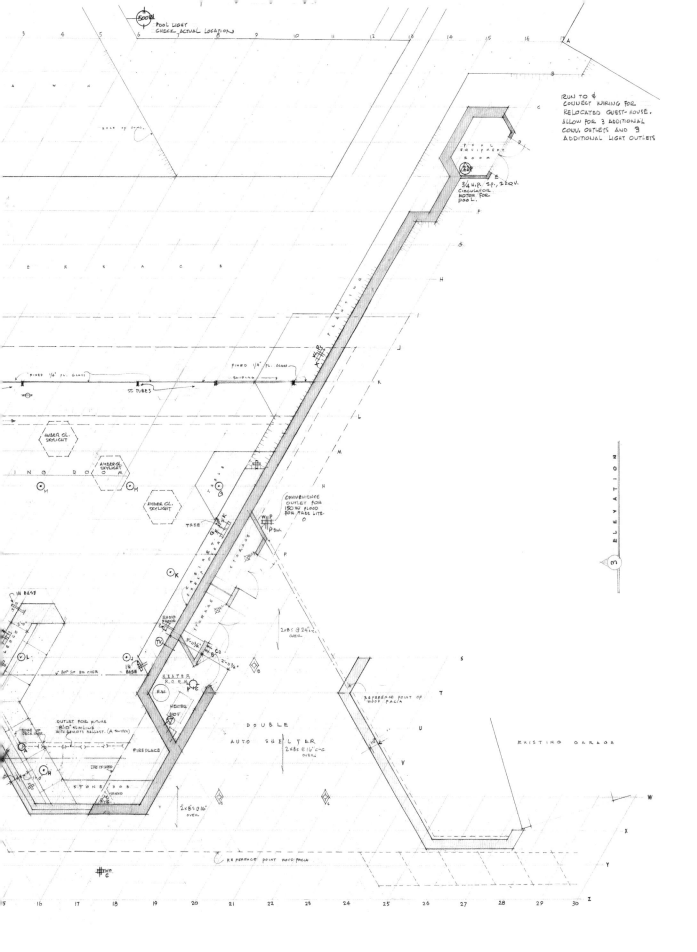

NINE OAKS

MAIN PLAN 1/4" = 1'-0"
SHEET 3

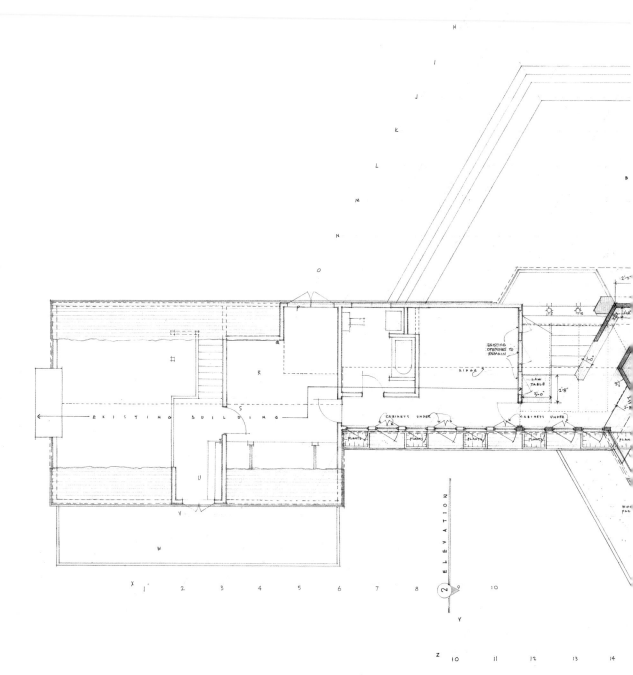

A

B

C

D

E

F

G

H

I

J

K

L

M

N

O

EXISTING BUILDING

ELEVATION ②

ELEVATION ①

X 1 2 3 4 5 6 7 8 ② 9 10

Y

Z 10 11 12 13 14

REMODELED RESIDENCE FO
MR. AND MRS. AARON G. GR
201 MT. HAMILTON AVENUE, PHONE WH 8 6540
LOS ALTOS, CALIFORNIA

AARON G. GREEN, A.I.A., A
319 GRANT AVENUE, PHONE YU 2 5149
SAN FRANCISCO, CALIFORNIA

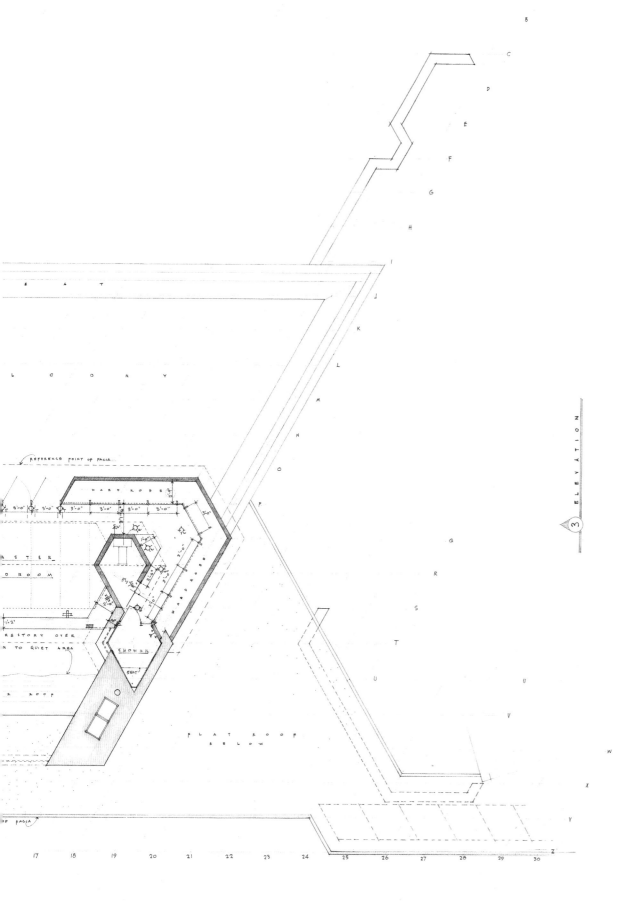

3 ELEVATION

2ᴺᴰ FL. PLAN   1/4" = 1'-0"

SHEET

4

the ground floor with a new master suite on the upper level. Green repurposed the original living room into his study and the addition of the third bedroom allowed the boys to take over both bedrooms in the existing house.

The new living space was a large, irregular shaped room that provided areas for various social and practical functions. The spacious room, large enough to accommodate multiple seating groups, opens onto a terrace and landscaped garden. A partially enclosed alcove, with a continuous built-in couch below bookshelves, continuous ribbon windows, and a low wood soffit, is arranged off the large stone fireplace providing a more intimate and sheltered area within the casual, informal space. James DeLong, in his *House Beautiful* magazine feature, describes the pavilion-like downstairs as, "a great flowing area that encompasses all kinds of family activity. It is a music room and entertaining room, gracefully accommodating large gatherings of guests. It is also, in its coved fireside area, a secluded retreat for con-

versation or reading. And from no part of this space is the outdoors far away, either visually or actually."[50]

Green used a thirty-/sixty-degree diamond unit system, four-foot on each of the four sides, to organize the reflex angles experienced throughout the entire composition. While the contrast between the formal original and the informal, more casual addition in plan provided an obvious contrast, Green was able to skillfully merge the two successfully as one.

The home was demolished circa 1988.

CHAPEL OF THE CHIMES

Green's project at the Chapel of the Chimes, located on Piedmont Avenue at the northwest end of Ramona Avenue in Oakland, was actually an addition to an existing crematory and columbarium that had been originally founded in 1909 and subsequently redesigned and expanded in 1928 by Julia Morgan (1872-1957). Morgan, the first woman licensed as an architect in California, became William

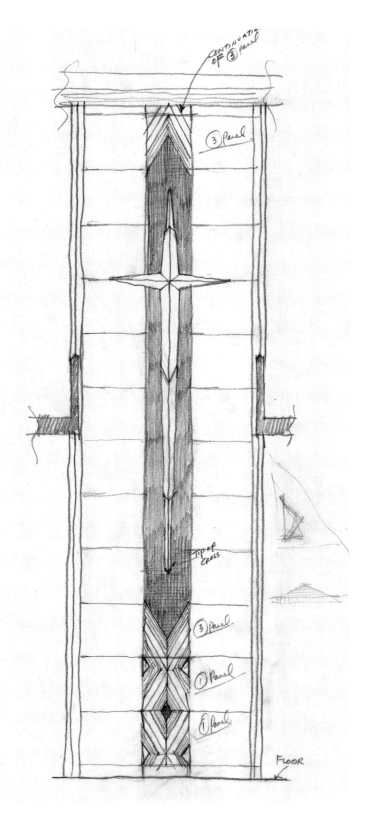

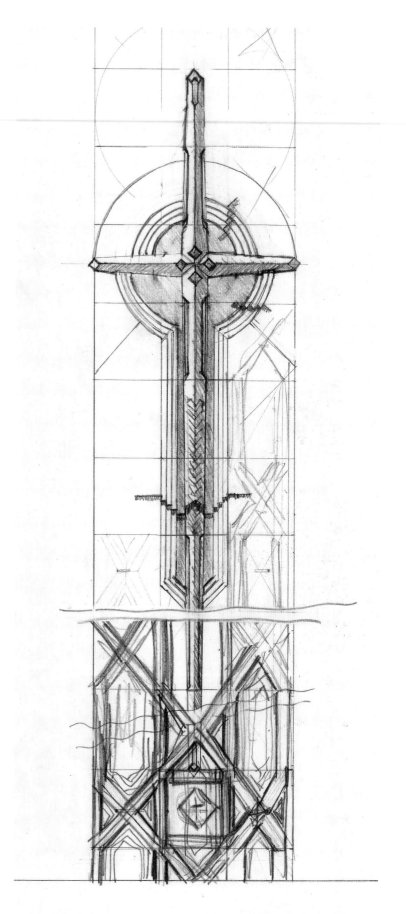

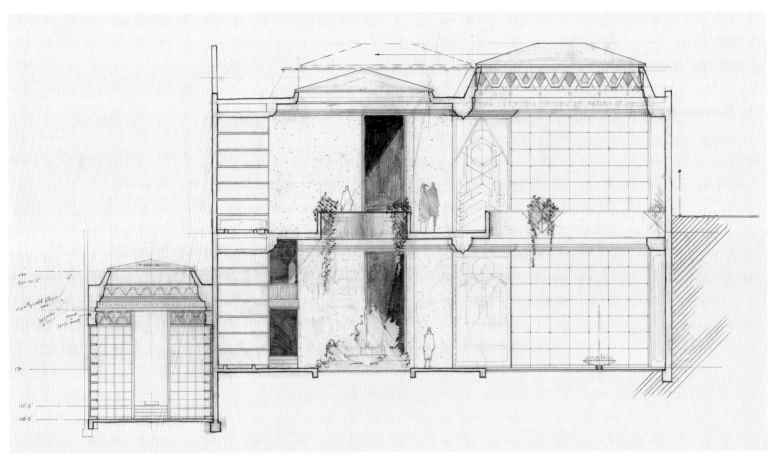

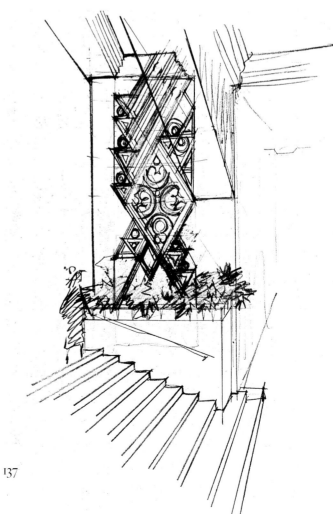

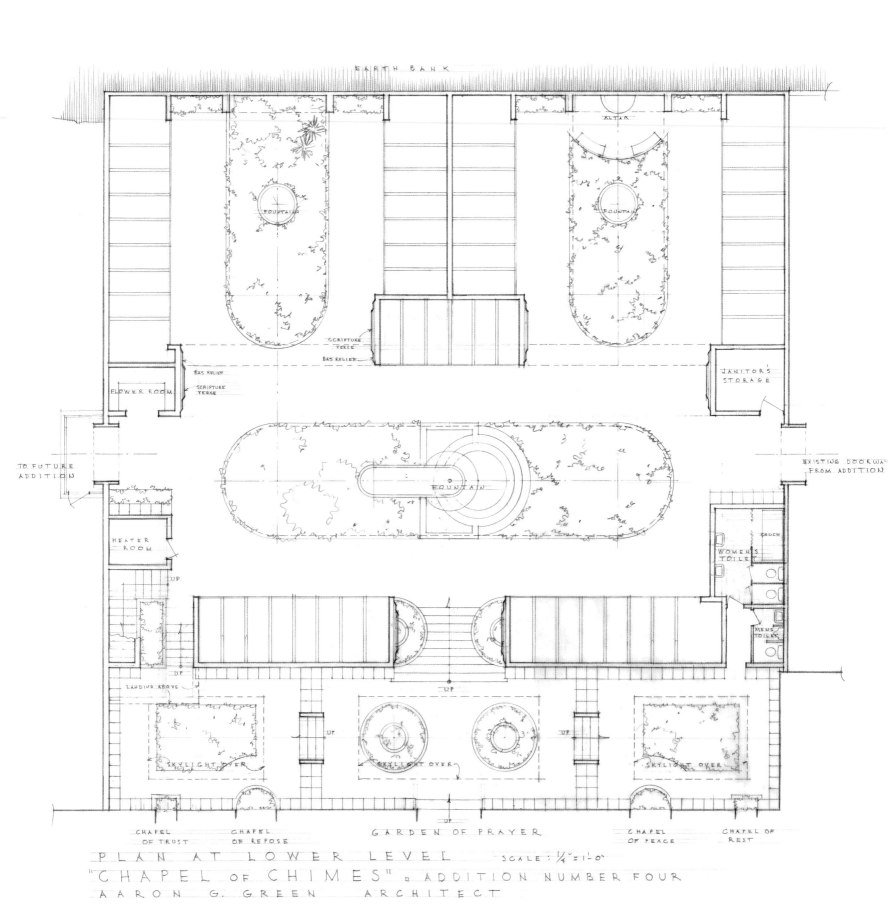

EARTH BANK

ALTAR

FOUNTAIN

FOUNTAIN

SCRIPTURE VERSE

BAS RELIEF

JANITOR'S STORAGE

BAS RELIEF

FLOWER ROOM

SCRIPTURE VERSE

FOUNTAIN

TO FUTURE ADDITION

EXISTING DOORWAY FROM ADDITION

HEATER ROOM

WOMEN'S TOILET

COUCH

UP

MEN'S TOILET

LANDING ABOVE

UP

UP

SKYLIGHT OVER

SKYLIGHT OVER

SKYLIGHT OVER

UP

CHAPEL OF TRUST

CHAPEL OF REPOSE

GARDEN OF PRAYER

CHAPEL OF PEACE

CHAPEL OF REST

PLAN AT LOWER LEVEL   SCALE: ¼" = 1'-0"

"CHAPEL OF CHIMES" • ADDITION NUMBER FOUR

AARON G. GREEN   ARCHITECT

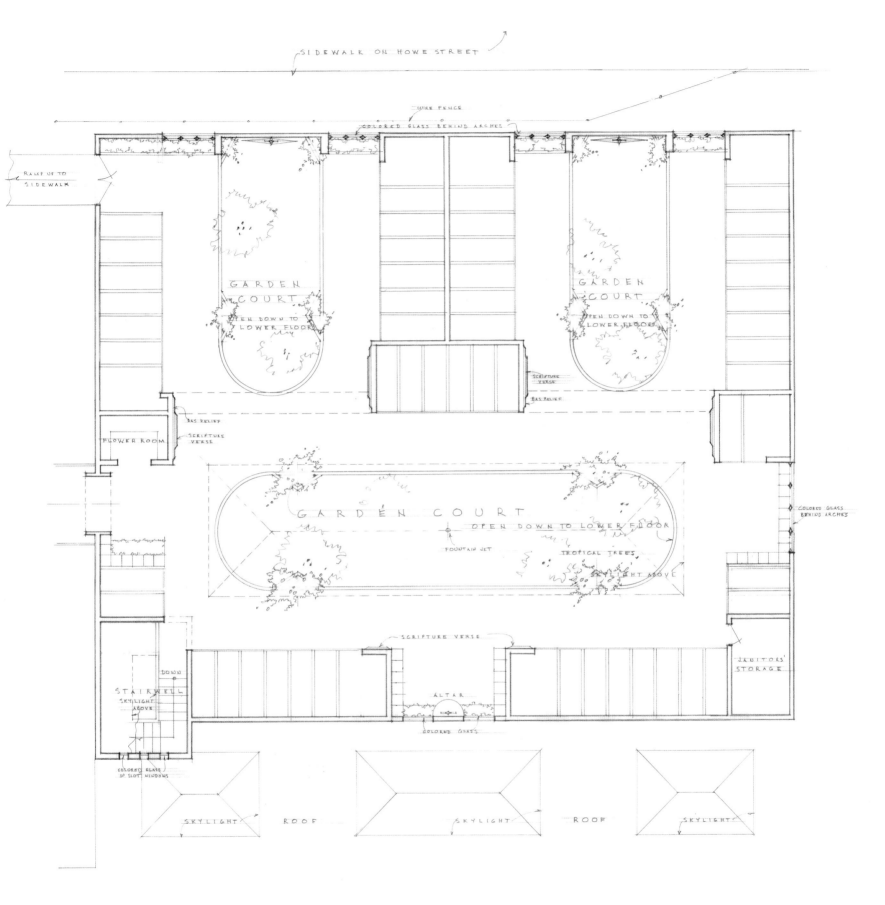

SIDEWALK ON HOWE STREET

WIRE FENCE

COLORED GLASS BEHIND ARCHES

RAMP UP TO SIDEWALK

GARDEN COURT
OPEN DOWN TO LOWER FLOOR

GARDEN COURT
OPEN DOWN TO LOWER FLOOR

SCRIPTURE VERSE

BAS RELIEF

BAS RELIEF

FLOWER ROOM

SCRIPTURE VERSE

COLORED GLASS BEHIND ARCHES

GARDEN COURT
OPEN DOWN TO LOWER FLOOR

FOUNTAIN JET

TROPICAL TREES

SKYLIGHT ABOVE

SCRIPTURE VERSE

JANITORS' STORAGE

DOWN

STAIRWELL
SKYLIGHT ABOVE

ALTAR

COLORED GLASS

COLORED GLASS IN SLOT WINDOWS

SKYLIGHT   ROOF   SKYLIGHT   ROOF   SKYLIGHT

PLAN AT UPPER LEVEL   SCALE: ¼"=1'-0"
"CHAPEL OF CHIMES"   ADDITION NUMBER FOUR
AARON G. GREEN   ARCHITECT

CHAPEL OF THE CHIMES

ADDITION NUMBER SEVEN

OAKLAND, CALIFORNIA

AARON G. GREEN ASSOCIATES, INC.   ARCHITECTS AND PLANNERS

Randolph Hearst's primary architect and is best known for the Hearst Castle in San Simeon. She went on to design more than 700 buildings in her long and prolific career.

Green obviously respected Morgan's extant Moorish and Gothic inspired work. His addition (and future additions) seamlessly blends with Morgan's work in reverential harmony. Bill Schwarz, an employee of Green's, described the work as a, "labyrinth of chapels, cloisters, sky-lit gardens and courts, including fountains, cast concrete, glass, mosaics, and antiquities, which exhibits Morgan's devotion to highest standards. Fresh, artful geometrics of Green's additions pay homage to Morgan's earlier Moorish-Gothic eclectic vision." [51] The experience provided by Green at the Chapel of the Chimes is a physical manifestation of a spiritual statement of sound and light that is consistent with his interment philosophy of providing a memorable experience for the living in the celebration of the life of the deceased.

Green's work at the Chapel of the Chimes began in 1955 and continued through multiple additions over the years until 1997. Jan Novie, Green's longstanding employee, reflected on the interment work and Green's ability to enlighten his clients:

Architecture for interment was of very special interest to Aaron. He felt that a great part of his own personal legacy in architecture related to the beauty of his work in that field. His basic concept was that you designed beautiful buildings for the living so that they would look forward to visiting their loved ones in a natural garden-like setting within beautiful timeless uplifting architecture. This is not easy to do. Interment work is historically done by clients who try to reduce their buildings to a bare minimum in terms of cost and architectural amenities. Most of Aaron's clients were different and quickly realized people were more than willing to pay the price to achieve a higher standard. They also realized they liked visiting the deceased in this fine architecture. [52]

■ MARIN CITY

■

■ The Housing Authority of Marin County announced in January 1957 that the design of the federally funded 300-unit Marin City, a low-rent housing project, was going to be a collaborative effort between Green and another San Francisco architect, John Carl Warnecke (1919-2010). The project represented the first phase of the redevelopment of Marin City, a community of workers created in 1942 to supply labor to construct ships for the war effort. A variety of apartment types would replace some of the temporary wartime housing.

It was a perfect storm for the project's designers, as the citizens of Marin County supported a project that would provide something of lasting value to the community and the federal government claimed to be promoting good design in their federal housing initiative. Green was the design architect for the master plan and housing units, with Warnecke's office being responsible for the architectural documents for construction. This was Green's largest project to date, estimated to cost approximately $4.3 million, and one of his first for a public governing body.

Green's approach towards Marin City was no different than any other project. His employee, Daniel Lieberman, offered, "He was very proud of it ... He really tackled it in a very noble way. There was nothing patronizing, that it wasn't important architecture or that he was going to build a bunch of barracks there. He was going to build permanent, fireproof, proud, handsome, concrete buildings."[53] Green's youth, growing up in the Deep South and having a liberal father who was, by example, tolerant of minorities while others in the south were racially prejudiced, provided him a basis for both empathy and respect for the future residents of Marin City.

The project's sloping hillside site, roughly L-shaped, contained almost thirty acres of land abutting Highway 101 on its east side and the Golden Gate National Recreation area to the south. Green implemented both low-rise buildings (three different types) and mid-rise, five-story towers (one type) in his design. Green's dramatic solution for the challenging site minimized grading; his buildings worked with the natural contours, stepping down the slope, set economically at right angles to the hill to eliminate drain-

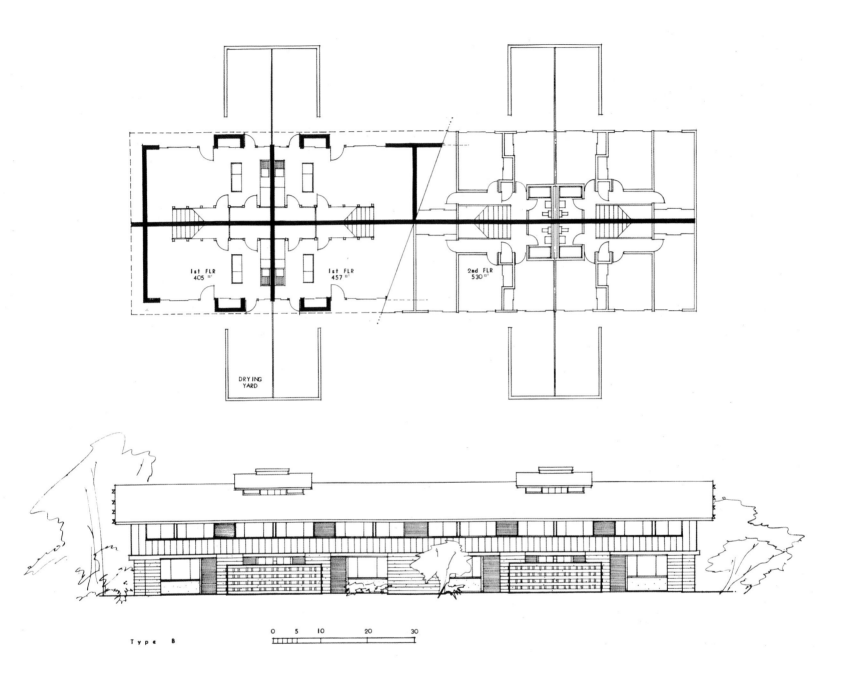

1st FLR
405 □'

1st FLR
457 □'

2nd FLR
530 □'

DRYING
YARD

Type   B

0   5   10   20   30

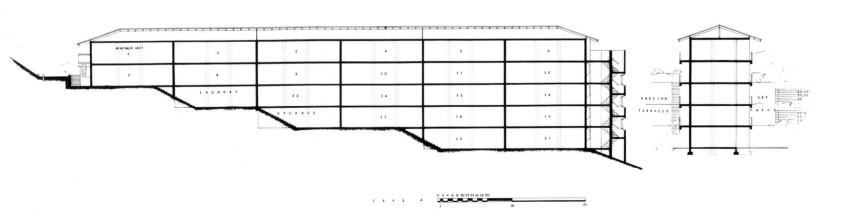

APARTMENT UNIT   1 | 2 | 3 | 4 | 5 | 6

7 | 8 | 9 | 10 | 11 | 12

LAUNDRY | 13 | 14 | 15 | 16

STORAGE | 17 | 18 | 19

20 | 21

PARKING
TERRACES

DRY
YARD

TYPE   A   0 2 4 6 8 10 12 14 16 18 20

1   30   60

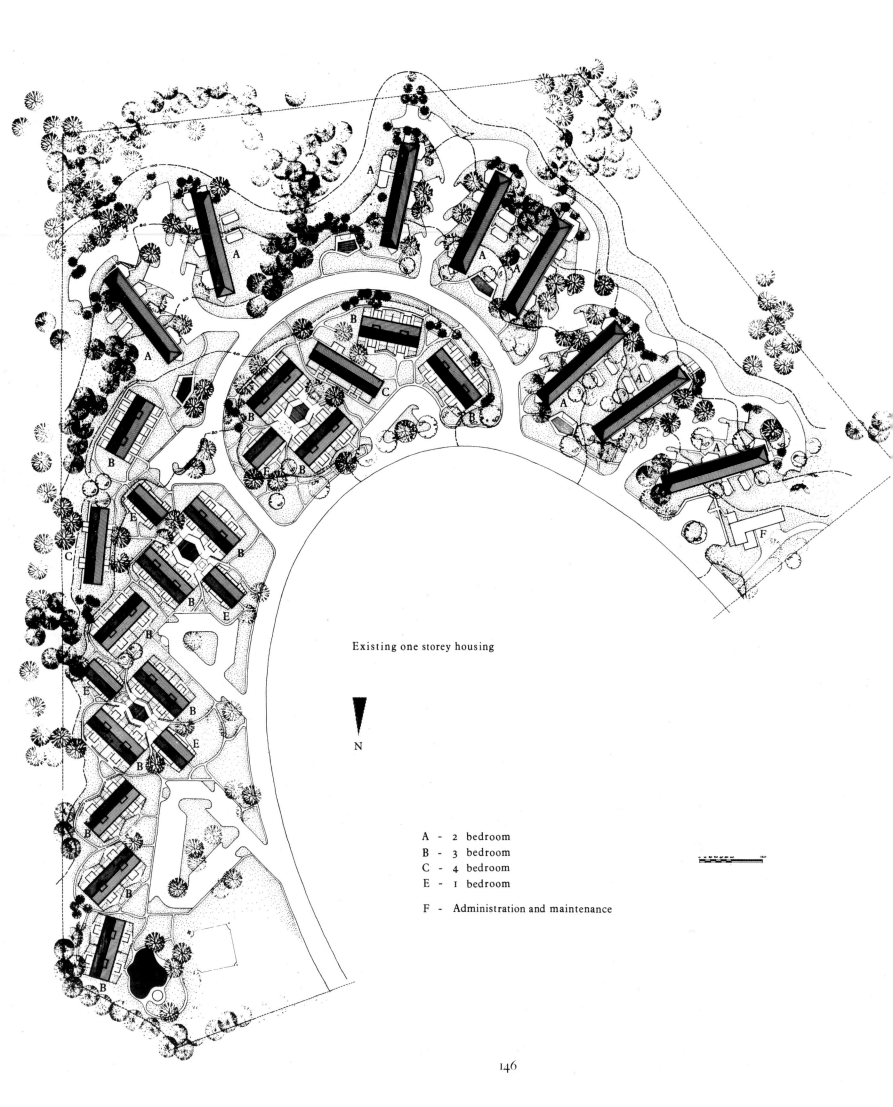

Existing one storey housing

N

A - 2 bedroom
B - 3 bedroom
C - 4 bedroom
E - 1 bedroom

F - Administration and maintenance

age issues, terracing, and retaining walls and providing ground level entry to all levels (eliminating the need for elevators). The dominant building materials for the tower buildings were cast-in-place concrete, patterned precast concrete, and red-clay tile roofs, while the low-rise buildings were a mix of integrally colored concrete masonry and wood frame construction.

The project, completed in 1961, received national acclaim, winning design awards from *Progressive Architecture* magazine and a First Honor Award by the Public Housing Administration in 1964 for design excellence, from more than 700 projects considered by a jury of architects and housing specialists. Ironically, it garnered negative attention as well because it didn't have the more typical and expected institutional appearance. Even though the project was built within the stipulated budget, it was publicly criticized by auditors of the U.S. General Accounting Office as a waste of the government's resources because of its unorthodox design and expensive elements, such as tile roofs and private balconies.

Of perhaps more importance, working with Marin County on Marin City helped open doors that enabled Green to bring Wright in as the architect for the Marin County Civic Center, which would become acknowledged as one of Wright's best works.

Green would later be involved in a much larger housing project with the San Francisco Redevelopment Agency. The Hunter's

Point project that began in 1966 was a new community with 2,000 low to moderate income dwelling units of varying sizes for approximately 10,000 residents on a 137-acre site with views of San Francisco and the Bay. Like Marin City, the site contained scores of temporary wartime housing units built by the federal government during World War II.

Green's master plan included a remarkably effective program of constructive citizen participation that sought to negate by design the scale and institutional character normally associated with mass housing that was expressly distasteful to the residents. According to Jan Novie, Green "took particular pride in providing the American Dream to these people in need. The goal was to learn as much as possible about their hopes and dreams as this was to become the true program for the project."[54]

◼ ANDERSON RESIDENCE

◼

◼   Curtis Besinger wrote about the Anderson residence for *House Beautiful* magazine,

> True, there is a roof overhead, and there are walls and mullions supporting it. But these do not seem so much to shut in and contain the space as to shelter it, give it definition, and suggest its use. The floor you see underfoot is a continuation of the exposed aggregate concrete pavement that is outside. The walls inside are the same as those outside. The same ceiling continues overhead. And, due to the way the glass has been set in many openings, there are not the usual lines of demarcation ... The absence of demarcation stems in large part from the fact that the inside and outside have been conceived and planned as one continuous area.[55]

Less than a half-mile from the iconic Wayfarers Chapel (designed by Frank Lloyd Wright's architect son, Lloyd Wright, ten years earlier), the site for the Judge F. (Judge was his first name, not his title or occupation) and Jeannie Anderson house presented a dichotomy of both challenge and opportunity. It was a small and extremely narrow, almost cliff-like parcel of land on the Palos Verdes Peninsula, dropping forty feet from Sea Cove Drive down to the beach below. On the other hand, its oceanfront advantage provided his clients a spectacularly overwhelming panoramic view of the Pacific Ocean. However, Green didn't open up the entire oceanfront face of the house to the view. As Besinger describes, Green, "makes it possible for its owners to savor the scene as they choose. It provides them with a full gamut of spaces and views and with a full range of experiences of the setting: from the complete openness of the terraces to the sequestered spaciousness of its deeply withdrawn interior; from the full sweep of the

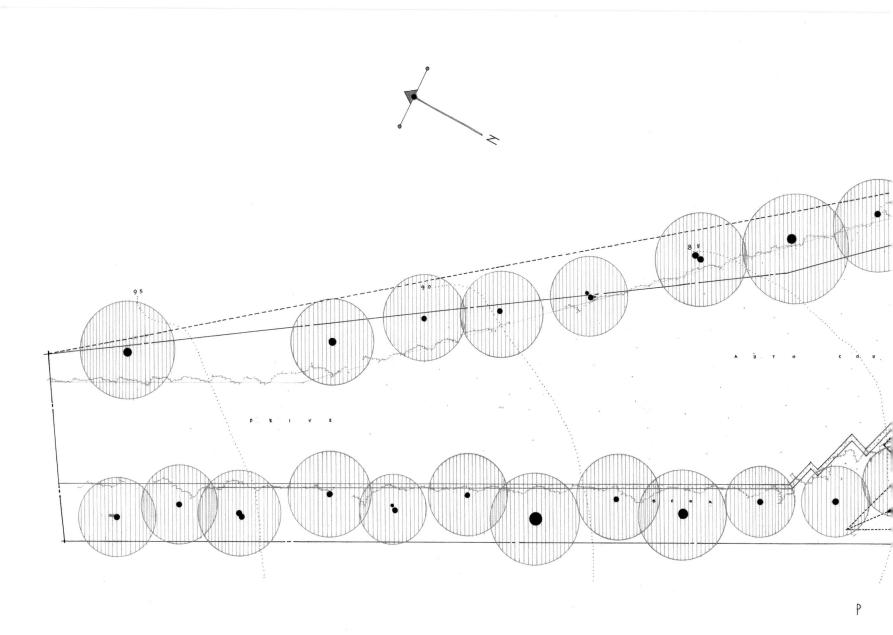

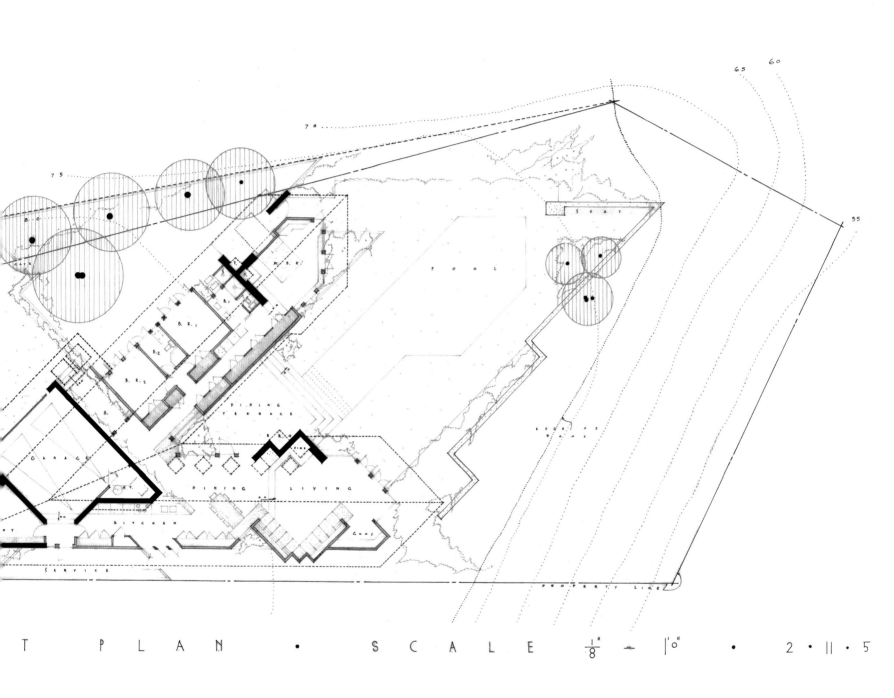

T   P L A N   •   S C A L E $\frac{1"}{8}$ = $1'0"$ •   2 • 11 • 5

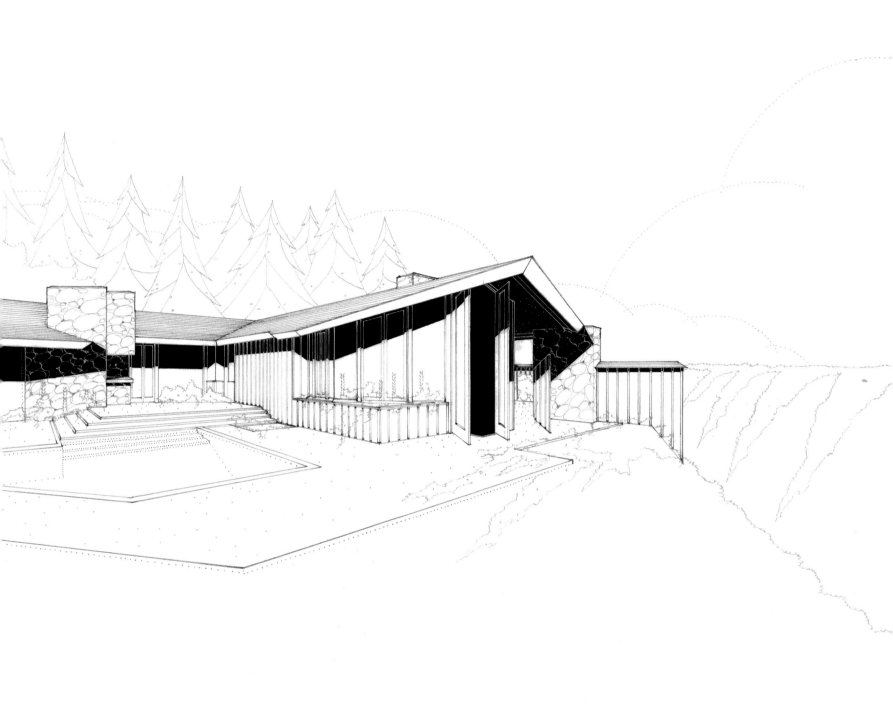

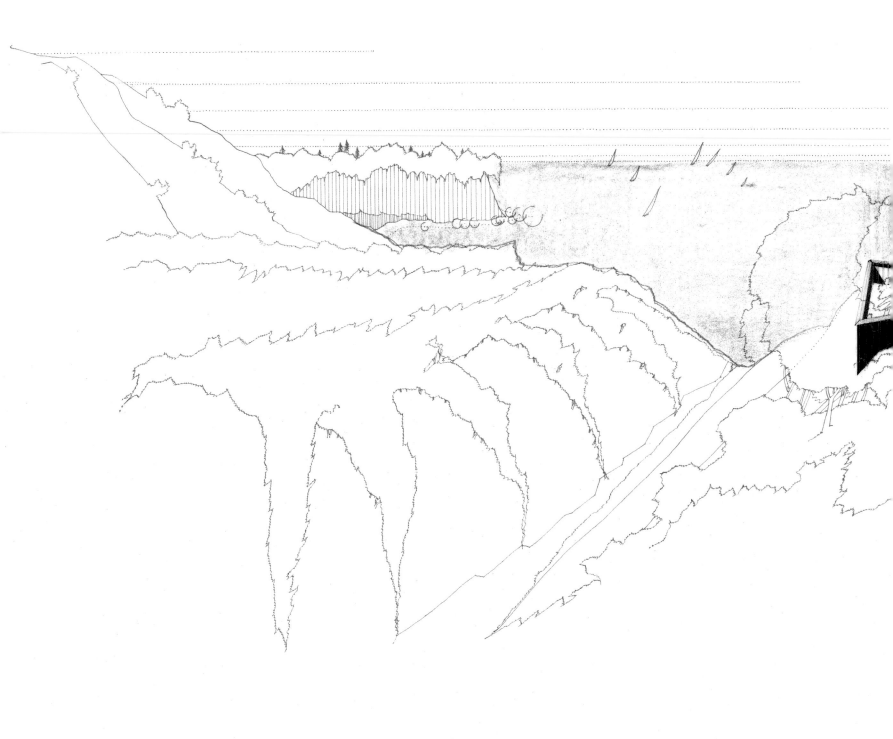

view to intriguing glimpses of smaller portions of it."[56] The Anderson opus is a collection and collaboration of sheltered and protected openness and deeply withdrawn, more intimate, private spaces.

The site and its natural features forced Green to design a tight V-shaped home. The plan, containing approximately 3,000 square feet, appears complicated while, in reality, it is essentially a compact home uniquely designed to deal with the site's serious challenges while enhancing its extraordinary opportunities. The single-story home provides subtle level changes in concert with the fall of the natural contours of the land. Again, the challenges of the site required steps but also allowed Green the opportunity to enhance the spatial quality of the interior.

Arriving in the motor court from the road, the home angles away and is partially hidden by a fenced-in walled garden. The entire composition presents an unassuming, solid face of stone and wood below an overreaching horizontal flat roof. Green deeply recessed the exterior entry and front door into a confined but sky-lit space, providing a sequencing of zones—moving from the public to the semi-public, and then into the semi-private interior "entrance hall" of the home. Once there, at the apex of the V, one is greeted by an interior garden—a design feature Green favored—and faces the choice of accessing the hall of the bedroom wing to the right or moving forward towards the wing of the living and dining spaces of the home.

It is also here that Green provides a glimpse of the overall view of the interior of the house and the vista beyond, as Besinger noted, "The unassuming exterior does not lead you to expect such spatial richness. All of it was achieved with the most modest of materials ... Although essentially open, the house offers a strong sense of shelter ... a seemingly continuous, yet sequestered space."[57]

The floor plan is based on a four-foot-square unit system. Like the interior space, the materials are relatively direct and simple – the walls of stone, irregularly coursed, wood, the floors of exposed aggregated concrete and some carpeting, and ceilings and soffits of buff colored plaster. Curiously, in the first sketches Green depicted the home's walls built of desert masonry, the method of construction utilizing stone and concrete that originated from Wright at his Arizona home, Taliesin West. This was eventually abandoned for the stone aesthetic similar to Taliesin, Wisconsin. Built-in furniture, cabinetry, shelving and trim, all designed by Green to both enhance and unify the interiors, were integrated.

The living area is an incredibly sophisticated chiseled space that provides for social occasions as well as quiet intimate seclusion. Above the two built-in sofas, Green integrated two large Oriental screens within the wood paneled walls. Unique in Green's career, his client, an avid gun enthusiast and collector, requested a room where he could store and shoot his guns. Green located the "gun room"

at the apex of the living area in a small, secluded corner. Here they devised a shooting range for target practice utilizing an underground storm drainpipe terminating at a catch basin at the curb. A rope and pulley system was created to move the target from the gun room at various lengths towards the catch basin at the street curb. Cleaning out the spent bullets was accomplished by removing the lid to the catch basin.

The home was built by Norwood & DeLong. The Andersons lived in the house for 36 years until 1994 when they sold it to family friends, William and Lynn Swank. The Swanks were wonderful stewards for more than twenty years; they sold the house in 2015.

LEE RESIDENCE

Philip Randolph Lee (1924–), a medical doctor, and his wife Catherine (1928–2005), an attorney, came to Green for the design of their house through their acquaintance with Green's wife Jean at Stanford University. Lee was the eldest of four sons of Russell Lee, a doctor who founded the Palo Alto Medical Clinic in the 1930s, which was one of the nation's first group practices. Because of the father's pioneering legacy in health policy, Philip would later become involved in the implementation of Medicare as Assistant Secretary of Health in the Department of Health, Education & Welfare in the Johnson administration.

Green's design for the large Lee family (they eventually had five children) was a linear plan on property that was part of an extended Lee family compound. The two-car carport terminated the home's

northeast end, with the library located at the opposing southwest terminus. In between was the large vaulted living and dining area along with the home's entrance and the four bedrooms and associated baths. A large terrace and expansive lawn to the southeast were accessed from the living area. The kitchen and laundry spaces were the only interruption to the linear plan, both projecting off the living zone in the northwest direction. The preliminary plan is evidence that Green considered the relationship of the home with the many large oak trees extant on the site when making the design.

The construction elements of the home were exposed, direct, and bold in statement of form, purpose, and materials. Four-inch high by sixteen-inch long adobe-like masonry was used for the walls and piers that supported the exposed wood beams of the roof, while

A   RESIDENCE   FOR   DR.   AND   MRS.   PHILIP   LEE
PORTOLA   VALLEY,
CALIFORNIA.
AARON   G.   GREEN,   A.I.A.,   ARCHITECT
SAN   FRANCISCO,
CALIFORNIA.

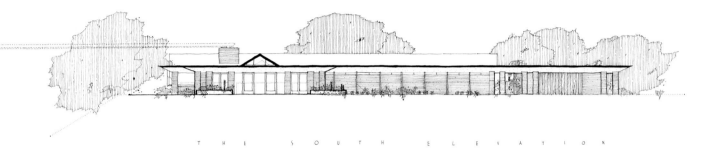

R E S I D E N C E   F O R   D R.   A N D   M R S.   P H I L I P   L E E

ORTOLA   VALLEY,

ALIFORNIA.

ARON   G.   GREEN,   A.I.A.,   ARCHITECT

AN   FRANCISCO,

ALIFORNIA.

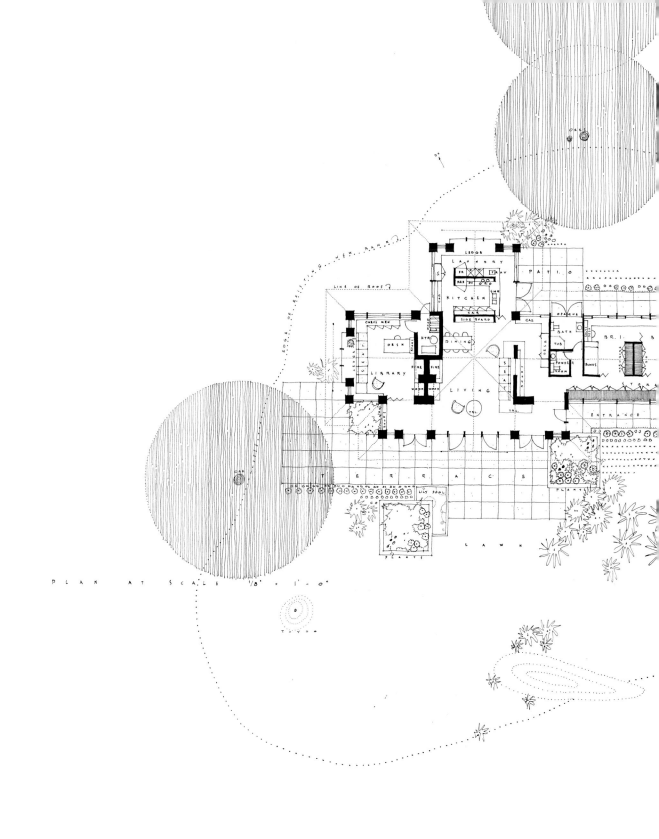

PLAN AT SCALE ⅛" = 1'-0"

A   R E S I D E N C E   F O R   D R .   A N

P O R T O L A   V A L L E Y,

C A L I F O R N I A .

A A R O N   G .   G R E E N,   A . I . A .,

S A N   F R A N C I S C O,

C A L I F O R N I A .

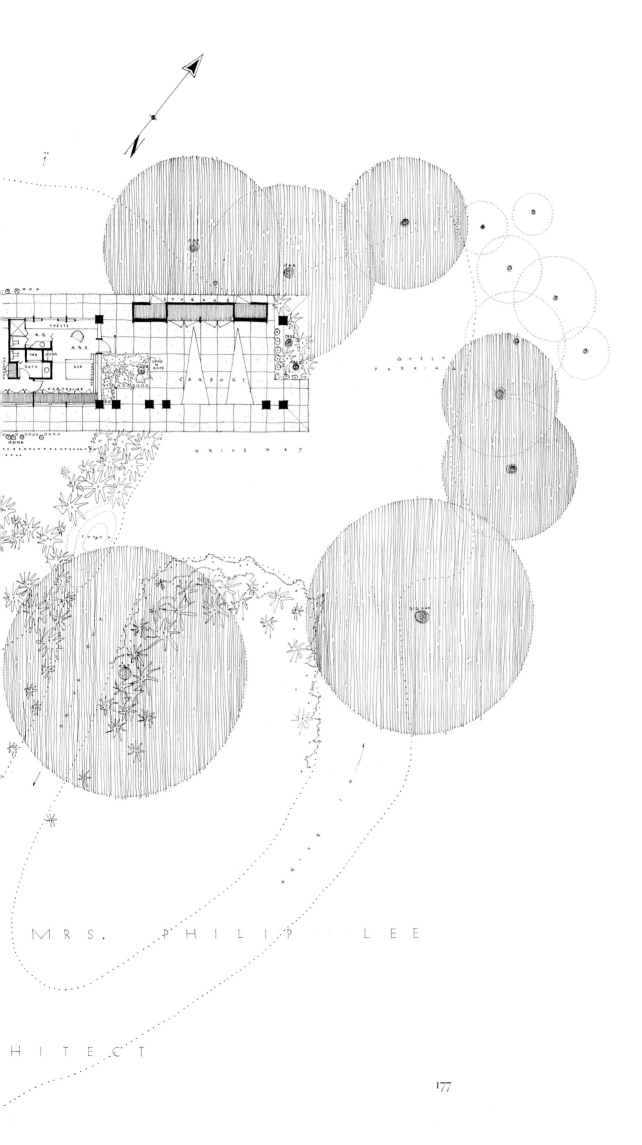

MRS. PHILIP LEE

HITECT

the ceilings were plaster. The sloped roof, with glazed gable ends, terminates onto a flat roofed "prow" encircling the home's perimeter that provides deep, sheltering overhangs to protect the home's interior from weather, penetrating sun, and glare. The prow's underside (i.e. soffit) actually sloped up towards the perimeter trim board, an unusual detail for Green. The majority of the floors were rough textured, colored concrete with the unit system expressed by the use of intersecting wood strips. Wood trim, shelving, casework, and built-in furniture were designed throughout, adding to the natural materials, textures, and patterns of the home that blended well with the natural setting in both the micro and macro environment.

After selling the home, Lee retained Green to design a complete condominium interior in Palo Alto. The home was eventually demolished along with the Paulsen residence next door by its new owner who had purchased both.

LENNERT RESIDENCE

One of Green's largest residential commissions was for Frank G. Lennert (1924–2013) and his wife Mary Ellen (1926–2007). Lennert was born in Hayward, California, and attended the University of California at Berkeley, graduating in 1947. In 1948 he was the first person with experience in electronics hired by the Ampex Corporation, a pioneering company in audio tape technology. He was an executive by the time he approached Green in 1959 to design a home for his impending retirement.

The site for this expansive home was a large parcel of wooded land in Woodside, which is on the San Francisco peninsula in San Mateo County. Green accounted for the heavily wooded site, and designed the home to nestle in amongst the redwoods in the south-west corner.

The plan of the single-story home, based on the four-foot-square module, was a modified T-shape, spreading out roughly in the north, east, and west directions. The center of the plan contained the dining and living spaces separated by five steps. This large space shared an expansive view to the southeast across the property. The north wing contained two guest bedrooms with their own bathrooms, and terminated with a three-bay carport. The east wing contained a study, music room, and a more secluded study at the far end. The western wing included the kitchen and laundry work spaces along with three additional bedrooms sharing a single bathroom, and the master bedroom suite.

Green's ingenious plan created multiple exterior areas for various functions – formal hard surfaced terraces, lawn terraces,

RESIDENCE FOR:

MR. AND MRS. FRANK G. LENNERT, WOODSIDE, CALIFORNIA.

AARON G. GREEN, A.I.A., ARCHITECT, SAN FRANCISCO, CALIFORNIA.

A   R E S I D E N C E   F O R :

MR. AND MRS. FRANK G. LENNERT,   WOODSIDE,   CALIFORNIA.

AARON   G.   GREEN,   A.I.A.,   ARCHITECT,   SAN   FRANCISCO,   CALIFORNIA.

fenced-in play areas, two pools, as well as many planters and areas designated for sculpture. Large expansive windows were designed along the southern side where the best views and privacy were secured. The floors were terrazzo with unit lines expressed by inlaid brass strips. Built-ins, as always, were installed throughout the home's interior.

The preliminary floor plan was unique in that gold ink was used to draw parts of it. Another unique feature, reminiscent of the golden spire at the Frank Lloyd Wright designed Marin County Civic Center, was a vertical spire that appears on the perspective drawings.

PLOT PLAN AND FLOOR PLAN   SCALE   1/8" = 1'-0"

A   R E S I D E N C E   F O R

M R.   A N D   M R S.   F R A N K   G.   L E N N E R T,   w

A A R O N   G.   G R E E N,   A. I. A.,   A R C H I T E C T

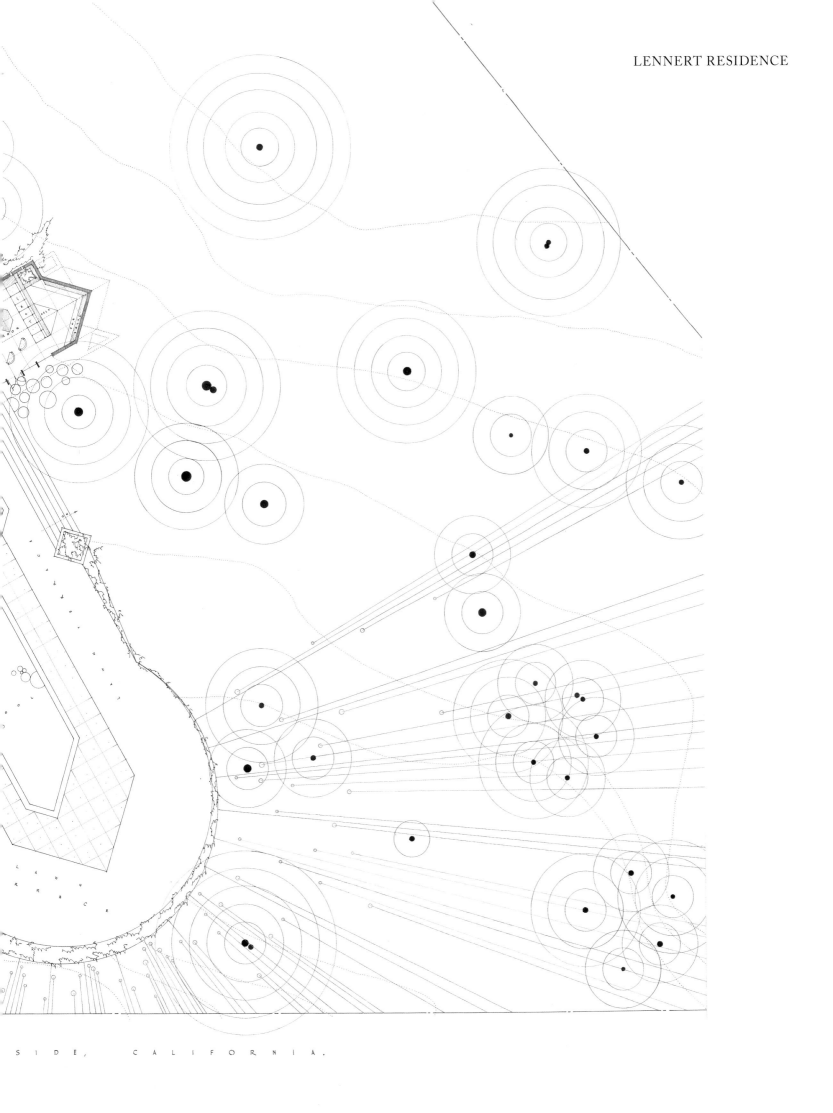

S I D E ,   C A L I F O R N I A .

A N   F R A N C I S C O ,   C A L I F O R N I A .

■ PAULSEN RESIDENCE
■

■ Besides being designed by Green, the Paulsen residence had many things in common with the Lee project designed two years earlier – both clients were doctors working in the same Palo Alto clinic, the properties were contiguous to each other, Paulsen's wife Margo was Philip Lee's sister, their architectural aesthetic and materials were quite similar, and, tragically, both homes have been demolished.

Green designed a large asymmetrical residence for James Paulsen, a psychiatrist, and his wife Margo, who was a physician, and their large family. It was built on a large, somewhat wild piece of property on Los Trancos Woods Road in the hills above Portola Valley, California, near Palo Alto. The steeply sloping, south facing panoramic view over the valley below was a primary ingredient in the

design of this elongated one-story L-shaped home. Typical of most of Green's work, this house quietly harmonizes with its site, naturally conforming to the general contours of the land.

Green's initial design manifested as a cross-shaped plan. The built version was more of an L-shaped plan with the two-car "car shelter" at the end of the short arm of the L. The intersection of the L is where the living spaces existed, with a large vaulted space containing a living area, piano alcove, and dining area off the kitchen. Both the living and piano alcove area projected outside the L.

Curtis Besinger, in his article published in *House Beautiful* magazine in July 1964, observed, "The living area is typical of the direct and open construction of the house. Its effectiveness as a place

R·E·S·I·D·E·N·C·E   F·O·R   D·R.   A·N·D   M·R·S.   J·A·M·E·S   P·A·U·L·S·E·N,   P·O·R·T·O·L·A   V·A·L·L·E·Y,   C·A·L·I·F·O·R·N·I

A·A·R·O·N   G.   G·R·E·E·N,   A·I·A.,   A·R·C·H·I·T·E·C·T,   S·A·N   F·R·A·N·C·I·S·C·O,   C·A·L·I·F·O·R·N·I·A

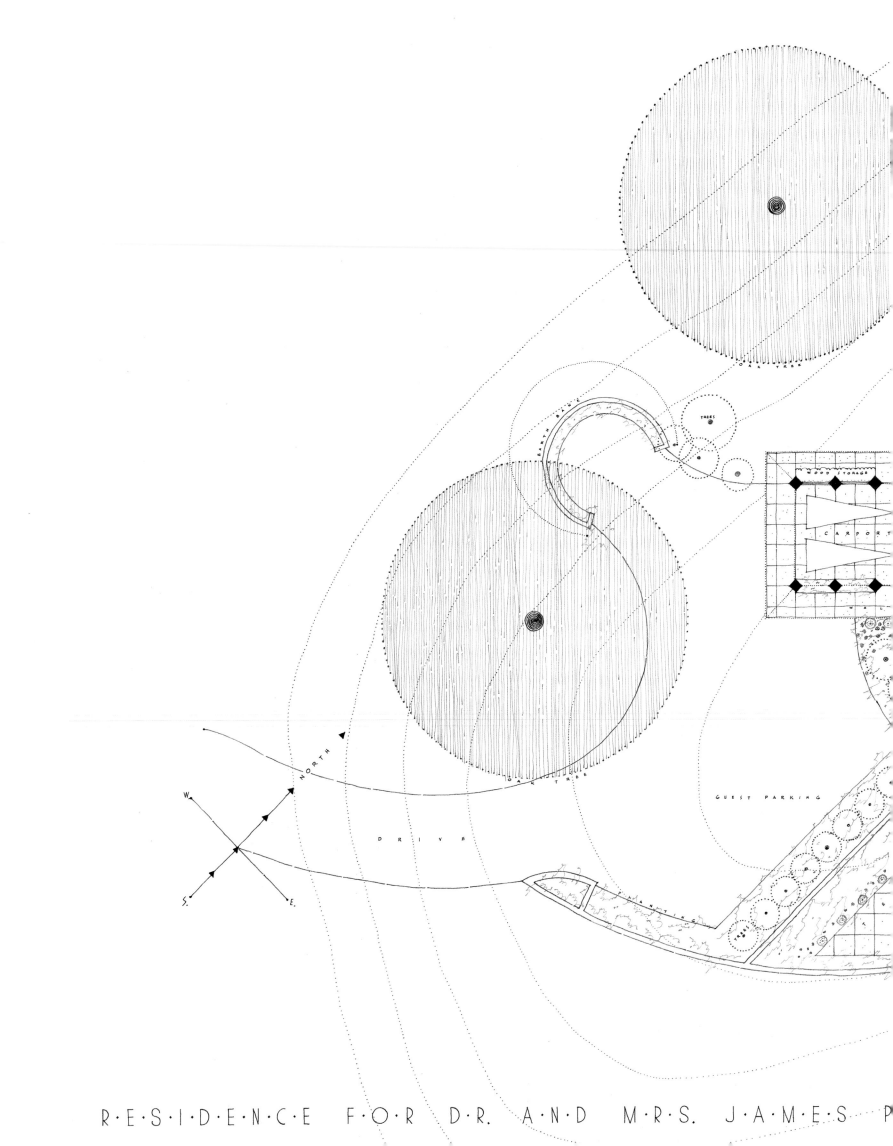

RESIDENCE FOR DR. AND MRS. JAMES P

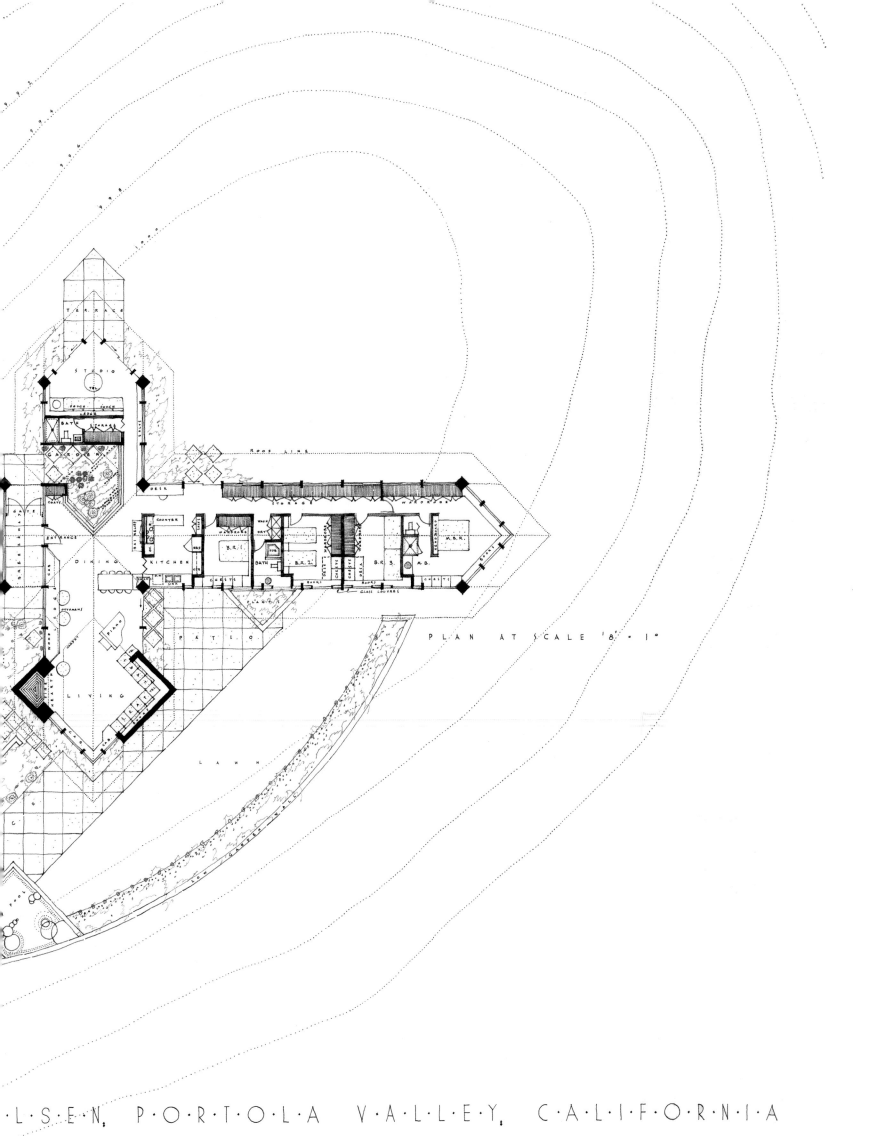

PLAN AT SCALE 1/8" = 1'0"

· L · S · E · N , P · O · R · T · O · L · A V · A · L · L · E · Y , C · A · L · I · F · O · R · N · I · A

in which to live is made up of elements that do not demand attention in themselves, but which, in a simple, direct manner provide a foreground frame for views of the landscape."[58] He continued, "Entering the main living area, you are presented with a broad panorama of the valley and the hills surrounding it. This view is framed between the counter forming the window sills, the piers supporting the roof, and the visor-like, flat roofed areas that pleasantly protects the viewer from the sunlight and glare."[59] The master bedroom suite, as well as three additional bedrooms and their associated bathrooms, were located in the long leg of the L. The short leg included the kitchen, a studio (with a bathroom), and the two-car carport. The client desired both coziness and spaciousness, which inspired Green's plan of the home as a grouping of alcoves.

Rotated piers constructed of four-inch by sixteen-inch adobe-like masonry capped with concrete support the wood beams and

tongue and groove wood roof decking above. The sloped roof with glazed gable ends terminated onto a flat roofed "prow" that encircled the home's perimeter and provided deep, sheltering overhangs to protect the home's interior from weather, penetrating sun, and glare. The majority of the floors are integrally colored concrete with the unit system scored into the surface.

The home's subsequent owner remodeled it without involving Green and, after purchasing the Lee house next door, chose to demolish both so that he could combine the properties and build a much larger home.

◼ ELDRED RESIDENCE
◼

◼   Green designed two different residential schemes for Dr. Roy Edward Eldred (1923–2004), a urologist, his wife Orchid Marcella (1926–2003), and their three children. The site was a steeply sloping waterfront site overlooking Richardson Bay in Belvedere, California. The first scheme in plan resembled a two-story solar hemicycle, however, instead of predominantly facing south for the best solar exposure it faced west to take full advantage of the views of Richardson Bay and the entire stretch of the Sausalito shoreline beyond. While distinctively unique in Green's portfolio, the design grew too large and proved to be cost prohibitive.

The 2,700-square-foot built version is a more compact rectilinear two-story plan, based on an eight-foot-square module. The primary axis of the linear home ran parallel to the contours of the site allowing the entire opus to nestle naturally into the hill. Green also recognized the site's paramount feature by orienting all the rooms along the west so that they would open out to the incredibly breath-taking views. After entering the home at its upper level from a bridge off an elevated street, the home dramatically opens up as a large volume with exposed wood beams and roof decking framing sweeping views of the Bay beyond. The principle living spaces are located on

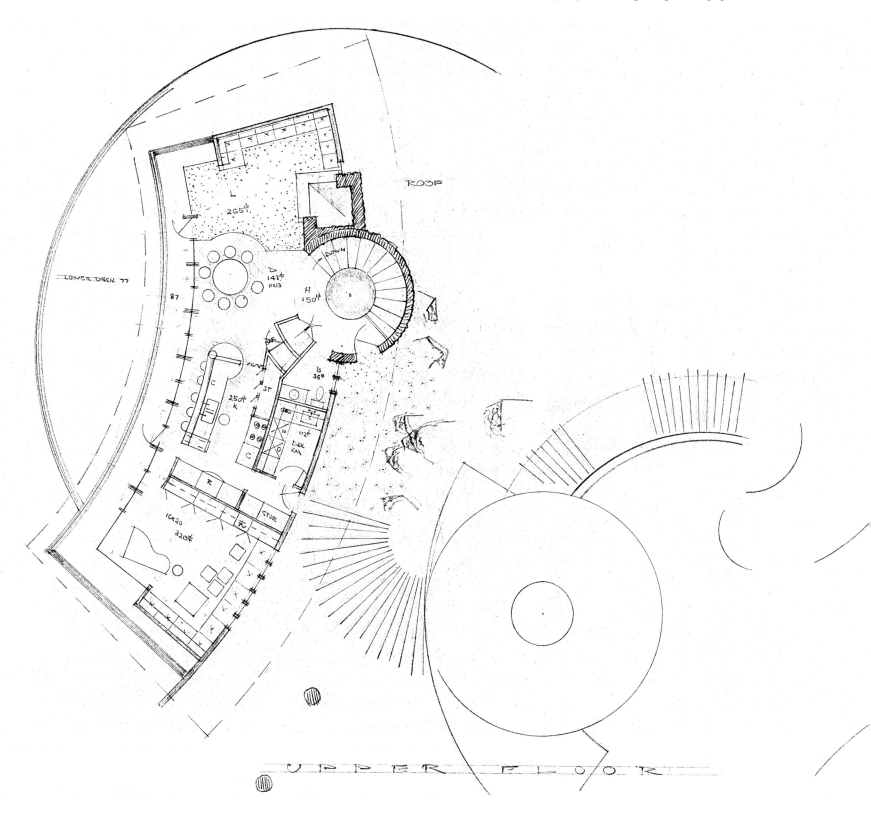

*The curvilinear plan on the left and following on pages 198–199 had
to be scrapped in favor of a more simple rectilinear concept.*

*Above, Aaron Green looks down at the completed residence from the
balcony of the carport, c. 1965.*

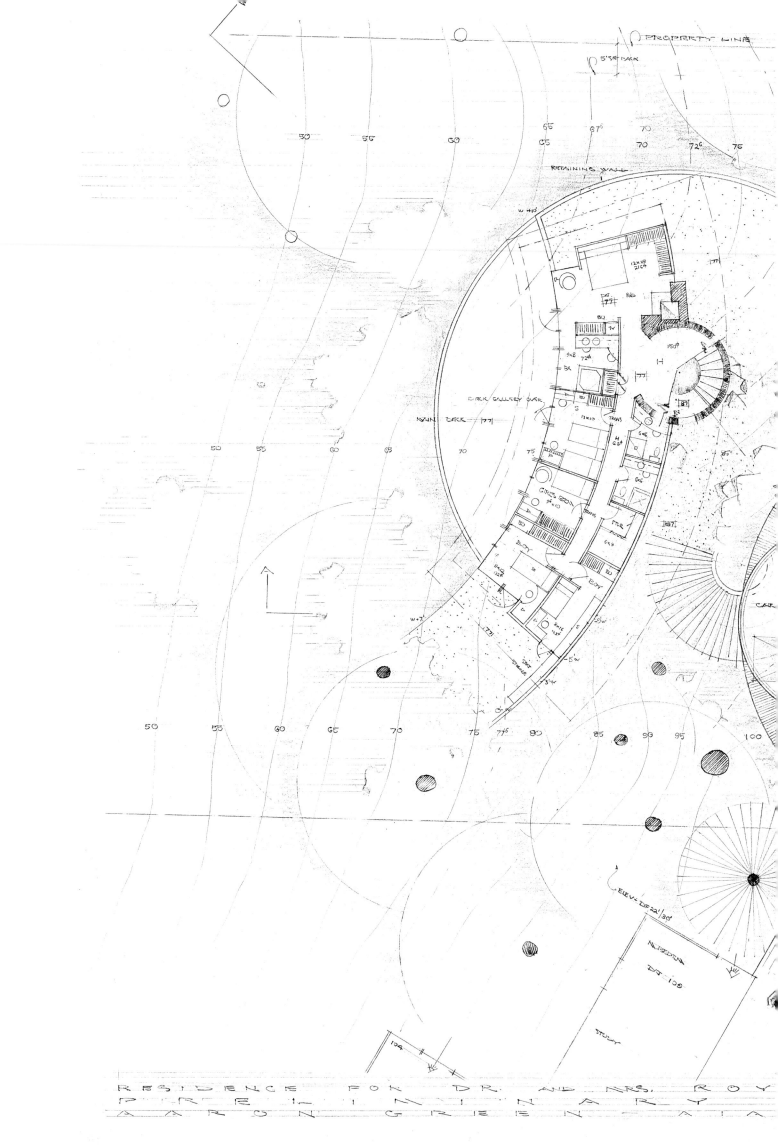

PROPERTY LINE

5' SETBACK

RETAINING WALL

RESIDENCE FOR DR. AND MRS. ROY
PRELIMINARY
AARON GREEN AIA

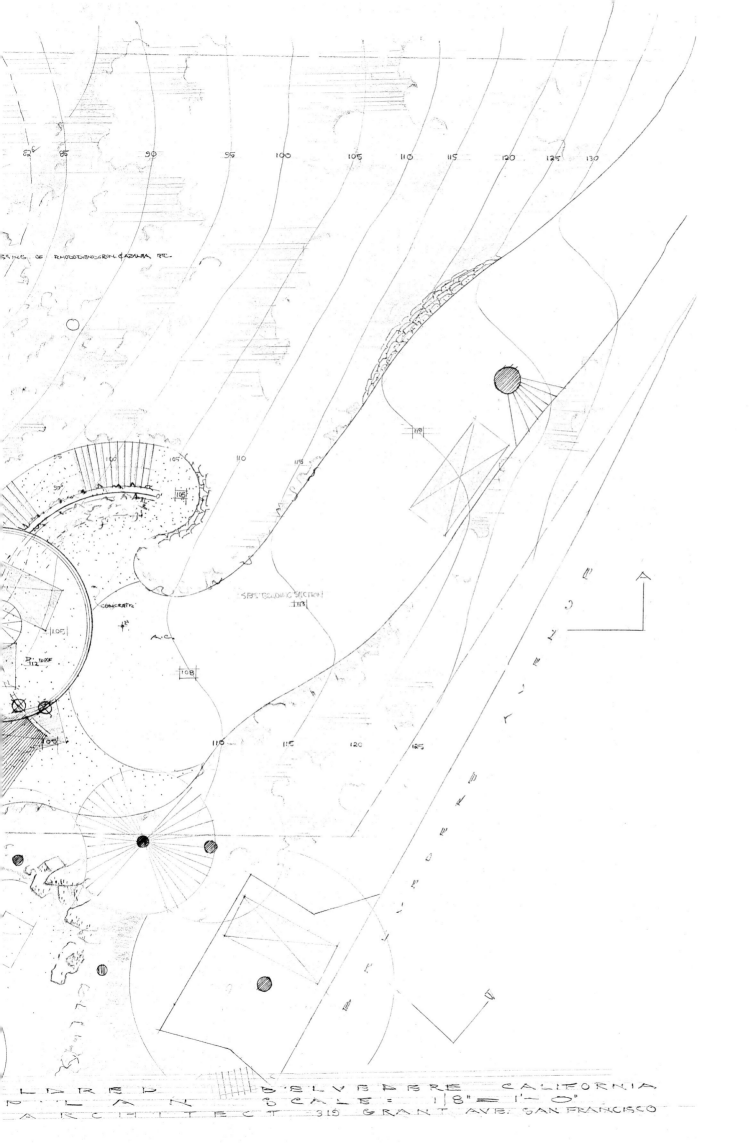

MASSING OF RHODODENDRON, AZALEA, ETC.

SEAT BACKING SECTION

CONCRETE

A.C.

B 12" ROOF

ALDREN   BELVEDERE   CALIFORNIA
PLAN   SCALE = 1/8" = 1'-0"
ARCHITECT 315 GRANT AVE. SAN FRANCISCO

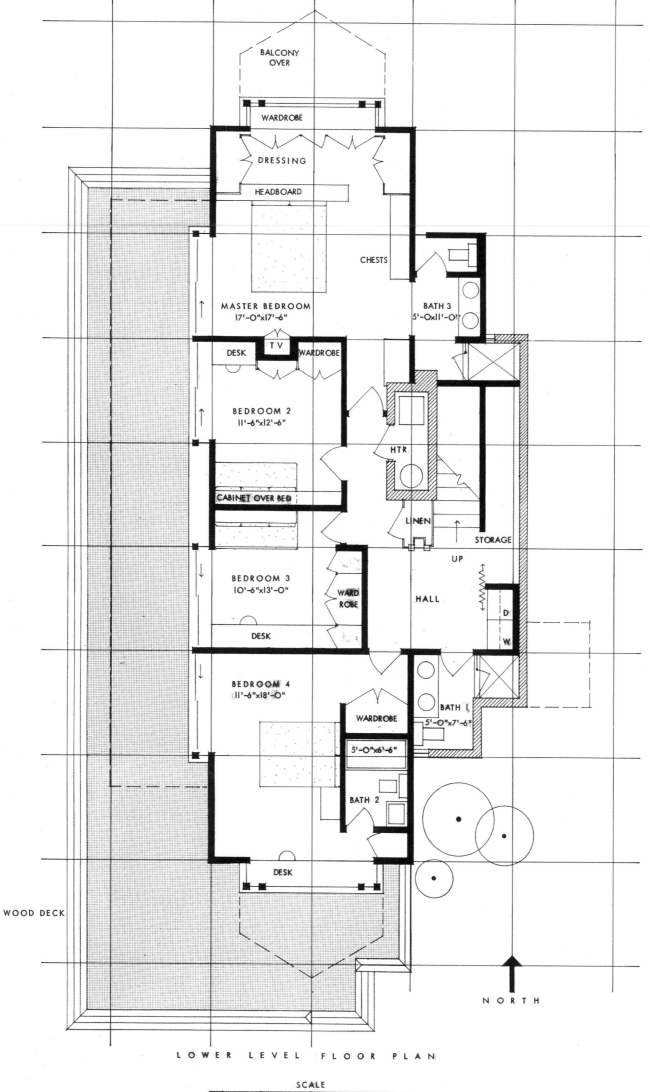

BALCONY
OVER

WARDROBE

DRESSING

HEADBOARD

CHESTS

BATH 3
5'-0x11'-0"

MASTER BEDROOM
17'-0"x17'-6"

DESK   T V   WARDROBE

BEDROOM 2
11'-6"x12'-6"

HTR

CABINET OVER BED

LINEN

STORAGE

UP

BEDROOM 3
10'-6"x13'-0"

WARD
ROBE

HALL

D

DESK

W

BEDROOM 4
11'-6"x18'-0"

WARDROBE

BATH 1
5'-0"x7'-6"

5'-0"x6'-6"

BATH 2

WOOD DECK

DESK

NORTH

LOWER LEVEL FLOOR PLAN

SCALE

0 1   4   8   16

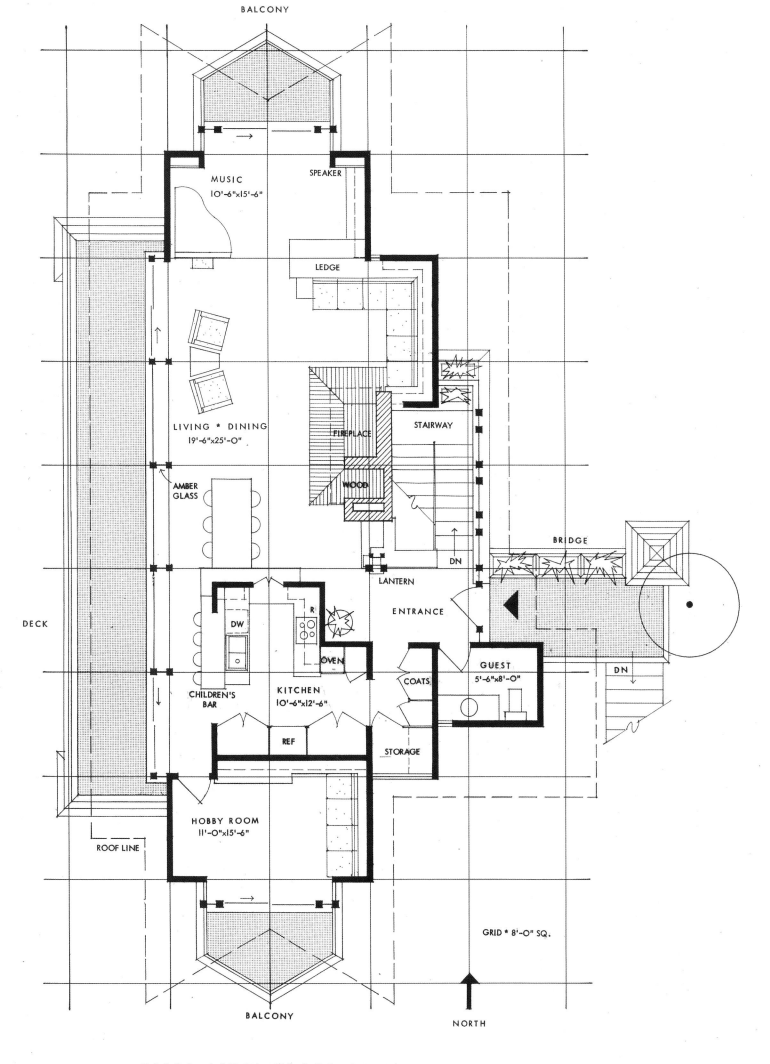

BALCONY

MUSIC
10'-6"x15'-6"

SPEAKER

LEDGE

LIVING * DINING
19'-6"x25'-0"

FIREPLACE

STAIRWAY

WOOD

AMBER
GLASS

DN

LANTERN

BRIDGE

ENTRANCE

DECK

DW

R

OVEN

CHILDREN'S
BAR

KITCHEN
10'-6"x12'-6"

COATS

GUEST
5'-6"x8'-0"

DN

REF

STORAGE

ROOF LINE

HOBBY ROOM
11'-0"x15'-6"

BALCONY

GRID * 8'-0" SQ.

NORTH

UPPER LEVEL FLOOR PLAN

SCALE

0 1   4   8   16

this upper level, and are organized as a single open space, masterfully delineated by its architecture, that provides areas for living, dining, and music. A large masonry fireplace serves this open room while anchoring the structure to the hillside. An interior, partially enclosed kitchen and work area divide the larger open living area from a smaller private study behind. Exterior decks at the north and south ends of the plan stretch the home's primary north south axis, and a third deck, forty feet long, is located along the majority of the west side. The lower level contains all four bedrooms and three bathrooms. All the bedrooms open out to the west onto an expansive wood deck.

Wood was the predominant material employed by Green for the house, exterior walls (horizontal redwood boards with vertical redwood battens), and roof (red cedar shingles). The low, sloped roof

provides sheltering overhangs to protect from the summer heat and inclement weather. Built-in cabinetry, furnishings, and custom lights were seamlessly incorporated.

SANTA CRUZ MEDICAL PLAZA

Iowa born Victor F. Bogard (1915–2002), after serving in World War II and receiving his discharge from the Navy, came to Santa Cruz, California, in 1947 and soon established Bogard Construction. His company began building homes but soon expanded beyond residential projects, building commercial and public buildings throughout Santa Cruz County. In 1962, acting as a developer for a group of doctors, he approached Green to design a medical complex at 550 Water Street in Santa Cruz, a rather flat site one mile northeast of the city's downtown. The names, noted on the drawings, were Doctors Ohta, Seftel, Monteith, Squire, Wileman, and Roussesau.

Green designed a casual master plan for the multi-building complex consisting of approximately 40,000 square feet made up of five buildings: four buildings surrounding the project's primary circular parking lot with a pavilion-like pharmacy building at its center. Three of the five buildings were built, the pharmacy building and two sprawling single-story structures containing the various doctor suites, both flanking the project's main entrance off Water Street. The two

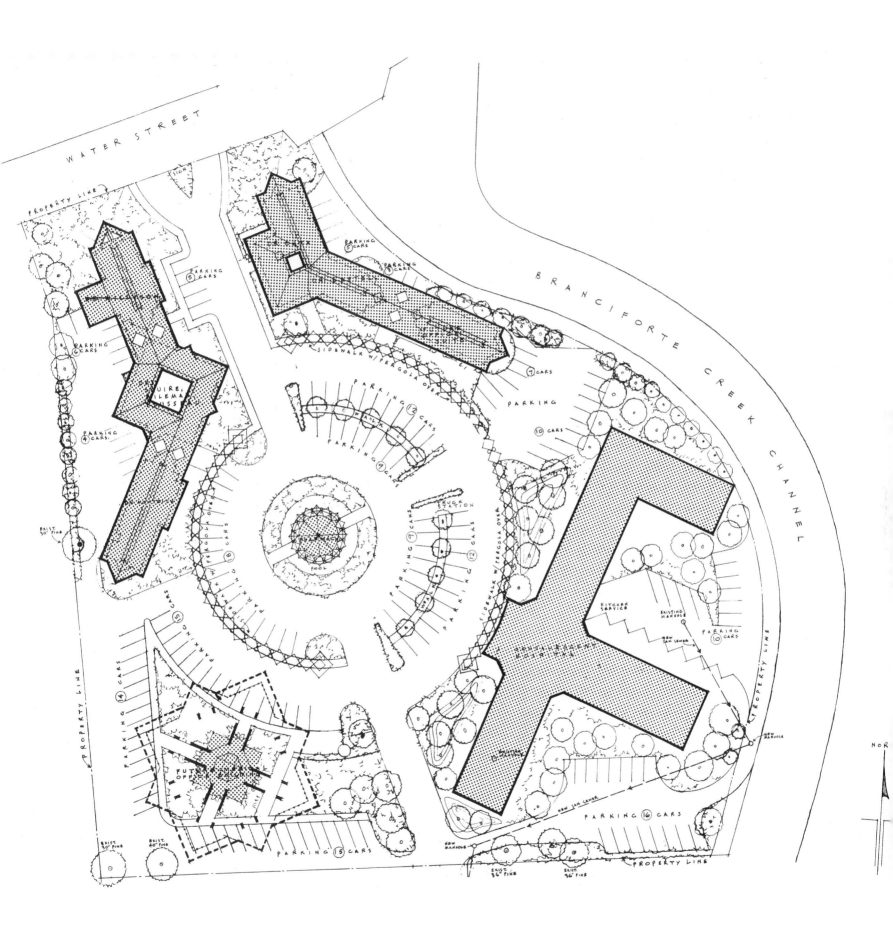

THE MEDICAL PLAZA FOR VICTOR BOGARD
SANTA CRUZ, CALIFORNIA   AARON G. GREEN A.I.A. ARCHITECT

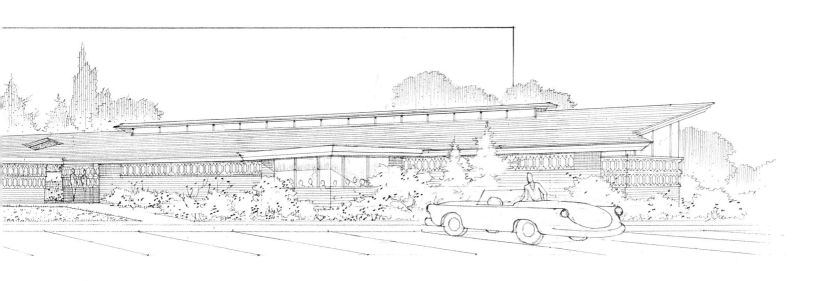

THE MEDICAL PLAZA FOR VICTOR BOGARD
SANTA CRUZ, CALIFORNIA   AARON G. GREEN A.I.A. ARCHITECT

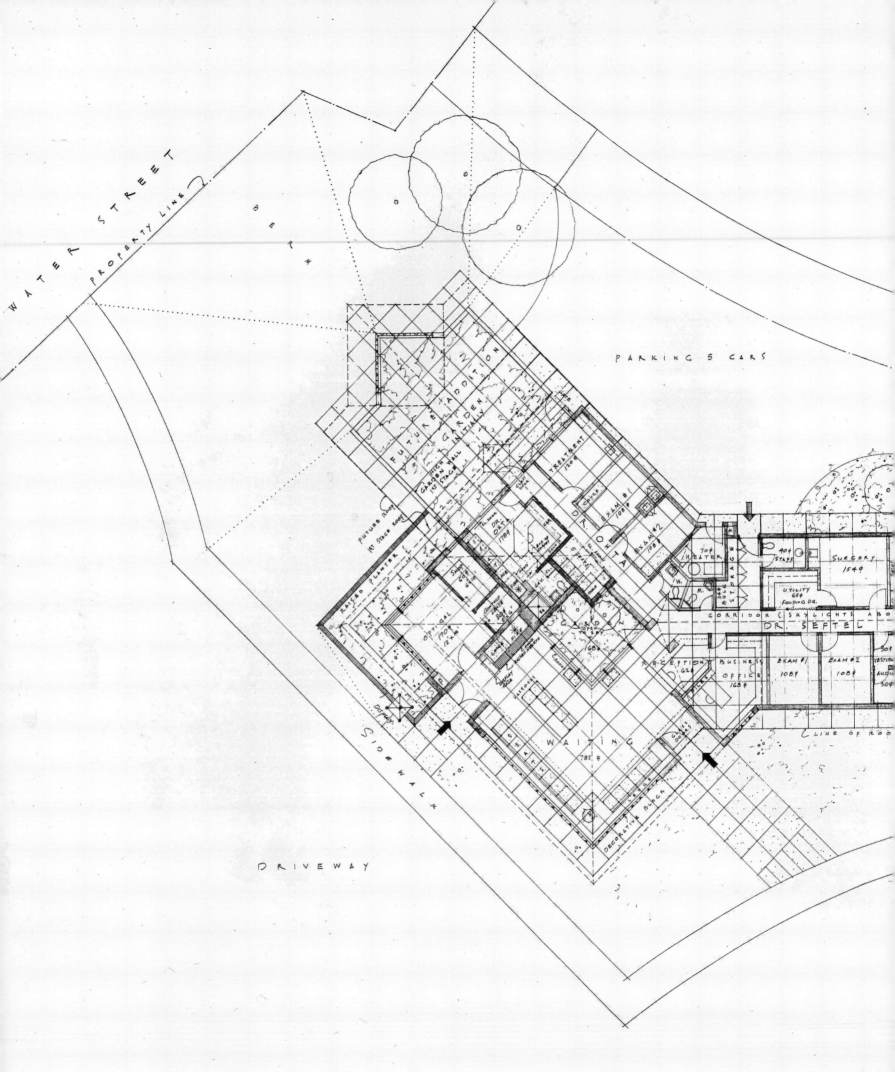

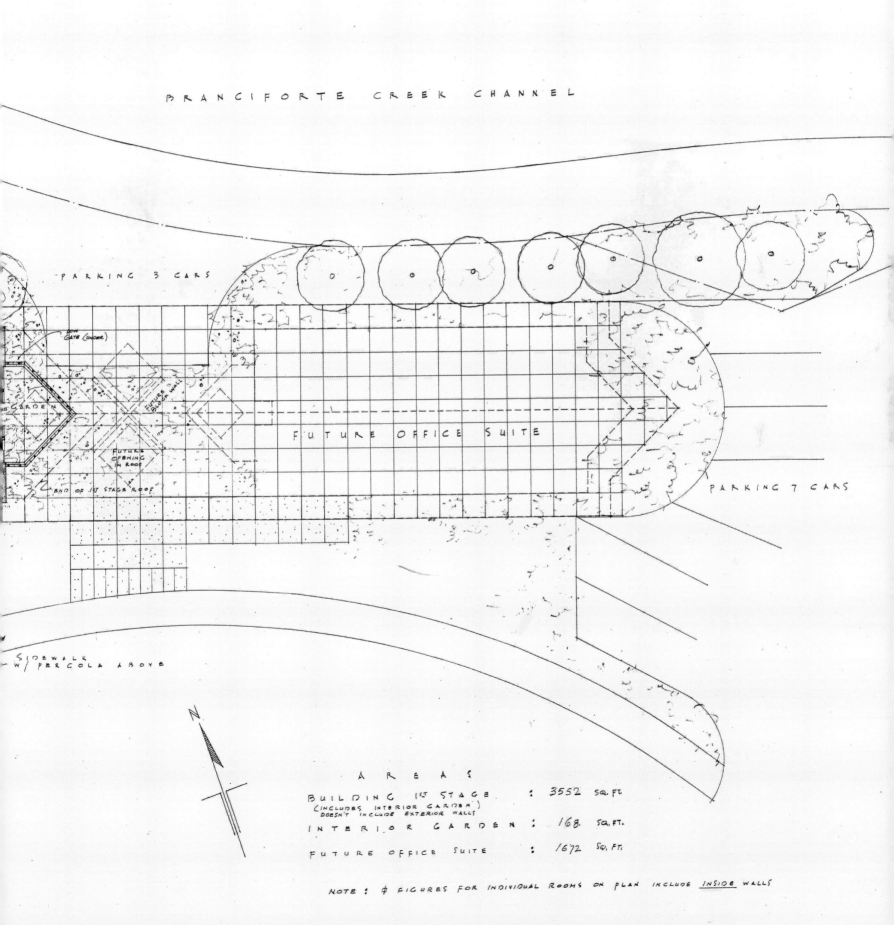

BRANCIFORTE CREEK CHANNEL

PARKING 3 CARS

LOW GATE (UNDER)

FUTURE PLAZA WALL

GARDEN

FUTURE OPENING IN ROOF

END OF 1ST STAGE ROOF

FUTURE OFFICE SUITE

PARKING 7 CARS

SIDEWALK
W/ PERGOLA ABOVE

N

A R E A S

BUILDING 1ST STAGE : 3552 SQ. FT.
(INCLUDES INTERIOR GARDEN)
DOESN'T INCLUDE EXTERIOR WALLS

INTERIOR GARDEN : 168 SQ. FT.

FUTURE OFFICE SUITE : 1672 SQ. FT.

NOTE: Ø FIGURES FOR INDIVIDUAL ROOMS ON PLAN INCLUDE INSIDE WALLS

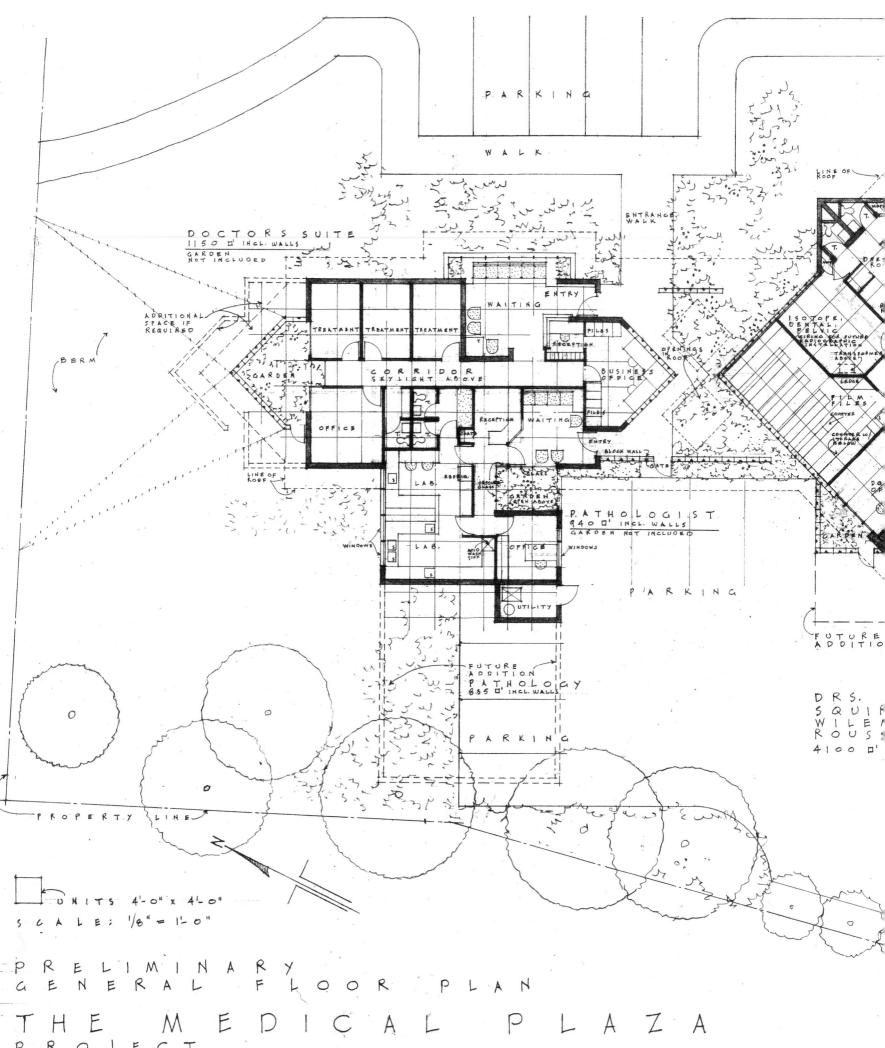

PARKING

WALK

LINE OF ROOF

ENTRANCE WALK

DOCTORS SUITE
1150 ☐' INCL. WALLS
GARDEN NOT INCLUDED

ADDITIONAL SPACE IF REQUIRED

BERM

WAITING   ENTRY

TREATMENT TREATMENT TREATMENT

FILES

RECEPTION

GARDEN

CORRIDOR
SKYLIGHT ABOVE

BUSINESS OFFICE

ISOTOPE,
DENTAL,
PELVIC
WIRING FOR FUTURE
REFRIGERATION
INSTALLATION

TRANSFORMER
ABOVE

LEDGE

OFFICE

RECEPTION   WAITING

FILES

FILM FILES

COUNTER

COUNTER W/
STORAGE
BELOW

ENTRY

COAT

LINE OF ROOF

BLOCK WALL
GATE

LAB.   REFRIG.

OBSCURE GLASS

GLASS

GARDEN
OPEN ABOVE

PATHOLOGIST
940 ☐' INCL. WALLS
GARDEN NOT INCLUDED

GARDEN

WINDOWS

LAB.

ACID
WASH
SINK

OFFICE

WINDOWS

PARKING

FUTURE
ADDITION

UTILITY

FUTURE
ADDITION
PATHOLOGY
835 ☐' INCL. WALLS

DRS.
SQUIR
WILEM
ROUSS
4100 ☐'

PARKING

PROPERTY LINE

N

☐ ⟶ UNITS 4'-0" x 4'-0"

SCALE: 1/8" = 1'-0"

PRELIMINARY
GENERAL FLOOR PLAN

THE MEDICAL PLAZA
PROJECT
FOR
VICTOR BOGARD
SANTA CRUZ, CALIFORNIA

A

SANTA CRUZ MEDICAL PLAZA

STORAGE

DIAGNOSTIC X-RAY N°2

DRESSING ROOMS

DARK ROOM

XEROMAT

CORRIDOR LIGHTS ABOVE

DIAGNOSTIC X-RAY N°3 TABLE

TRANSFORMER

FILES

RECEPTION

BUSINESS OFFICE

TYPING & MED. RECORDS

FILES

WAITING

ENTRY

CONSULTATION & OFFICE

X-RAY THERAPY 296 □'

LINE OF ROOF

PARKING

FUTURE ADDITION

ENTRANCE WALK

PARKING

OPENINGS IN ROOF

FILES

BUSINESS OFFICE 220 □'

RECEPT.

ENTRY

TOILET

UTILITY

EXAM 150 □'

ALTERNATE SINK LOCATION

EXAM 96 □'

DOCTOR'S OFFICE 144 □'

WAITING 442 □'

SKYLIGHT ABOVE

STORAGE

MED. UTILITY

EXAM 96 □'

DOCTOR'S OFFICE 144 □'

LINE OF ROOF

ADDITIONAL DOCTOR'S SUITE 850 □' INCL. WALLS

ENTRANCE WALK

DR. MONTEITH
2015 □' INCL. WALLS

EXAM 96 □'

EXAM 96 □'

DOCTOR'S & AMBUL. ENTRY

STORAGE

TREATMENT

TREATMENT

OFFICE

WAITING

ENTRY

RECEPTION

BUSINESS OFFICE

EXISTING 30" PINE

N G. GREEN A.I.A. ARCHITECT

MARCH 30, 1962
REVISED: APRIL 10, 1962
DR. MONTEITH
DRS. SQUIRE,

ENTRANCE PERSPECTIVE
THE MEDICAL PLAZA FOR VICTOR BOGARD
SANTA CRUZ , CALIFORNIA   AARON G. GREEN A.I.A. ARCHITE

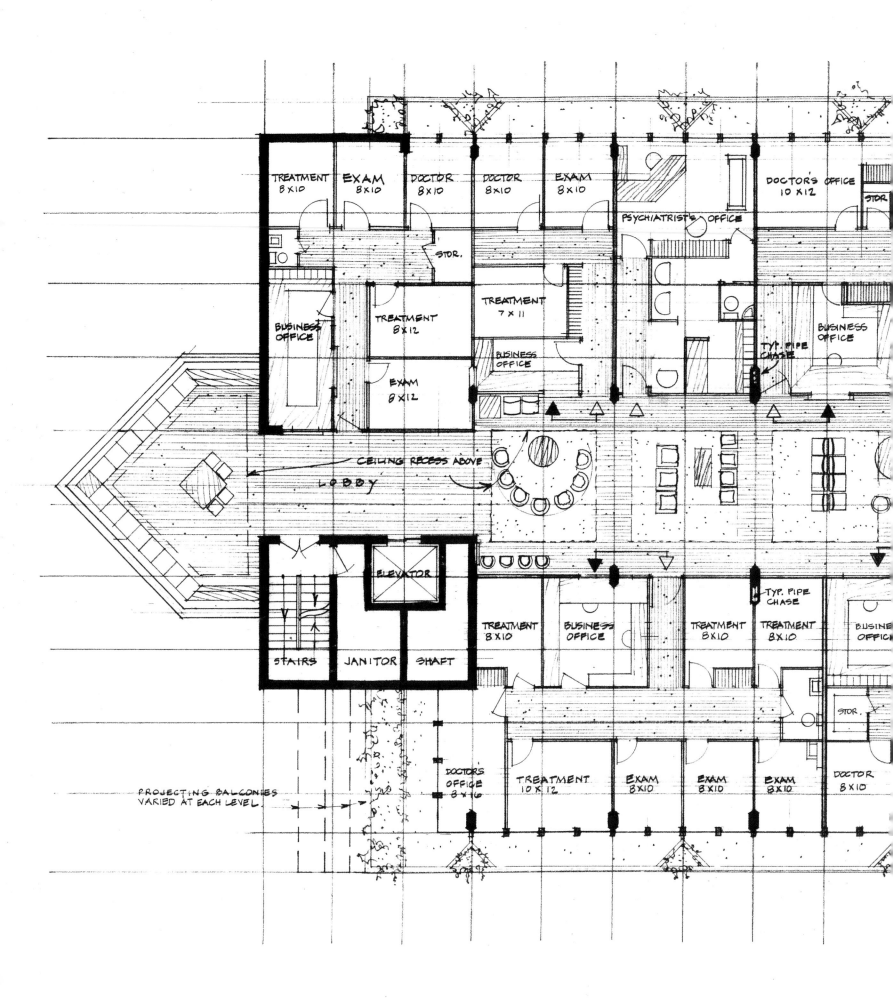

TREATMENT
8 X 10

EXAM
8 X 10

DOCTOR
8 X 10

DOCTOR
8 X 10

EXAM
8 X 10

DOCTOR'S OFFICE
10 X 12

STOR.

PSYCHIATRIST'S OFFICE

STOR.

BUSINESS OFFICE

TREATMENT
8 X 12

TREATMENT
7 X 11

TREATMENT
8 X 12

BUSINESS OFFICE

BUSINESS OFFICE

EXAM
8 X 12

TYP. PIPE CHASE

CEILING RECESS ABOVE

LOBBY

ELEVATOR

TREATMENT
8 X 10

BUSINESS OFFICE

TREATMENT
8 X 10

TREATMENT
8 X 10

BUSINESS OFFICE

TYP. PIPE CHASE

STAIRS

JANITOR

SHAFT

DOCTORS OFFICE
8 X 10

TREATMENT
10 X 12

EXAM
8 X 10

EXAM
8 X 10

EXAM
8 X 10

DOCTOR
8 X 10

STOR.

PROJECTING BALCONIES
VARIED AT EACH LEVEL

PROFESSIONAL OFFICE BUILDING FO

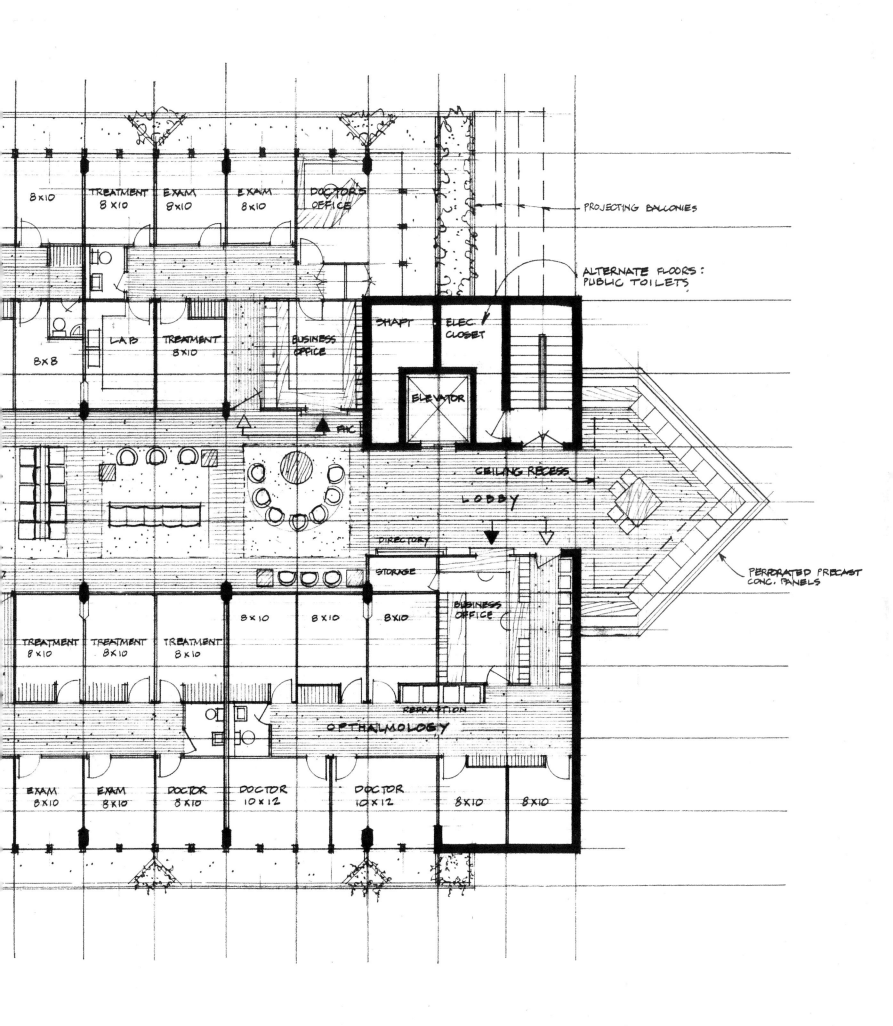

8x10   TREATMENT   EXAM   EXAM   DOCTOR'S
        8x10   8x10   8x10   OFFICE

PROJECTING BALCONIES

ALTERNATE FLOORS:
PUBLIC TOILETS

LAB   TREATMENT   BUSINESS   SHAFT   ELEC.
        8x10   OFFICE   CLOSET

8x8   ELEVATOR

8x8   CEILING RECESS

                                       LOBBY

                                       DIRECTORY

                                       STORAGE
                                                        PERFORATED PRECAST
                                                        CONC. PANELS

                                       BUSINESS
                                       OFFICE

TREATMENT   TREATMENT   TREATMENT   8x10   8x10   8x10
  8x10   8x10   8x10

                                    REFRACTION

                        OFTHALMOLOGY

EXAM   EXAM   DOCTOR   DOCTOR   DOCTOR   8x10   8x10
8x10   8x10   8x10   10x12   10x12

MR. VICTOR BOGARD   SCALE 1/8" = 1'-0"
                           NOVEMBER 30, 1970

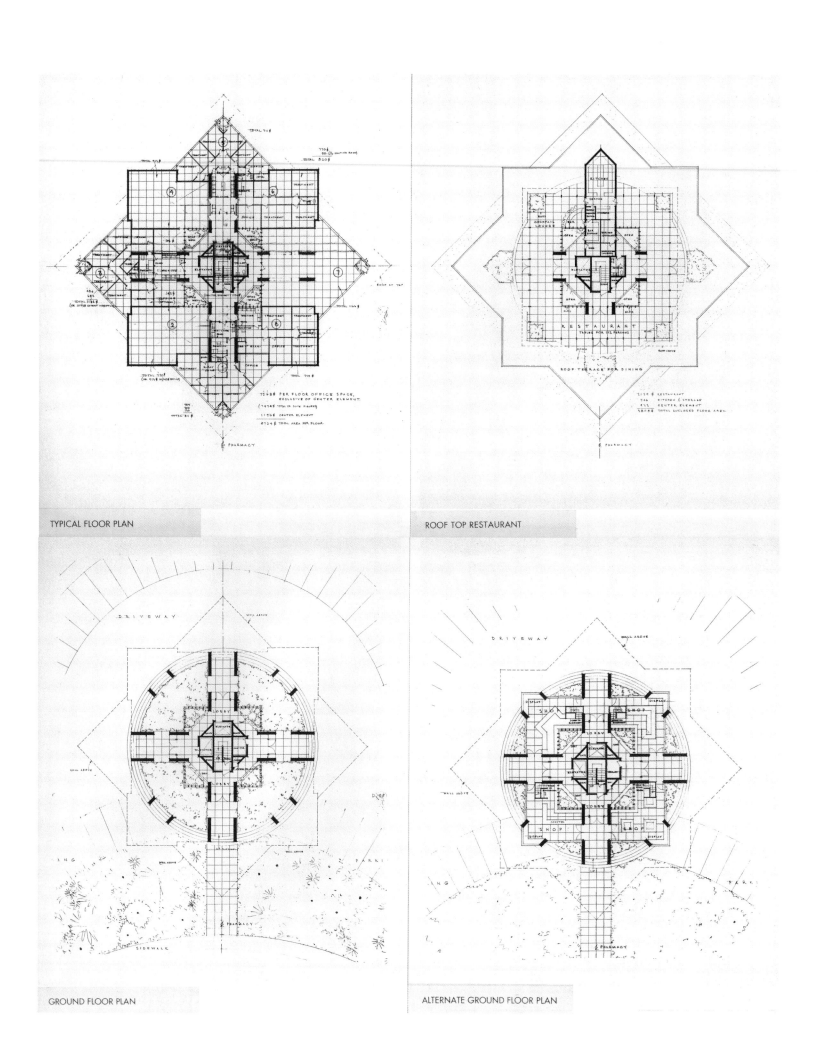

TYPICAL FLOOR PLAN

ROOF TOP RESTAURANT

GROUND FLOOR PLAN

ALTERNATE GROUND FLOOR PLAN

ROFESSIONAL OFFICE BUILDING
PRELIMINARY STUDY   SANTA CRUZ, CALIFORNIA
THE MEDICAL PLAZA FOR VICTOR BOGARD
AARON G. GREEN, A.I.A. ARCHITECT

buildings that weren't built were a large rambling convalescent hospital and a rather compact seven-story office tower. The latter (indicated as future) was planned as a medical office building on floors two through six, with four small shops surrounding the elevator core at the ground floor and a rooftop restaurant, with space to accommodate more than 120 persons, as its seventh floor.

Green sought to provide a calming, familiar, and comfortable experience for the patients, as opposed to the more institutional and sterile layouts found in most medical buildings. With its informality and overall warmth, this project was not too dissimilar from many of the homes he designed. The architecture of the single-story structures is unquestionably residential in scale and character with the buildings all laid out on a predominant eight-foot-square module. A large square component anchored each of the two sprawling buildings with smaller, narrower wings extending out. Consistent exterior materials provided a cohesive palette: four-inch by sixteen-inch brick-red "combed-face" masonry blocks, windows shuttered with perforated wood panels in geometric patterns, and tile roofs. The low-sloping, sheltering roofs dramatically projected beyond their terminating walls. The interiors contained terra cotta colored concrete floors (with radiant heating) and plaster walls and ceilings. Each building contained a garden atrium and fireplace that were planned for future

expansion. The diminutive pharmacy building at the core of the development (figuratively and literally) is an octagonal building topped with a pyramid roof. Along the perimeter of the circular parking, Green designed a playful steel pergola structure that was supported by steel columns and complete with integral lighting that enveloped the circular sidewalk.

■

■

■

■ LILIENTHAL RESIDENCE
■

■   Little is known about this project beyond a property survey and two partially completed preliminary sketches – one of the floor and the other a framing plan. What does exist suggests a project that quite possibly was Green's most daring departure from his more practiced and comfortable vernacular, transcending his own typology learned from Wright, with a uniquely curvilinear plan that organized its structure. Green himself recognized this, as he selected it to be illustrated as an example of his work in a book that featured work by Frank Lloyd Wright apprentices.

In 1962, Dorothy Fries Lilienthal (1892–1971), widow of financier Jesse W. Lilienthal, Jr. (1887–1952), commissioned Green

to design a house to be built on her family property, a 3.3-acre parcel at 40 Baywood Avenue in Hillsborough, California (interestingly, the line between San Mateo and Hillsborough bisected the property). The new house was to replace the long-standing family homestead built in 1902.

The house was actually the interstitial spaces contained within an arrangement of partial circles (possibly a response by Green to save several large trees on site). Green's free flowing plan was anchored in the center by a dominating masonry core consisting of the fireplace and chimney and two bathrooms. Rotating around this core was the entrance gallery feeding the living and dining rooms and ter-

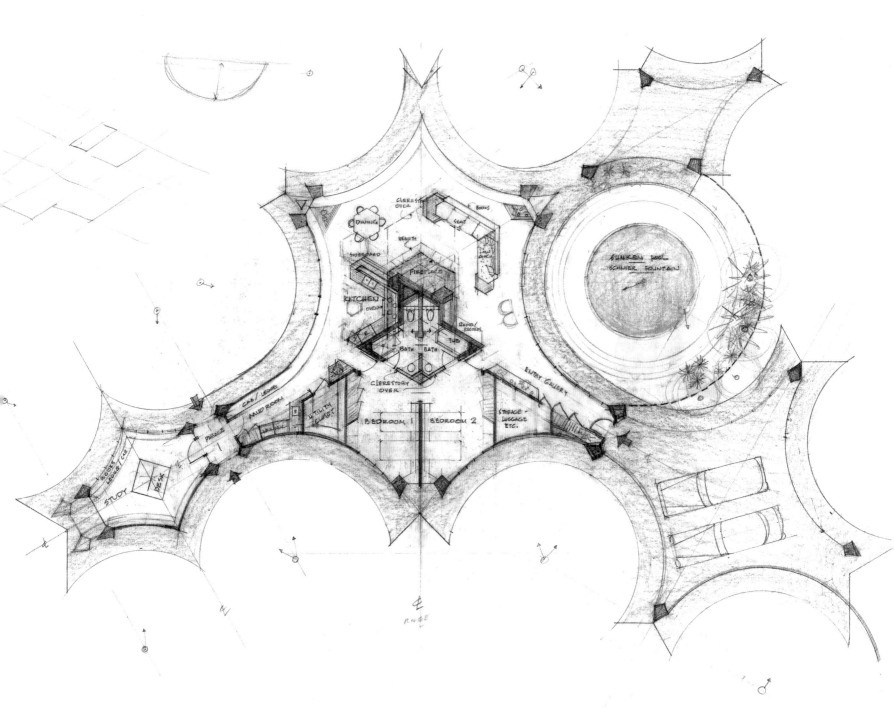

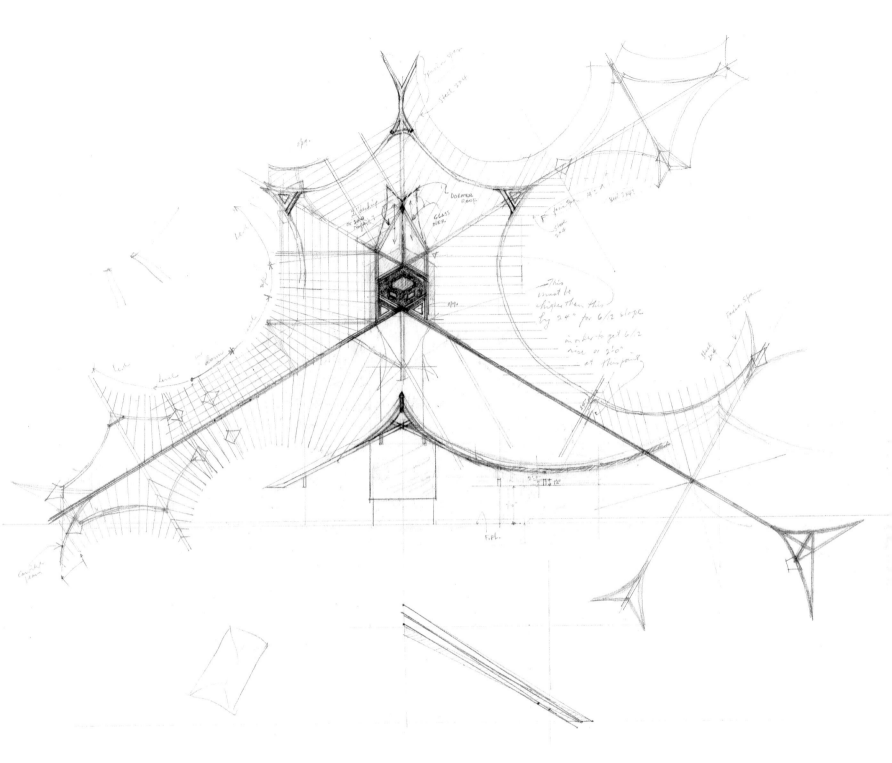

minating at the kitchen. In the opposite direction was a study and second entrance with a mud room that terminated at the kitchen as well. Two bedrooms and a study completed the composition. Off the main entry gallery, and in full view from the living room, Green designed a large, exterior, sunken circular pool featuring a "Schnier sculpture."[60]

The overall plan, while free flowing, was rather compact. The framing plan for the roof suggests that Green was thinking of heavy timbers, glue laminated beams, wood, and steel, while the curving fascia was to have been built up with 3/8-inch-thick wood strips. No further sketches or drawings exist to suggest the materials Green contemplated for the exterior, although the floor plan indicates large expanses of glass.

Atypical to his standard operating procedure of showing the client designs only after they were completely resolved, Green was quite excited about this particular design direction, yet apprehensive as to whether the client would share his enthusiasm. So he decided to share the incomplete floor plan, basically a drawn-to-scale, rough sketch, with Mrs. Lilienthal. Her reaction was not at all positive, and Aaron was, as Jan Novie recalled, "pretty much fired on the spot."

IVES DENTAL OFFICE

In 1956, Green designed a modest residence for Dr. Harold Nathan Ives (1918–1997) and his wife Elinor on a hillside site overlooking a tree filled valley just north of Cloverdale, California. It was a single-story modified T-shaped plan with a broad reaching, sheltering, wood-shingle roof. The terminals of two legs ended in rotated squares, one containing the large living and dining room and the other the master bedroom suite. The third leg was the two-car carport. The building was constructed of glass, concrete masonry, and redwood board with batten walls; construction finished in 1958.

Five years later, in 1963, Ives approached Green for a new building to house his dental practice on a small lot at 114 North Main Street in Cloverdale, within a mile of his home. While the project wasn't large, Green delivered a gem for his loyal client. The

single-story rectangular building was, like Ives' house, based on a four-foot-square module. Upon entering you came to a waiting room and reception desk, and the remainder of the building housed a business office, five operating rooms, a lab, and a private office for Ives. The operatory rooms faced small, enclosed gardens. Rich Lowry, who worked for Green in the 1960s recalled, "Dr. Ives was a solo practitioner. The entire dental building was designed with great care around the way Dr. Ives preferred to practice."[61]

The exterior was straightforward with minimal materials – concrete masonry and glass. The concrete masonry was laid with narrow vertical slits that allowed light to enter but restricted the view. The roof was flat and featured a wide overhang with an uninterrupted, deep, redwood fascia broken up by vertical wood batten strips. A

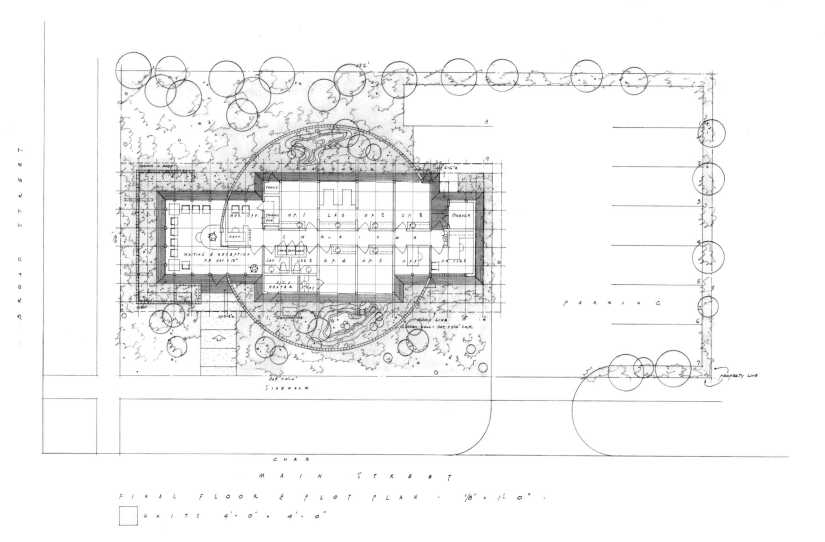

DENTAL   OFFICE   BUILDING   FOR   DR.   HAROLD   N.   IVE

CLOVERDALE,   CALIFORNI

AARON   G.   GREEN,   AIA,   ARCHITECT

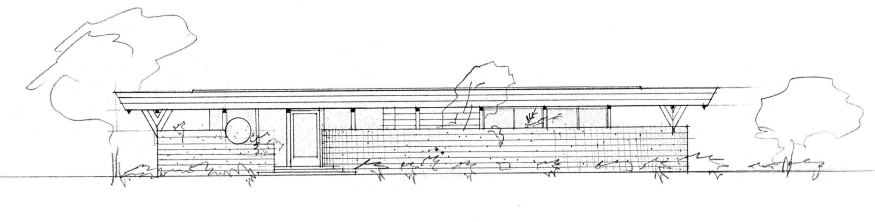

FRONT ELEVATION   APR 17

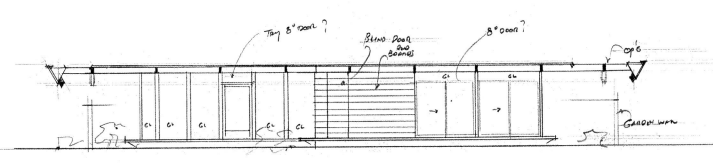

INSIDE GARDEN SECTION

APR 7

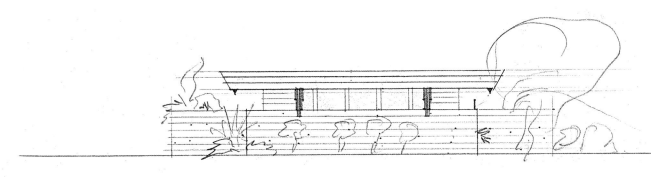

SIDE ELEVATION

APR 17

234

unique aspect of Greens design was a circular garden wall constructed of concrete masonry units that was integrated with the building's rectangular geometry. The circular wall was a device to provide privacy for the patients from onlookers on the street while allowing them views into the surrounding gardens between the exterior building wall and circular masonry wall. The calming view into the gardens for the patients was obviously important in Green's design.

ORIENTAL GARDENS SHOPPING CENTER

Peter J. Pasetta (1904–1979) and his wife Alice P. (1906–1999) were well-known Santa Clara builders and developers. In 1961 they commissioned Taliesin Associated Architects, Frank Lloyd Wright's successor firm, to design a project christened the "Court of the Seven Seas" on a forty-acre oceanfront site on West Cliff Drive in Santa Cruz overlooking Monterey Bay. It was to consist of an international trade center, hotel, motel, conference center, theater, gallery, and chapel. Designed by William Wesley Peters, President of the Taliesin Associated Architects, its estimated cost was in the neighborhood of $4,000,000 and was never built. Green did not play a part in this California venture, however, two years later, in 1963, the Pasettas approached Green to design a shopping center on thirteen acres at the northwest corner of Monroe Street and Scott Boulevard.

The shopping center consisted of a Safeway supermarket anchoring numerous smaller retail spaces, a lounge and restaurant (with a banquet center), a drugstore, a bank, and a hardware store. The bank became a liquor store as the design continued to be developed. Beyond the hardware store, Green placed an automobile service station on the perimeter of the property facing Monroe Street. Green received prototypical drawings for their preferred store layout from the corporate offices of Safeway, a supermarket chain founded in 1911. Over objections from Safeway, Green modified the provided plans to suit the site, project's exterior concept and materials for continuity with the entire shopping center.

The design aesthetic undertook many manifestations while the geometrically strong master plan remained relatively similar in all iterations. The overall plan was V-shaped, with the supermarket anchoring one wing and the hardware store the other. The lounge and restaurant were located at the apex of the V. For the enjoyment of the shoppers, Green developed lush areas of planting in the body of the V, including a water feature and two bridges. They eventually settled on a theme for the shopping center. Initially referred to on the design drawings as the Garden Shopping Center it evolved into the "Oriental Gardens Shopping Center" with the interior garden area becoming more in line with a true Japanese garden. Green adjusted the exteriors to reflect an Asian-island aesthetic, mostly modifying the roof forms, slopes, and elements. The deep overhangs of the roof and their steeply raked wood fascias were paramount throughout the complex providing shelter from sun and inclement weather for the shoppers. Green used storefront glass and brick red concrete ma-

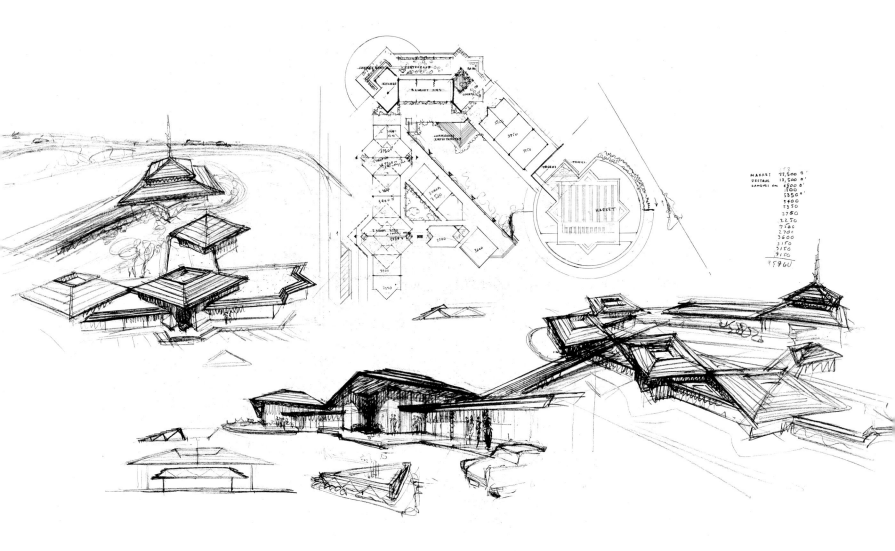

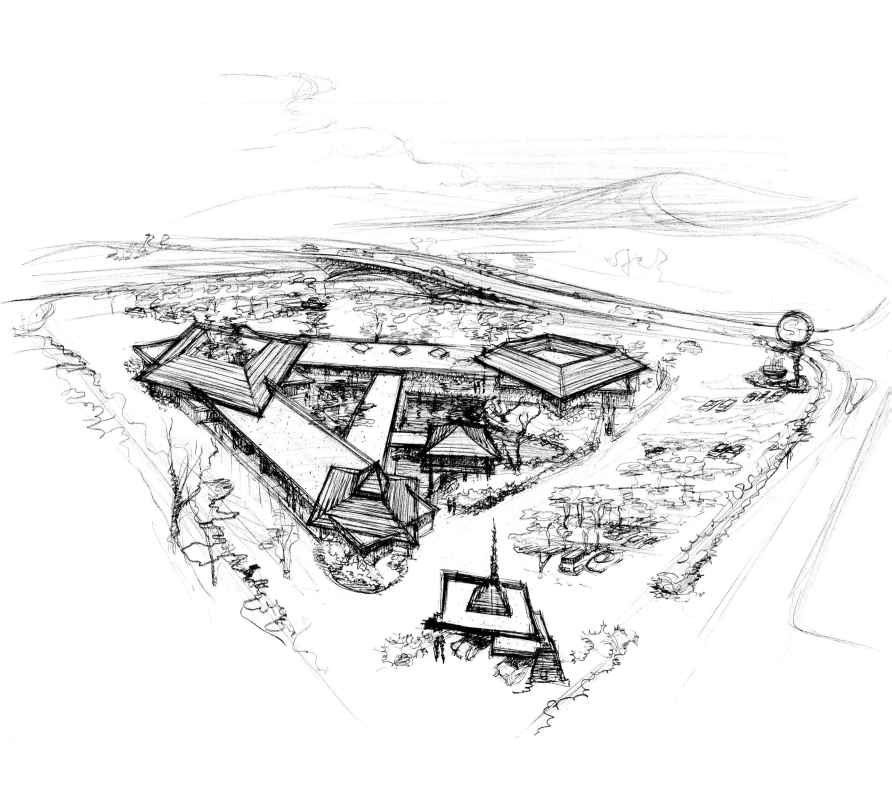

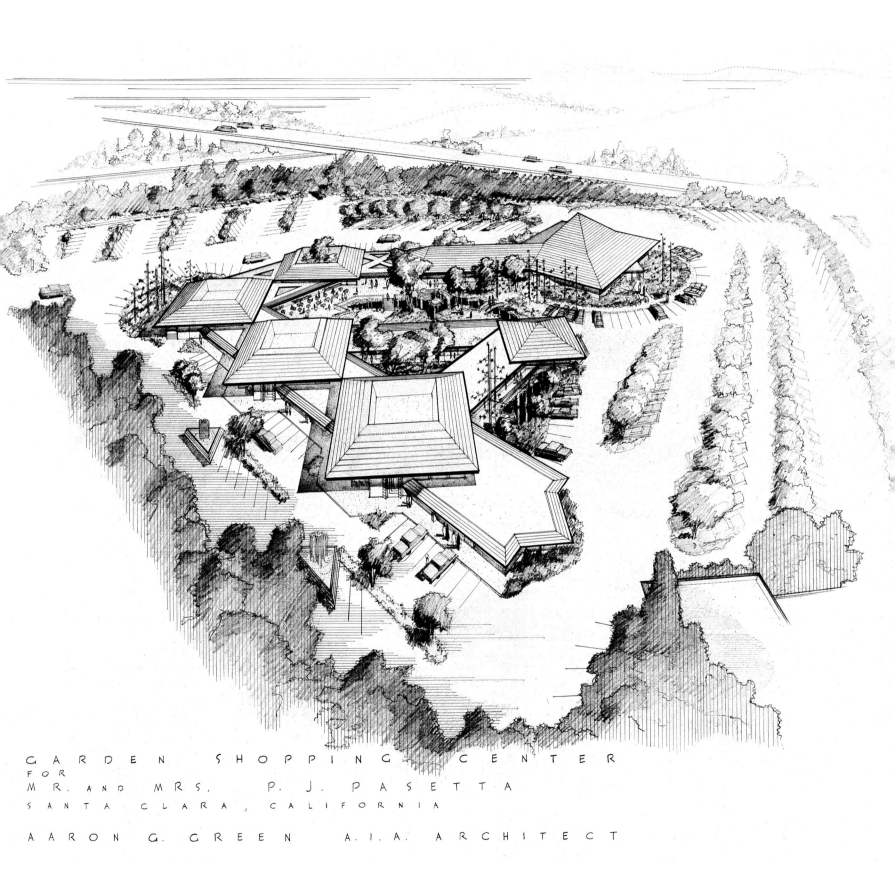

GARDEN SHOPPING CENTER
FOR
MR. AND MRS. P. J. PASETTA
SANTA CLARA, CALIFORNIA

AARON G. GREEN A.I.A. ARCHITECT

ORIENTAL GARDEN SHOPPING CENTER
SANTA CLARA   CALIFORNIA
AARON G GREEN   A·I·A·   ARCHITECT

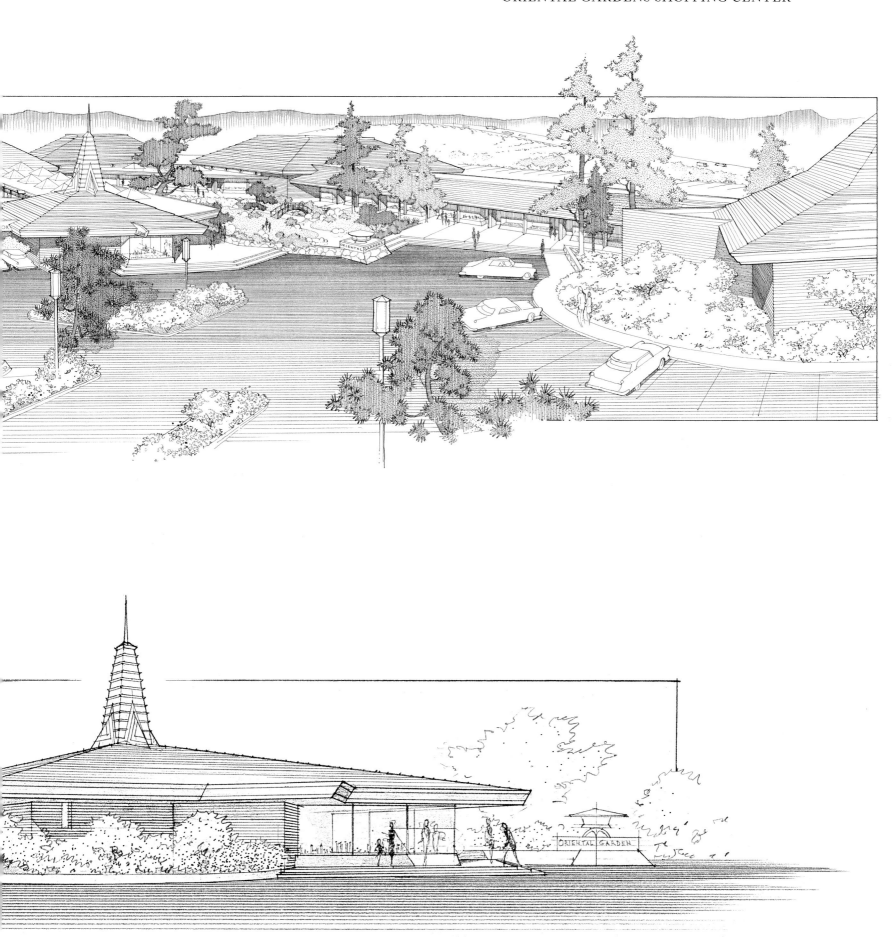

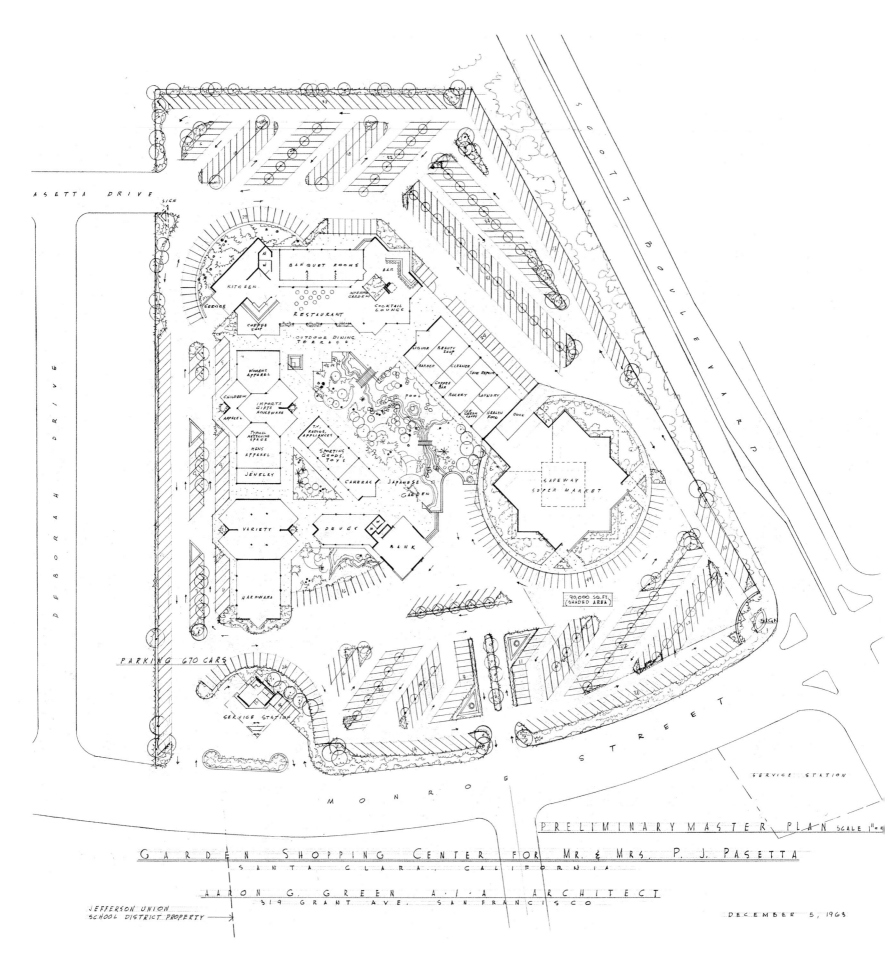

ASETTA DRIVE

SCOTT BOULEVARD

DEBORAH DRIVE

BANQUET ROOMS

BAR

KITCHEN

INTERIOR GARDEN

SERVICE

COCKTAIL LOUNGE

RESTAURANT

COFFEE SHOP

OUTDOOR DINING TERRACE

LIQUOR

BEAUTY SHOP

BARBER

CLEANER

SHOE REPAIR

COFFEE BAR

BAKERY

LAUNDRY

WOMENS APPAREL

CHILDREN APPAREL

IMPORTS GIFTS HOUSEWARE

POOL

HEALTH FOOD

FRESH CANDY

DOCK

TV RADIOS APPLIANCES

TYPICAL RETAILING SPACE

MENS APPAREL

SPORTING GOODS TOYS

JEWELRY

CAMERAS

JAPANESE GARDEN

SAFEWAY SUPER MARKET

VARIETY

DRUGS

BANK

HARDWARE

90,000 SQ. FT. (SHADED AREA)

PARKING 670 CARS

SIGN

SERVICE STATION

MONROE STREET

SERVICE STATION

PRELIMINARY MASTER PLAN SCALE 1"=5

GARDEN SHOPPING CENTER FOR MR. & MRS. P. J. PASETTA

SANTA CLARA, CALIFORNIA

AARON G. GREEN A.I.A. ARCHITECT

319 GRANT AVE. SAN FRANCISCO

JEFFERSON UNION SCHOOL DISTRICT PROPERTY →

DECEMBER 5, 1963

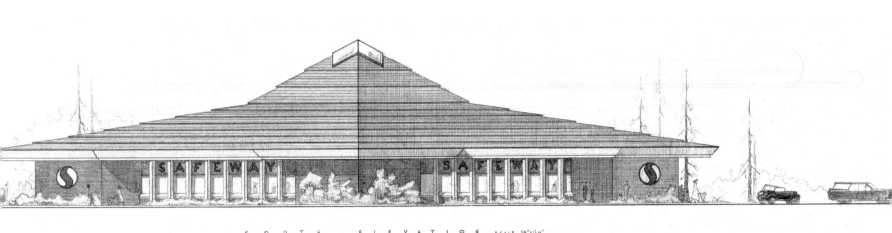

S O U T H   E L E V A T I O N   SCALE 1/8"=1'-0"
S A F E W A Y   S T O R E   # 6 9 9
O R I E N T A L   G A R D E N   S H O P P I N G   C E N T E R

sonry for the exterior walls and incorporated patterned, cast-in-place concrete elements as contrast while exposing the structural glue-laminated wood beams to view. Flat red interlocking concrete tiles were used for the roofing shingles.

Construction of the Safeway began in June 1965. While the shopping center served the area's population for many years it was eventually demolished and replaced with an apartment complex. Incredibly, Green's diminutive but striking gas station has quietly survived (just east of Deborah Drive). It is the only service station Green designed that was actually built in his entire oeuvre.[62]

■

■

■

WEIR OFFICE BUILDING

Robert Howard Weir (1922-), an attorney, established his law practice in 1957. Early in 1963 he approached Green to design an office building for his small practice with space built for future expansion. Green's design was an exercise on how to maximize rentable space for his client.

The project was located at 93 West Julian Street, north of San Jose's downtown core. The small, slightly sloping, narrow parcel was hemmed between West Julian Street to the south, Market Street to the west, and Little Market Street to the east. From Julian Street the lot widened somewhat until the parcel ended against an existing building to its north. Green, wanting to provide the largest building footprint possible, elevated the building over a partially below-grade parking level. This allowed the building to be built to the setbacks, maximizing rentable area while still providing the necessary amount of parking. Around the perimeter of the site, outside the building setbacks, Green added planted earthen berms and expansive landscaping to screen the cars.

The rectangular building was almost 4,800 square feet in size. Its plan was based on a three-foot-square module, an atypical choice for Green. The design provided nine private offices for the attorneys around the building's perimeter, each with a skylight and high windows that provided light while maintaining privacy. An unusual feature of this project was that the offices, each approximately twelve feet by eighteen feet, contained both a work area and a conference area that could be separated by an accordion door. A larger private office, located in the building's northwest corner, included a fireplace with a raised hearth. Support staff areas, a library, and a large conference room were located in the building's core area with the reception and waiting area at the building's south end. Throughout the offices Green detailed built-in furnishings, casework, and shelving. His building seamlessly integrated the necessary and functional building systems while providing interior light coves, changes in ceiling planes, and other elements that promoted a comfortable working environment.

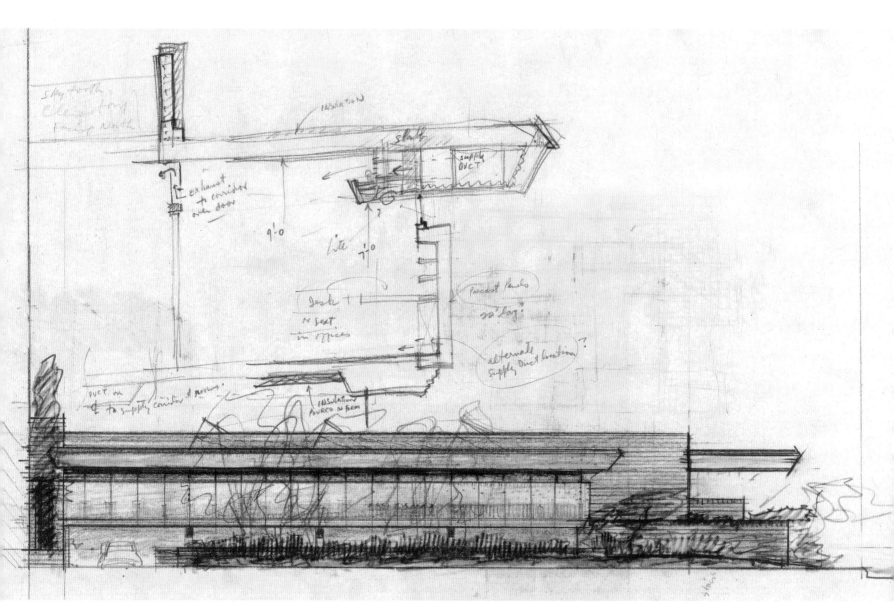

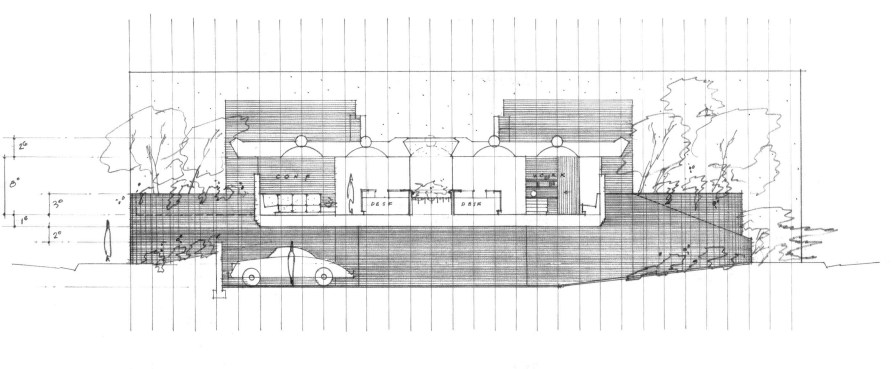

UNITS 3'-0" x 3'-0"

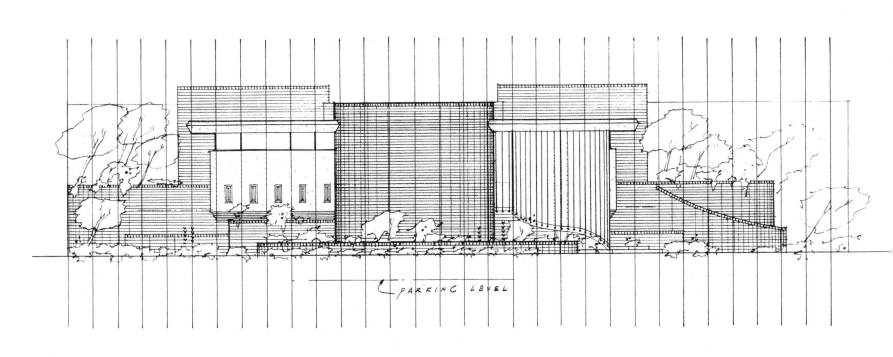

JULIAN STREET ELEVATION
SCALE 1/8" = 1'-0"

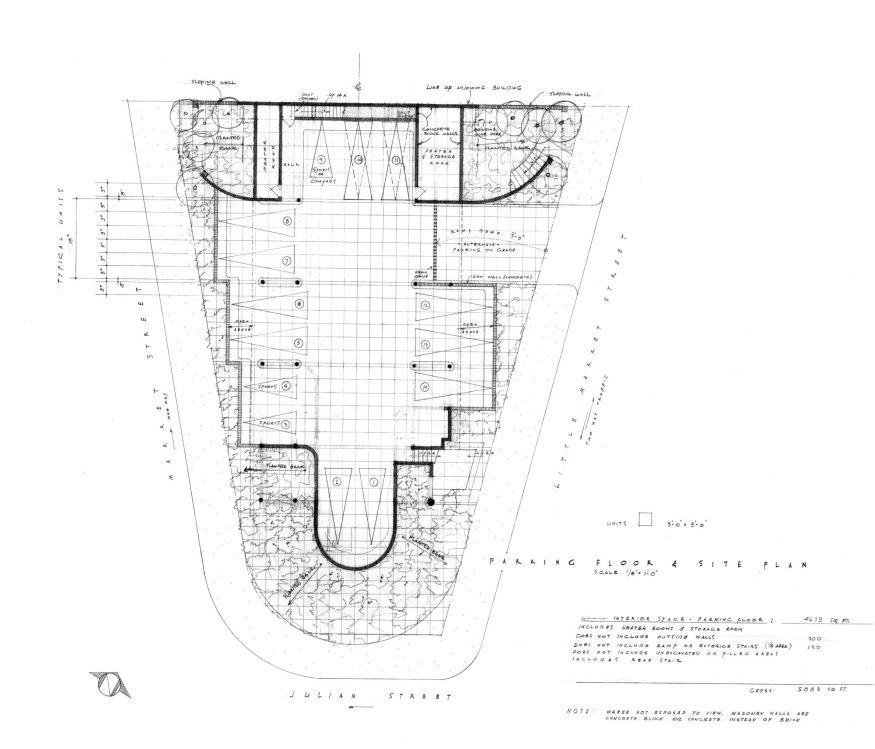

PARKING FLOOR & SITE PLAN
SCALE 1/8"=1'-0"

UNITS ☐ 3'-0" X 3'-0"

INTERIOR SPACE - PARKING FLOOR : 4633 SQ. FT.
INCLUDES HEATER ROOMS & STORAGE ROOM
DOES NOT INCLUDE OUTSIDE WALLS   300
DOES NOT INCLUDE RAMP OR EXTERIOR STAIRS (1/4 AREA) 150
DOES NOT INCLUDE UNEXCAVATED OR FILLED AREAS
INCLUDES REAR STAIR

GROSS   5083 SQ. FT.

NOTE: WHERE NOT EXPOSED TO VIEW, MASONRY WALLS ARE
CONCRETE BLOCK OR CONCRETE INSTEAD OF BRICK

JULIAN STREET

OFFICE BUILDING FOR MR. ROBERT H. WEIR, SAN JOSE, CALIFORNIA

AARON G GREEN AIA ARCHITECT
SAN FRANCISCO CALIFORNIA

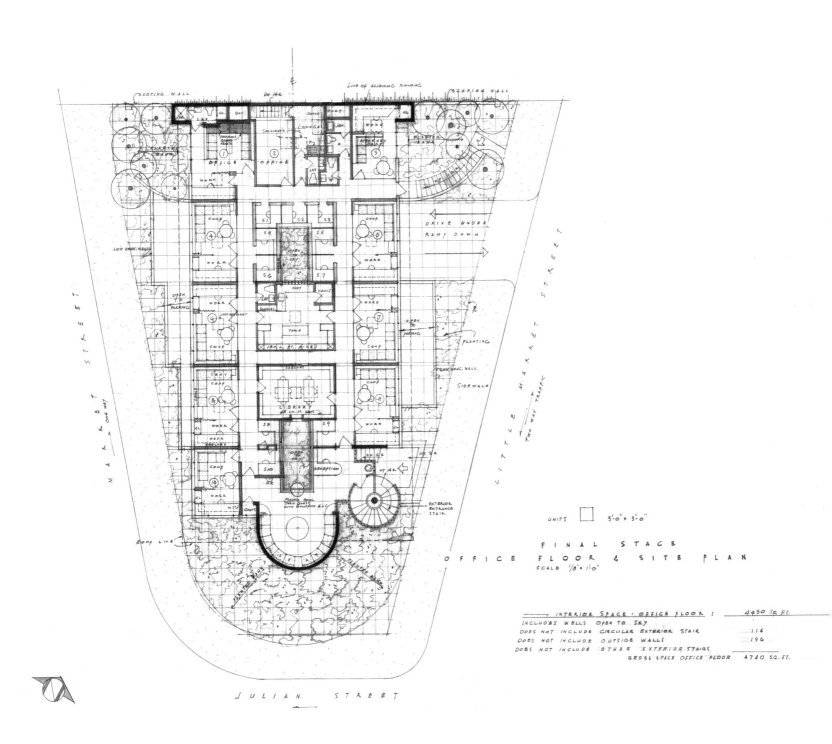

FINAL STAGE
OFFICE FLOOR & SITE PLAN
SCALE 1/8" = 1'0"

UNITS ☐ 3'-0" x 3'-0"

INTERIOR SPACE · OFFICE FLOOR :	4430 SQ. FT.
INCLUDES WELLS OPEN TO SKY	
DOES NOT INCLUDE CIRCULAR EXTERIOR STAIR	114
DOES NOT INCLUDE OUTSIDE WALLS	196
DOES NOT INCLUDE OTHER EXTERIOR STAIRS,	
GROSS SPACE OFFICE FLOOR	4740 SQ. FT.

JULIAN   STREET

FFICE   BUILDING   FOR   MR.   ROBERT   H.   WEIR,   SAN JOSE, CALIFORNIA

ARON G GREEN AIA ARCHITECT

AN FRANCISCO CALIFORNIA

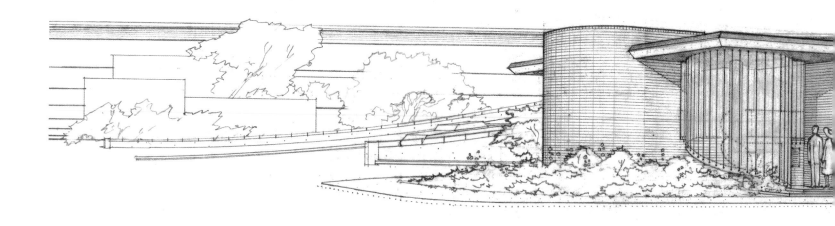

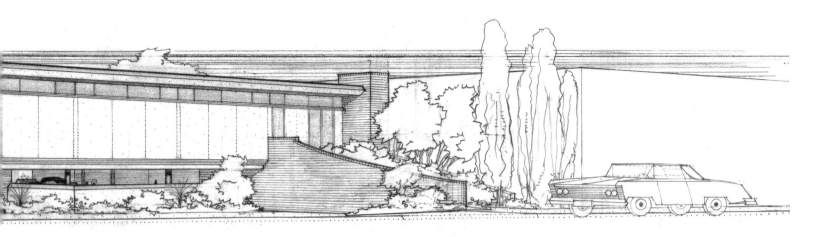

The exterior materials for the building were simple and few – masonry, stucco, and glass. Green's earliest designs explored ornamentation on the plain stucco surfaces but they were eventually eliminated, opting for a more simplistic style. Playing off the building's basic rectilinear shape, at the southeast corner, Green incorporated an open, circular stair that led to the building's public entrance, the reception area, and, enclosed by solid masonry, a waiting area with a circular, built-in couch. A second entrance for the attorneys and staff was located on the northern end of the Little Market Street side. The flat roof, separated from the solid wall below by a narrow band of glass, overhung the building to dramatic effect.

The building served Weir's law practice well until the 1990s when the building was demolished to make way for a large, high-density apartment project.

OHTA RESIDENCE

In 1964, Green designed a large single-story house for the prominent Santa Cruz ophthalmologist Dr. Victor M. Ohta (1925–1970), his wife Virginia (1927–1970), and their four children. It was built on a ten-acre ridge top parcel off Rodeo Gulch Road in the Soquel area of the Santa Cruz Mountain Range, five miles south of Santa Cruz. The home provided the Ohta family rural tranquility while allowing them to take full advantage of a commanding, uninterrupted view over a second, tree-lined ridge of Monterey Bay and the Pacific Ocean in the distance. On the opposite side of the view, Green located a natural shaped pool surrounded by an extensive terrace and Japanese garden. Consistent in Green's work was the ease at which the elongated house and the site were integrated as the house nestled harmoniously into the steep hill site. Construction began in

1965 with Victor Bogard, who had completed the construction of Ohta's medical office complex in Santa Cruz the previous year.

The clients voiced a desire that they, "want the house to be gentle in spots and strong in other spots … want to find our own little island."[63] The house enclosed approximately 3,800 square feet of living space. The linear plan, based on the four-foot-square module, stretched more than 150 feet along the ridgeline. An anchoring, central core balanced the two wings, the shorter one housing the master suite and the longer one containing a hobby room, three bedrooms, and a combination studio/bedroom along with the requisite closets and bathrooms. The central core was a large, high ceiling volume with a living area, dining area, and kitchen included within, each revolving around a stone masonry element incorporating a kitchen range, oven,

PRELIMINARY   DESIGN
RESIDENCE   FOR   DR   AND   MRS   VICTOR   M   OHTA
SANTA   CRUZ   COUNTY   CALIFORNIA
MARCH   1964
AARON   G   GREEN   AIA   ARCHITECT

barbeque, fireplace, and enclosed laundry room. The three-car carport, shop, and the primary entry were the only elements that violated the dominant linear nature of the plan. A caption in the October 1965 *House Beautiful* magazine described the house as, "Triangular variations from a basic theme of disciplined rectangles gives this house a reflexive, free flowing shape that will allow it to fit easily into the natural contours of the site."[64] Despite the home being large, the design provided many intimately scaled areas within.

Rough beige Arizona Kaibab stone was the consistent material of the walls, inside and out, contrasting with redwood and plaster as well as on the interior surfaces. The floors were of flagstone, exposed concrete, or carpeting. The low, sloped roof, covered with cedar shingles, provided shelter from the heat and inclement weather with deep overhangs. However, at certain strategic locations the overhangs cut back to provide sun and light patterns within. Along with the design of the building, Green designed copious built-in furnishings, cabinetry, and millwork, supervised the landscaping of the property, and selected the carpets, drapery, and upholstery fabrics.

The collaboration of a trusting and faithful client and a creative architect brought forth a beautiful and successful design, one of Green's finest residential works. Fortunately the current owner has carefully and fully restored the home and gardens, as indicated by the color photographs (taken in 2016) alongside the black and white images from 1968.

■

■

■

■ LUM YIP KEE, LTD. OFFICE BUILDING
■
■

■ Aaron Green rarely received commissions outside of California. One exception was a multi-tenant, multi-story office building he designed in 1965 for Lum Yip Kee Limited. It was to replace their existing two-story building, occupied in 1910, at 80 North Kings Street between Smith Street and Maunakea Street, near Chinatown, in downtown Honolulu.

Just how the commission came to Green is currently unknown. Lum Yip Kee (1866–1943) was born in China but immigrated to Hawaii in 1884. He was one of Hawaii's pioneers in agriculture, merchandising, banking, and land development. With his son Yin

Tai (Y. T.) Lum, they founded the Lum Yip Kee Limited real estate investment company in 1932.

Green produced several variations of this project, including a two-story design, a four-story design, and a five-story design, the latter expanding from the company's current site to merge with the property on the corner at Smith Street. Each design included offices for the client, an additional space for a large financial institution on the street level floor, and a smaller rental space. Jack Howe produced numerous rendered studies for the three options. Other than the number of stories, the designs were similar and used a consistent

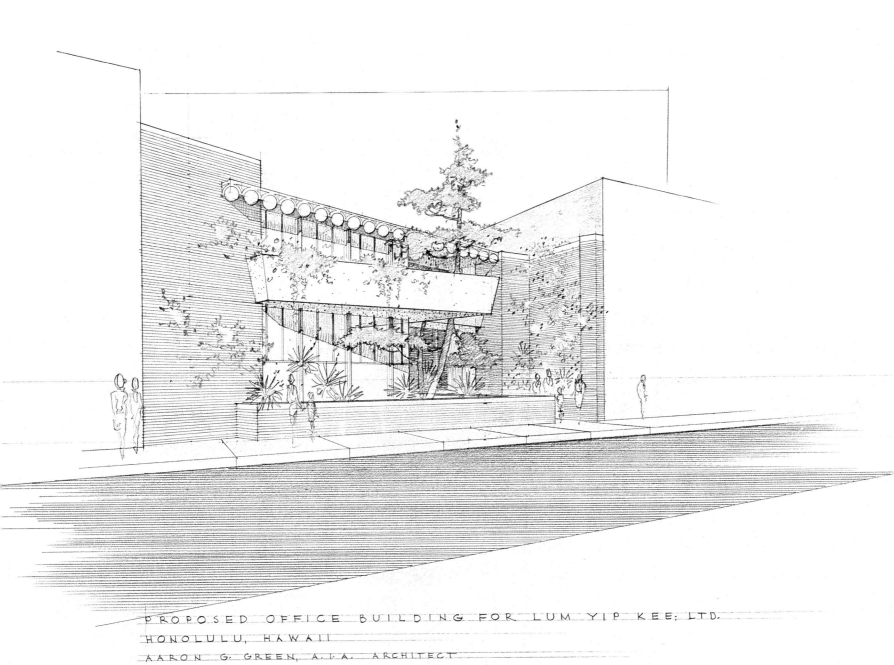

PROPOSED OFFICE BUILDING FOR LUM YIP KEE, LTD.
HONOLULU, HAWAII
AARON G. GREEN, A.I.A. ARCHITECT

PROPOSED OFFICE BUILDING FOR LUM YIP KEE, LTD.
HONOLULU, HAWAII
AARON G. GREEN, A.I.A. ARCHITECT

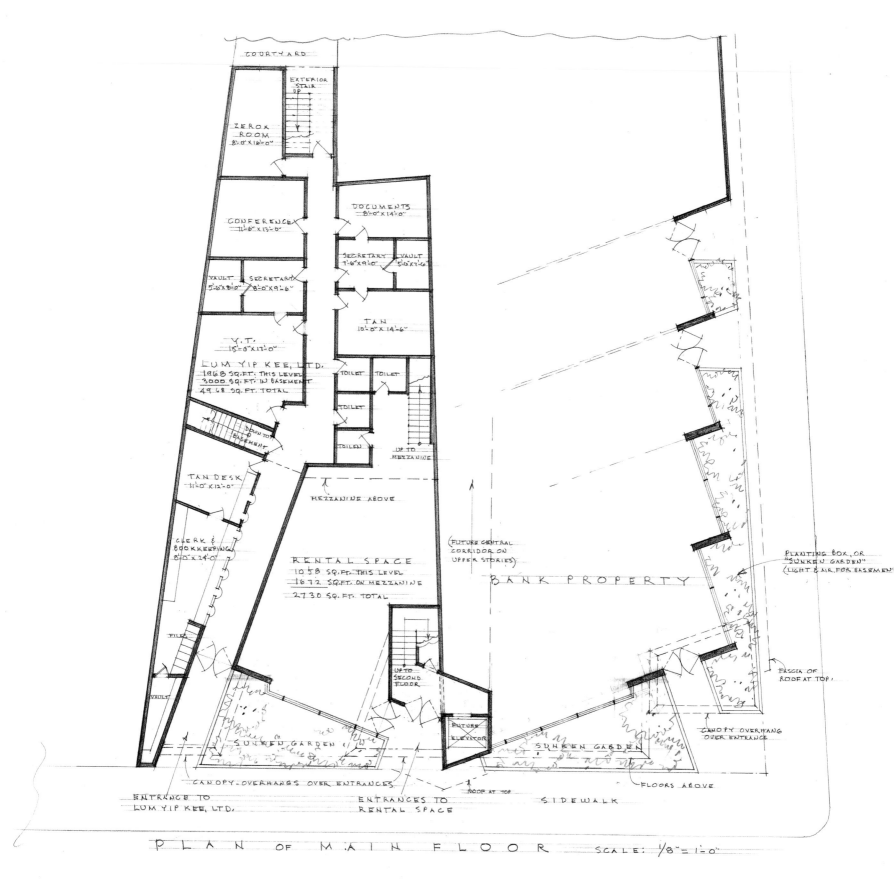

COURTYARD

EXTERIOR STAIR UP

ZEROX ROOM
8'-0" X 18'-0"

CONFERENCE
11'-6" X 13'-0"

DOCUMENTS
8'-0" X 14'-0"

SECRETARY
7'-6" X 9'-0"

VAULT
5'-0" X 7'-6"

VAULT
5'-6" X 8'-0"

SECRETARY
8'-0" X 9'-6"

TAN
10'-0" X 14'-6"

Y. T.
15'-0" X 17'-0"

LUM YIP KEE, LTD.
1968 SQ. FT. THIS LEVEL
3000 SQ. FT. IN BASEMENT
4968 SQ. FT. TOTAL

TOILET   TOILET

DOWN TO BASEMENT

TOILET

TAN DESK
11'-0" X 12'-0"

TOILET

UP TO MEZZANINE

MEZZANINE ABOVE

CLERK & BOOKKEEPING
8'-0" X 24'-0"

RENTAL SPACE
1058 SQ. FT. THIS LEVEL
1672 SQ. FT. ON MEZZANINE
2730 SQ. FT. TOTAL

(FUTURE CENTRAL CORRIDOR ON UPPER STORIES)

BANK PROPERTY

PLANTING BOX, OR "SUNKEN GARDEN" (LIGHT & AIR FOR BASEMENT)

FILES

UP TO SECOND FLOOR

VAULT

FUTURE ELEVATOR

FASCIA OF ROOF AT TOP.

SUNKEN GARDEN

SUNKEN GARDEN

CANOPY OVERHANG OVER ENTRANCE

CANOPY OVERHANGS OVER ENTRANCES

ROOF AT TOP

FLOORS ABOVE

ENTRANCE TO
LUM YIP KEE, LTD.

ENTRANCES TO
RENTAL SPACE

SIDEWALK

PLAN OF MAIN FLOOR   SCALE: 1/8" = 1'-0"

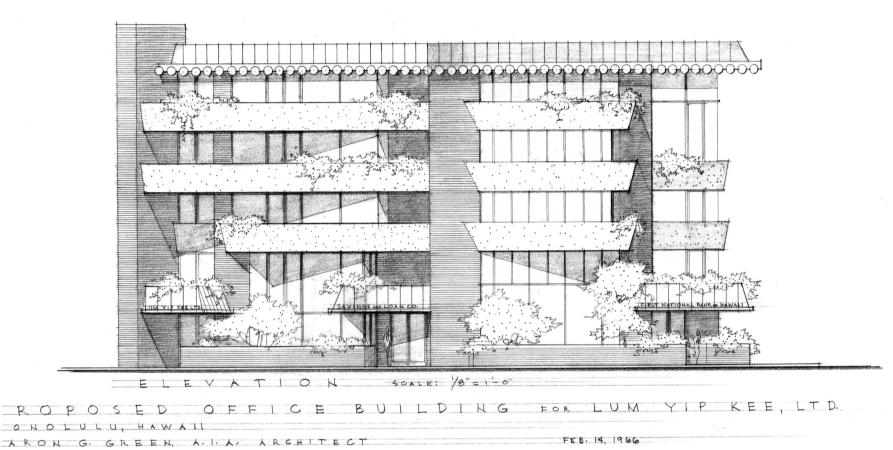

ELEVATION SCALE: 1/8" = 1'-0"

PROPOSED OFFICE BUILDING FOR LUM YIP KEE, LTD.

HONOLULU, HAWAII

AARON G. GREEN, A.I.A., ARCHITECT   FEB. 14, 1966

palette of materials—glass, brick, stucco, and copper—and featured projecting horizontal stucco balconies and planter boxes across the solid vertical brick walls. At the uppermost roof Green included an ornamented, scalloped fascia replete with spheres marching along the lower edge, a detail similar to that used at Wright's Marin County Civic Center, and a detail that Green was certainly familiar with.

Why the project never went beyond the design phase is unknown. The original two-story building remains with its façade updated in the 1970s, and still houses the offices of Lum Yip Kee, Ltd.

■ WOELFFEL YOUTH CENTER
■

■ In 1965 the Santa Clara County Peace Officers became incorporated as a non-profit, non-political, fraternal organization of law enforcement officers, personnel, and their families. According to Howard DeSart, who wrote a short history of the Santa Clara County Peace Officers Association, it was, "Hailed as a much needed organization by law enforcement officials, the Association will have as its primary goals the establishment of a police training academy, youth center, and recreational and social facilities for the members and their families."[65]

Blanche Woelffel, a local business woman whose deceased husband, Richard Woelffel, had owned a local cannery, donated the property for the project. The site was forty-two acres of sloping land at 23000 West Stevens Creek Road north of Cupertino, which presented a challenge to Green with its 200-foot-elevation change. The organization swiftly retained Green who, on June 22 of that year, presented his Architect's Program Analysis for the project. Green's thorough report and subsequent visual master plan design brilliantly responded to the client's laudatory mission to provide a youth center, a training center, and a building for the association's 500 members (the former two buildings named after Woelffel). The estimated cost to construct the project was $2,500,000.

Green's master plan placed the first two components close to each other while the third was located in a more remote location of the site. Green identified and augmented other natural areas on the site for passive recreation, including parks, picnicking, playgrounds, hiking trails, and even a small children's zoo.

At the lower area of the property Green located the Woelffel Youth Center. It was actually two buildings, a 14,500-square-foot multi-purpose facility for large gatherings and a 15,500-square-foot gymnasium, connected by an extensive terrace. Exterior and proximal to both buildings were outdoor recreational and athletic areas for tennis, handball, volleyball, basketball, and baseball, a quarter-mile track, and a twenty-five-meter swimming pool.

The 55,000-square-foot Woelffel Police Officer's Training Academy was broken up into three distinct buildings that were interconnected by covered breezeways that stepped up the steep slope. The program of the training center specified classrooms, offices, a large multi-purpose space, conference rooms, a mock courtroom, small kitchen, lecture hall, library, police museum, and dormitories for 120 inhabitants. The Santa Clara County Peace Officers Association building was placed apart from the other two buildings, near the summit of the property. The bold linear building, sitting along a

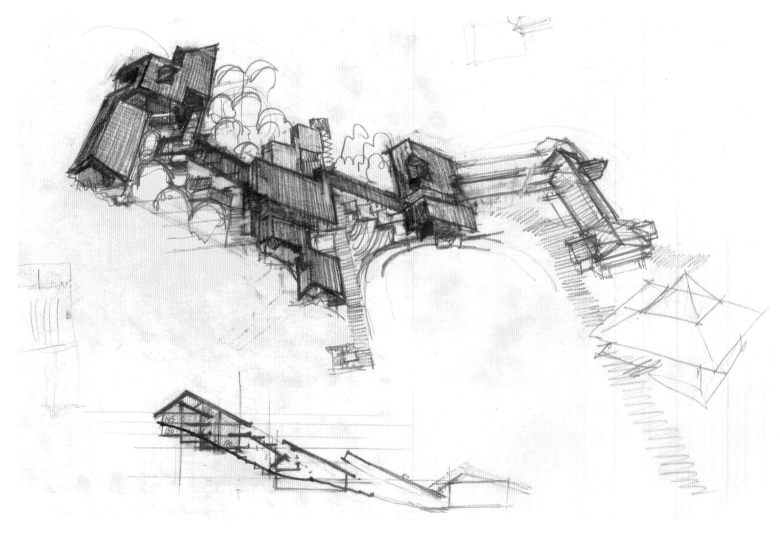

SANTA CLARA COUNTY PEACE OFFICERS ASSOCIATION
ASSOCIATION BUILDING

AARON G GREEN · AIA · ARCHITECT

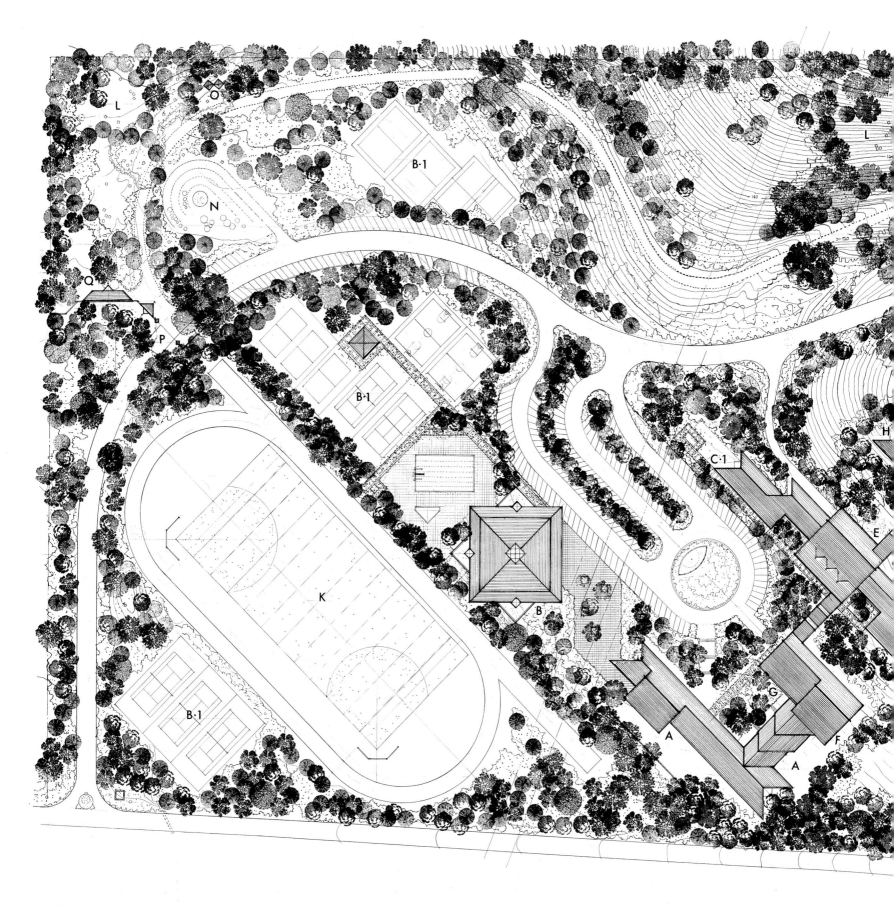

THE WOELFFEL YOUTH CENTER

SANTA CLARA COUNTY PEACE OFFICERS ASSO

AARON G GREEN ∗ AIA ∗ ARCHITECT

MASTER PLAN

LEGEND			PHASE
A	WOELFFEL YOUTH CENTER		I
B	GYMNASIUM		I
B·1	OUTDOOR COURTS		I
C	CLASSROOMS		I
C·1	CLASSROOMS		II
D	OFFICES & ADMINISTRATION		I
E	MULTIPURPOSE ROOM		I
F	LECTURE HALL		II
G	LIBRARY & MUSEUM		I & II
H	DORMITORY		I
H·1	DORMITORY		II
J	ASSOCIATION BUILDING		I
K	ATHLETIC FIELDS		I
L	PICNIC & B.B.Q. AREAS		I & II
M	CHILDREN'S ZOO & TRAILS		II
N	CHILDREN'S PLAYGROUND		I
O	OUTDOOR RESTROOMS		II
P	MAIN ENTRANCE		II
Q	CORPORATION YARD		II
R	PARK & RECREATION		II
S	POND		II

NORTH

SCALE
0   50   100

ATION

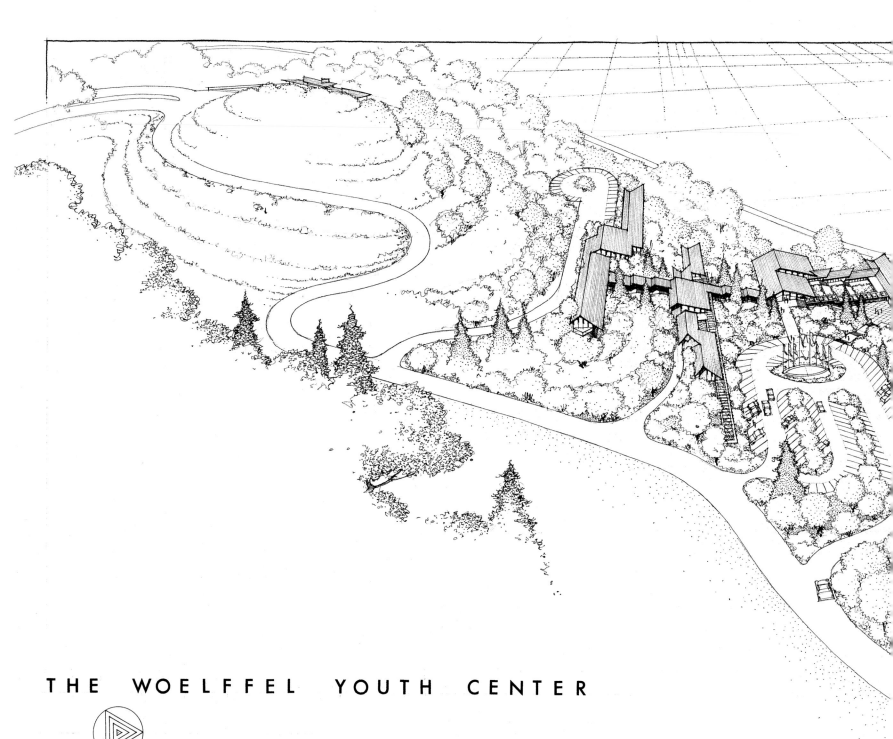

THE WOELFFEL YOUTH CENTER

SANTA CLARA COUNTY PEACE OFFICERS ASSO

AARON G GREEN   AIA   ARCHITECT

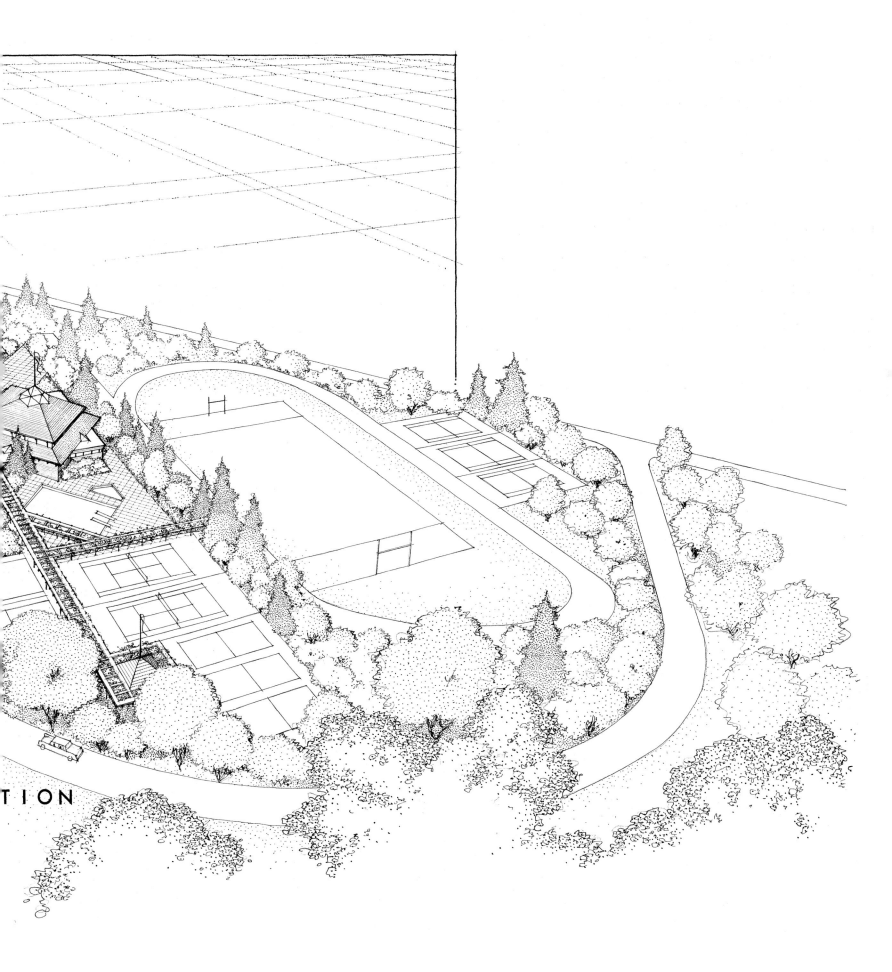

TION

THE WOELFFEL YOUTH CENTER

SANTA CLARA COUNTY PEACE OFFICERS ASSOCIATION

AARON G GREEN ▪ AIA ▪ ARCHITECT

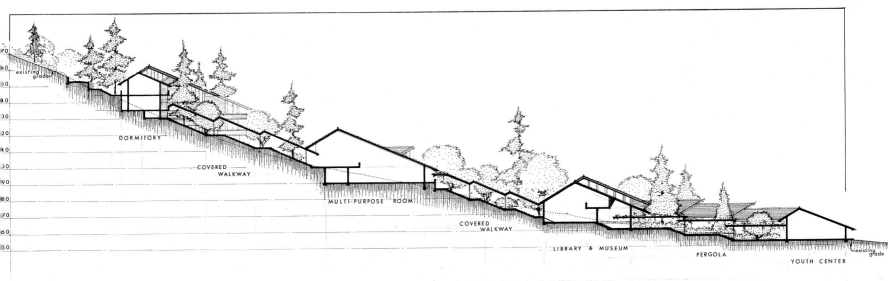

HE WOELFFEL YOUTH CENTER   CROSS SECTION

ANTA CLARA COUNTY PEACE OFFICERS ASSOCIATION

ARON G GREEN · AIA · ARCHITECT   SCALE : 1″ = 20′

Within the cross section, the following labels appear: existing grade, DORMITORY, COVERED WALKWAY, MULTI-PURPOSE ROOM, COVERED WALKWAY, LIBRARY & MUSEUM, PERGOLA, YOUTH CENTER, existing grade.

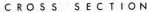

natural ridge, had wide views and was approximately 35,000 square feet and included a dining area with a kitchen and service areas, a recreation room with a fireplace, and offices.

While the architectural forms varied with the building units, the architectural aesthetic and materials were designed to provide visual continuity, unifying the various human-made parts with the natural environment to create a relatively quiet but inventive project. Preliminary plans hinted at buildings of masonry and glass sheltered with low-sloped, gable roofs and a decorative, celebratory finial detail for the ridge beams. Numerous project renderings were drawn for fundraising purposes by John ("Jack") Howe (1913–1997) who left the Taliesin Fellowship and Taliesin Associated Architects to work with Green from October 1964 until mid-1967, at which time he departed San Francisco for Minnesota to start his own independent practice. Howe had been a charter member of the Taliesin Fellowship at its inception in 1932 and was Frank Lloyd Wright's chief draftsman – later becoming known as "the pencil in Wright's hand."

In an attempt to accommodate his client's lack of capital, Green deferred his fee until the project became fiscally possible. Jan Novie suggests that this wasn't unusual for Green. "Aaron would have been willing to work *pro bono* and accept the risk with hopes of recouping most or all the fees if it went forward. Green's office overhead was low and Jack was incredibly fast so that if things did not work out he could accept the financial loss."[66]

Unfortunately the project never reached a point of financial fitness. Woelffel's stipulation that monies could be obtained only through private donations and not from federal or state grants restricted the Association in securing adequate funding to move the project forward. Adding to their frustration, Woelffel further stipulated they needed to have $100,000 in hand and an additional $500,000 in pledges by May 1, 1968. In January 1968 the Association voted to return the property to Woelffel and the project died.

NEWARK COMMUNITY CENTER

In 1966 the City of Newark, California, commissioned Green to design a new community center, and, in 1982, they returned to Green for a new library, a separate police annex, a remodel of the existing office building annex, and a state of the art City Council Chamber on the upper floor of the existing City Office Building Tower. The one-acre parcel for the community center fronts Cedar Boulevard less than two miles north of the city center, and is alongside a seventeen-acre city park. The latter project was located adjacent to the City's existing eight-story civic center building on Civic Terrace Avenue off Newark Boulevard. Both projects stand as examples of Green's ingenious manner of providing for the desired functions in civic buildings that are free of any institutional temperament.

Green's 17,000-square-foot community center building is a lodge-like, L-shaped plan anchored at the intersection of the legs with a significant double-sided masonry fireplace. The legs of the L shelter an expansive private terrace bordered with an arbor. The plan, based on a eight-foot-square units, provides a multitude of spaces, including a large social hall, lounge, arts and crafts studio, game room, meeting rooms with associated storage, mechanical spaces, and a catering kitchen. Green once again incorporated planting areas and strategically placed skylights to bring nature and light into the building. The circulation is efficient while informal, subtle level changes provide further definition of zonal nuances and the more public, social spaces look out onto the protected, articulated terrace. The terrace also acts as an expansion of the social hall in accommodating weather.

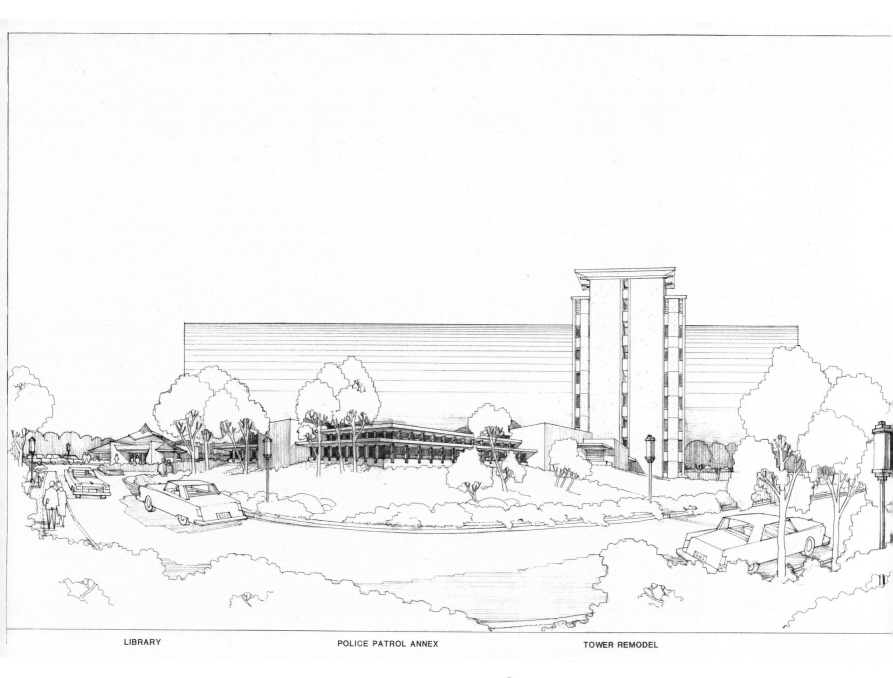

LIBRARY   POLICE PATROL ANNEX   TOWER REMODEL

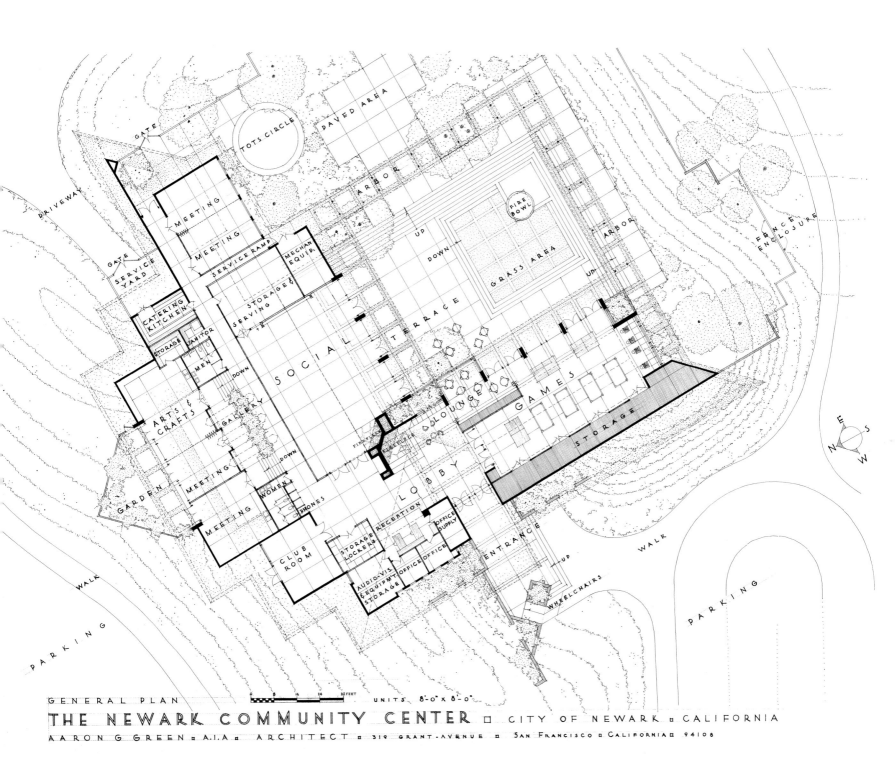

THE NEWARK COMMUNITY CENTER □ CITY OF NEWARK □ CALIFORNIA

GENERAL PLAN

UNITS 8'-0" X 8'-0"

AARON G GREEN □ A.I.A. □ ARCHITECT □ 319 GRANT AVENUE □ SAN FRANCISCO □ CALIFORNIA □ 94108

THE NEWARK COMMUNITY CENT

AARON G GREEN ¤ A.I.A ¤ ARCHITECT ¤ 319 GRANT

R □ CITY OF NEWARK □ CALIFORNIA

NUE □ SAN FRANCISCO □ CALIFORNIA □ 94108

THE NEWARK COMMUNITY CE

AARON G GREEN ¤ A.I.A ¤ ARCHITECT ¤ 319 GRA

ER □ CITY OF NEWARK □ CALIFORNIA

AVENUE □ SAN FRANCISCO □ CALIFORNIA □ 94108

THE NEWARK COMMUNITY CENTER □ CITY OF NEWARK □ CALIFORNIA

AARON G GREEN □ A.I.A □ ARCHITECT □ 319 GRANT AVENUE □ San Francisco □ California □ 94108

THE NEWARK COMMUNITY CENTER □ CITY OF NEWARK □ CALIFORNIA

AARON G GREEN □ A.I.A □ ARCHITECT □ 319 GRANT AVENUE □ SAN FRANCISCO □ CALIFORNIA □ 94108

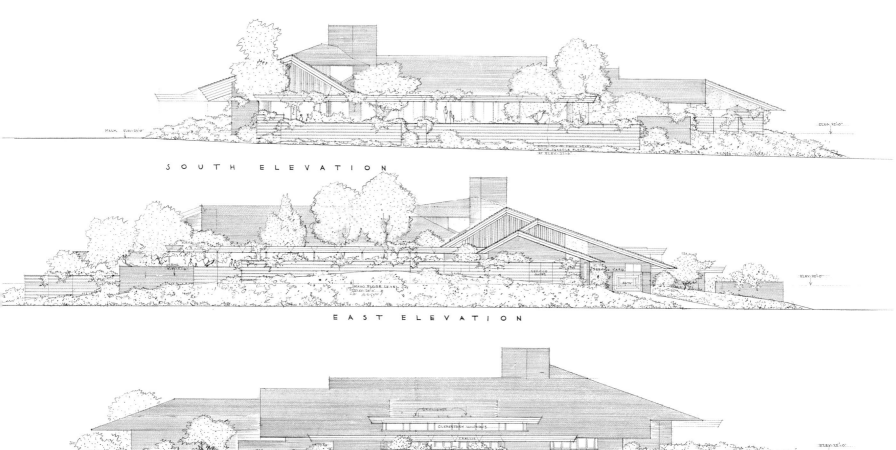

SOUTH ELEVATION

EAST ELEVATION

NORTH ELEVATION

WEST ELEVATION   Scale: ⅛"=1'-0"

THE NEWARK COMMUNITY CENTER □ CITY OF NEWARK □ CALIFORNIA

AARON G GREEN □ A.I.A. □ ARCHITECT □ 319 GRANT AVENUE □ SAN FRANCISCO □ CALIFORNIA □ 94108

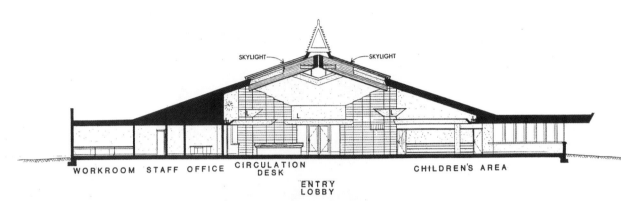

SKYLIGHT   SKYLIGHT

WORKROOM   STAFF OFFICE   CIRCULATION DESK   CHILDREN'S AREA

ENTRY LOBBY

Ⓑ SECTION B·B

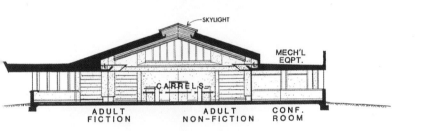

SKYLIGHT

MECH'L EQPT.

CARRELS

ADULT FICTION   ADULT NON-FICTION   CONF. ROOM

Ⓒ SECTION C·C

L = TYPICAL INDIRECT H.I.D. LIGHTING UNIT. (LOCATED IN ALL LIGHT DECK AREAS).

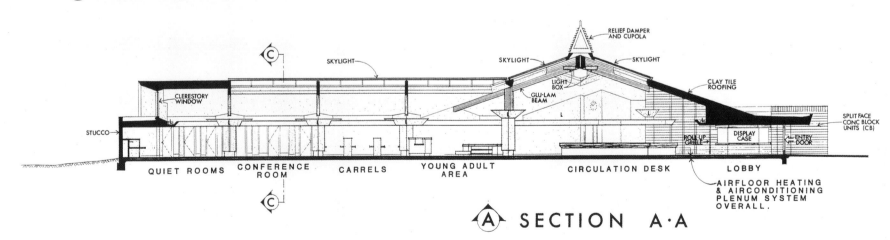

RELIEF DAMPER AND CUPOLA

SKYLIGHT   SKYLIGHT   SKYLIGHT

LIGHT BOX

CLAY TILE ROOFING

CLERESTORY WINDOW

GLU-LAM BEAM

STUCCO

SPLIT FACE CONC BLOCK UNITS (CB)

ROLL UP GRILLE   DISPLAY CASE   ENTRY DOOR

QUIET ROOMS   CONFERENCE ROOM   CARRELS   YOUNG ADULT AREA   CIRCULATION DESK   LOBBY

AIRFLOOR HEATING & AIRCONDITIONING PLENUM SYSTEM OVERALL.

Ⓐ SECTION A·A

LIBRARY CROSS SECTIONS

GRAPHIC SCALE:
0'   8'   16'   24'

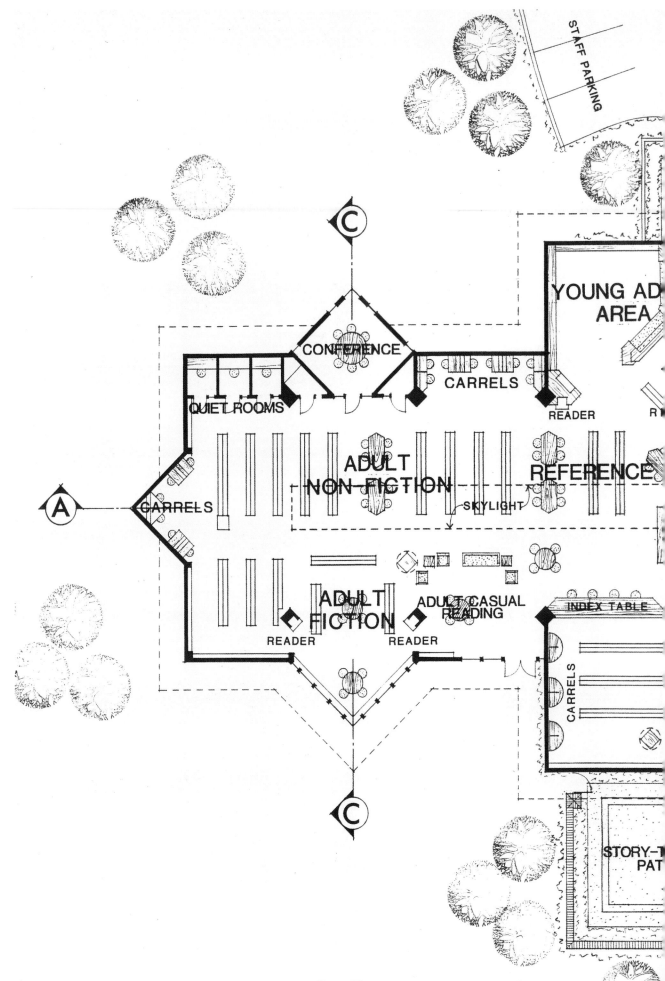

STAFF PARKING

C

YOUNG AD
AREA

CONFERENCE

CARRELS

QUIET ROOMS

READER

R

A CARRELS

ADULT
NON-FICTION

REFERENCE

SKYLIGHT

ADULT
FICTION

ADULT CASUAL
READING

INDEX TABLE

READER

READER

CARRELS

C

STORY-T
PAT

LIBRARY FLOOR PLAN

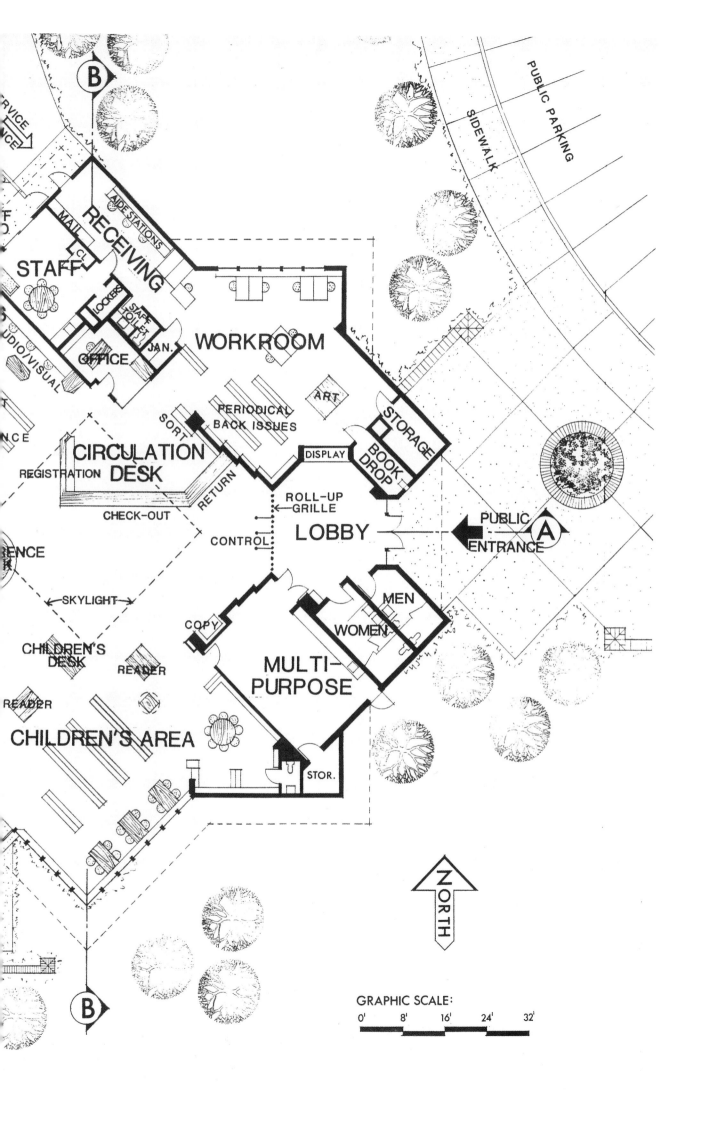

PUBLIC PARKING

SIDEWALK

B

SERVICE
ENTRANCE

STAFF

RECEIVING

AIDE STATIONS

MAIL

CL

LOCKERS

STAFF TOILET

JAN.

OFFICE

STUDIO/VISUAL

WORKROOM

ART

STORAGE

PERIODICAL
BACK ISSUES

SORT

DISPLAY

BOOK DROP

CIRCULATION
DESK

REGISTRATION

RETURN

CHECK-OUT

ROLL-UP
GRILLE

REFERENCE

CONTROL

LOBBY

PUBLIC
ENTRANCE

A

SKYLIGHT

COPY

MEN

WOMEN

CHILDREN'S
DESK

READER

MULTI-
PURPOSE

READER

CHILDREN'S AREA

STOR.

NORTH

B

GRAPHIC SCALE:

0'   8'   16'   24'   32'

ENTRANCE

Green's aesthetic for the building is an expression of compatibility, being principally residential in nature to relate to the surrounding neighborhood. Even though the building is much larger in plan and has larger interior spaces, its exterior presents a palatable human scale. Green incorporated materials that required low or no maintenance, including red masonry blocks for the exterior walls and cedar shingles for the low-sloped, sheltering, hipped roofs. The interiors were a mix of the masonry and plaster with exposed wood trusses that provided further interest in the more open areas of the social hall and game room. The massive fireplace in the entrance lobby provides a symbolic gesture of warmth and familial community.

The City of Newark's governmental offices were housed in an eight-story, vertical city hall that was built in the 1960s. In 1982 they approached Green to design a new annex to the tower for the police department, to do interior updates to the plan to fill the voids and update spaces left unoccupied by the relocation of the police department, and to renovate and remodel other interiors within the tower (including the design for a new city council chamber). Separately, they asked Green to design a new city library on the same property.

The police annex building was an 8,000-square-foot, irregularly shaped structure added onto the base of the tower. Green wanted to minimize the building's impact on the existing park-like setting so he partially buried and bermed the building into the hillside and provided a generous setback from the new Civic Terrace Avenue that was constructed to reach the library site. The success of the building is that while serving its purpose it is a quiet, unobtrusive neighbor to the new library and adjoining city park.

The library is rather isolated from the busier traffic on Newark Boulevard and nestles seamlessly into the contiguous Civic Center Park and acts as the civic center's focal point. Green's 15,000-square-

foot library for Newark basically, in plan, comprises two similar sized squares superimposed upon each other, with one rotated 45 degrees. A shorter, similar composition is attached to the larger volume opposite the entrance. While the simple, rotated geometry provides for an efficient structural system, the resultant exterior and interior are both bold and direct. The all encompassing clay tile roof, with its spire-shaped cupola and widespread skylights, are the building's predominant forms, structured using heavy timber and glue laminated wood frame construction exposed to the interior's vaulted open space. The human scale of the exterior, created by the skilled manipulation of proportion and materials, provides little clue as to the unexpected but exhilarating spatial excitement of the library's interiors.

BRIDGE TOWNHOUSES

Lucy Frances Bridge (1891–1999), a widower since her husband's death in 1958, came to Green in late 1966 wanting to develop a parcel of prime real estate on the southeastern edge of Tiburon, a town located on a peninsula in Marin County. The elevated property between Linda Vista Avenue and Mar East Street allowed views to the southeast towards nearby Angel Island and wider views across the San Francisco Bay to Richmond to the northeast, Berkeley to the east, the city of San Francisco directly south and the Golden Gate Bridge to the southwest. The design of the project was underway in 1967, with preliminary drawings dated February 5th.

Green's project was an assemblage of three townhouse buildings that were specifically designed to take full advantage of both the sloping hilltop site and the expansive views. While trying to maximize the number of units for his client, Green sensitively located the buildings to enhance the natural setting, and designed them to be fully integrated into the property's slope. Two of the buildings contained four units each with the third having only two units. Detached, covered parking structures were included for the residents along with a half circle swimming pool, an elevated deck that overlooked the bay, and a larger terrace feature with a fountain and fire pit located lower on the property for resident gatherings and activities. The units were all split foyers, entering the townhouses mid-level between the upper living level and the lower sleeping level. The floor plan was organized on a four-foot-square grid. A half bath and laundry room were located at the top of the stairs that led to the lower sleeping level. Off the tight entry Green located a two-story tall garden element that spatially expanded the entry experience. The living spaces were on the upper level, containing spaces for eating and cooking and studies that doubled as guest rooms. An interesting feature seen in one of Green's schemes was exterior scooped dormers

ELEVATION FROM SOUTH · MAR EAST STREET

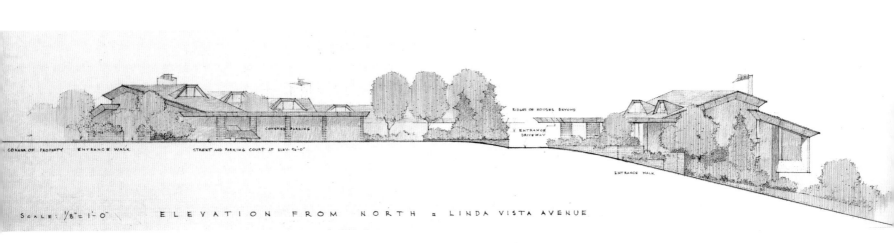

SCALE: 1/8" = 1'-0"   ELEVATION FROM NORTH · LINDA VISTA AVENUE

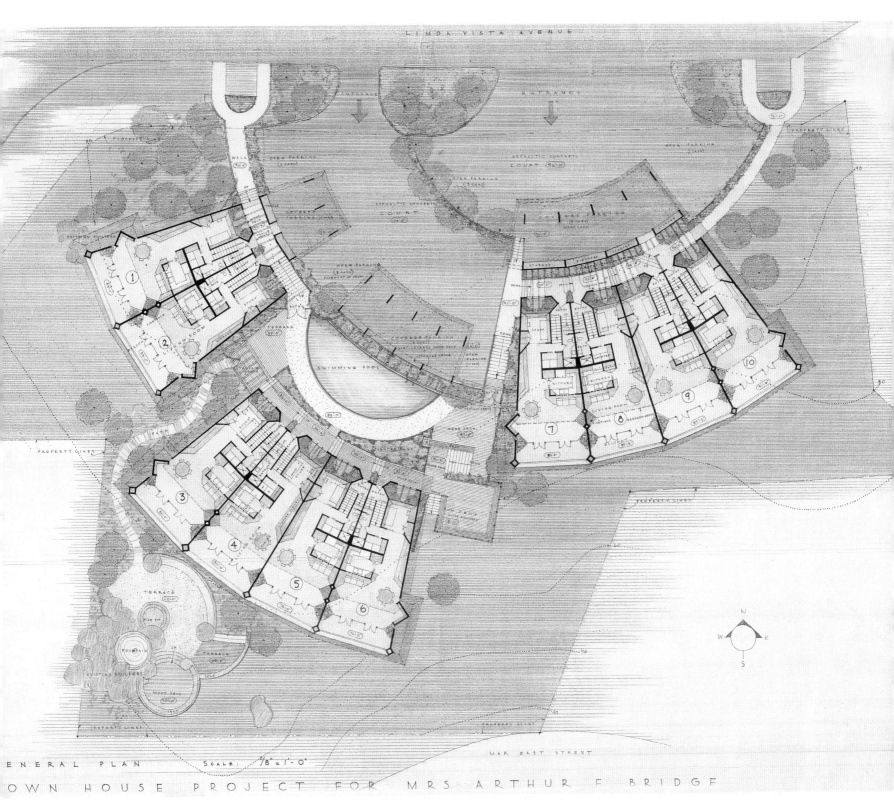

LINDA VISTA AVENUE

ENTRANCE

GENERAL PLAN   SCALE: 1/8" = 1'-0"

TOWN HOUSE PROJECT FOR MRS. ARTHUR F. BRIDGE

VIEW LOOKING SOUTHEAST

TOWN HOUSE PROJECT FOR MRS.
TIBURON, CALIFORNIA
AARON G. GREEN A.I.A. ARCHITECT

THUR F BRIDGE

VIEW LOOKING NORTHEAST
FROM CENTRO EAST DRIVE

TOWN HOUSE PROJECT FOR MRS. ARTHUR F. BRIDGE
TIBURON, CALIFORNIA
AARON G. GREEN A.I.A. ARCHITECT

VIEW LOOKING NORTHEAST FROM CENTRO EAST DRIVE

TOWN HOUSE PROJECT FOR MRS ARTHUR F BRIDGE
TIBURON, CALIFORNIA
AARON G. GREEN A.I.A. ARCHITECT

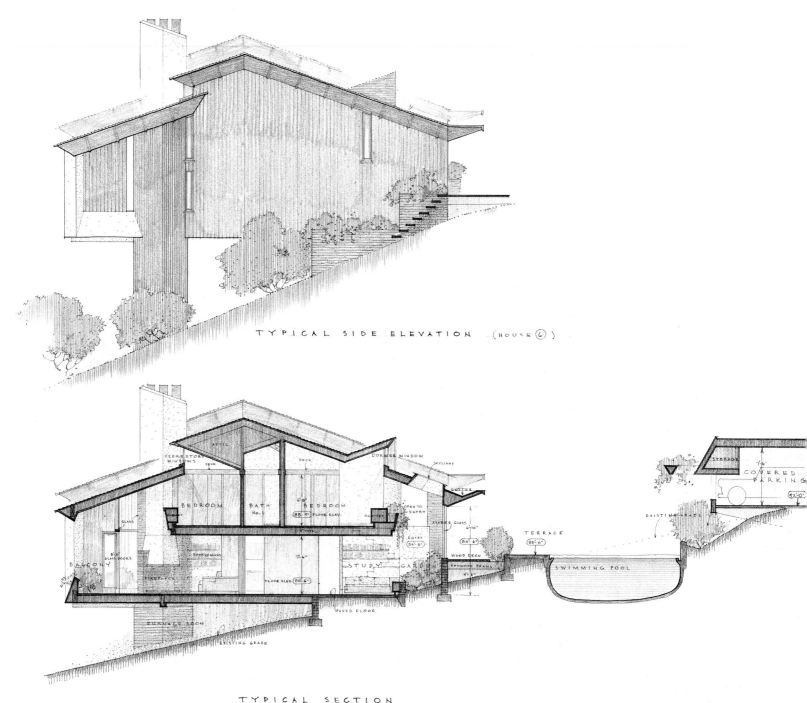

TYPICAL SIDE ELEVATION (HOUSE ⑥)

TYPICAL SECTION

(HOUSE ⑥)

SECTION AND ELEVATION OF TYPICAL TOWNHOUSE   SCALE: 1/4" = 1'-0"

TOWN HOUSE PROJECT FOR MRS. ARTHUR F. BRIDGE

TIBURON, CALIFORNIA

AARON G. GREEN   A.I.A.   ARCHITECT

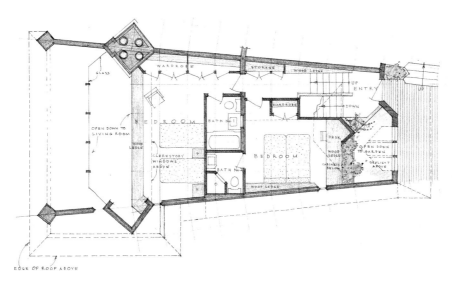

UPPER FLOOR

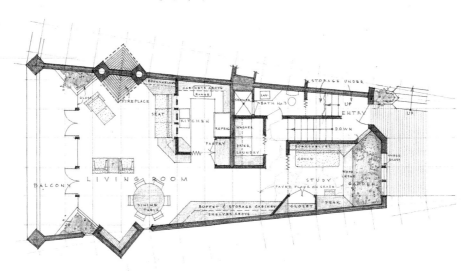

LOWER FLOOR

PLANS OF TYPICAL TOWN HOUSE   SCALE: 1/4" = 1'-0"   UNITS 4'-0" x 4'-0"

TOWN HOUSE PROJECT FOR MRS. ARTHUR F. BRIDGE

TIBURON, CALIFORNIA

AARON G. GREEN A.I.A. ARCHITECT

that were introduced to the roof line above the study/guest rooms that captured more light for the interior bedroom.

The primary living space had full height glass along the exterior wall, providing expansive views and manipulating the space to allow the bedroom above to overlook the living area. This also provided a vertical counterpoint accentuated by a fireplace that was anchored with a built-in couch and a two-story masonry and plaster chimney element. At the rear of the units, on the lower level, Green provided a private, roofed sun deck across the entire width of each unit. The lower sleeping level contained two bedrooms, each with a

bathroom. The exterior was primarily colored concrete masonry block and vertical redwood siding with plaster stucco elements. At least two schemes were developed for this project, but despite the high quality, efficient and cost effective design, the project was never built.

CITY OF SAUSALITO LIBRARY

In the mid-1960s the City of Sausalito pursued the construction of three municipal projects – a fire station, a corporation yard, and a public library. The city wanted cost effective and functional public buildings of the highest quality and design. Green designed the $45,000 concrete masonry and wood corporation yard building, proving to the community that good design need not cost more than the prefabricated metal building they had originally considered. After that success, the city retained Green for the last of the three projects, the public library, to be financed with public bonds. In December 1966, the Sausalito Public Library Board of Trustees and the librarian provided Green a seven-page service program along with a fourteen-page building program, describing the need for a building of approximately 10,000 square feet, holding 40,000 volumes,

as the basis for the design. He presented his preliminary design drawings in January 1967 for the $400,000 project.

The city owned site for the library was in a prominent location, a park-like, picturesque setting along the edge of Richardson Bay adjacent to the Sausalito Yacht Club and close to the town plaza, with unobstructed views of nearby Belvedere and Angel Islands and to San Francisco across the Bay. The design of the uniquely shaped angular building was primarily driven by the triangular geometry of the property. The five-sided, elongated, chevron-formed single-story building was elevated above the existing grade to protect it from potential flood conditions, being right at the water's edge. The building's plan was based upon a modified eight-foot-square grid. Generally repeating the shape of the floor plan below the low-sloped,

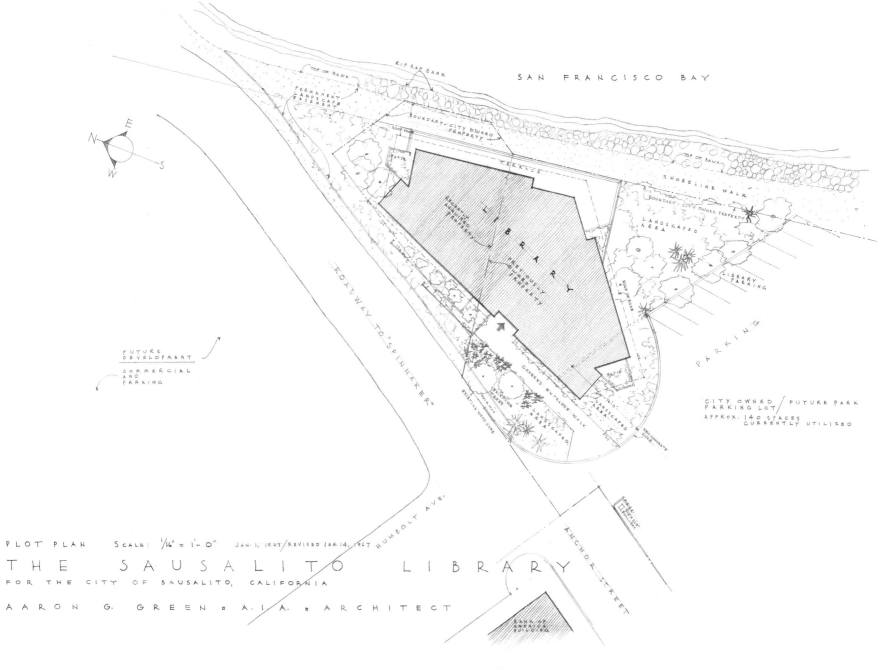

PLOT PLAN   SCALE: 1/16" = 1'-0"   JAN. 1, 1967/REVISED JAN. 14, 1967

THE SAUSALITO LIBRARY
FOR THE CITY OF SAUSALITO, CALIFORNIA
AARON G. GREEN ▪ A.I.A. ▪ ARCHITECT

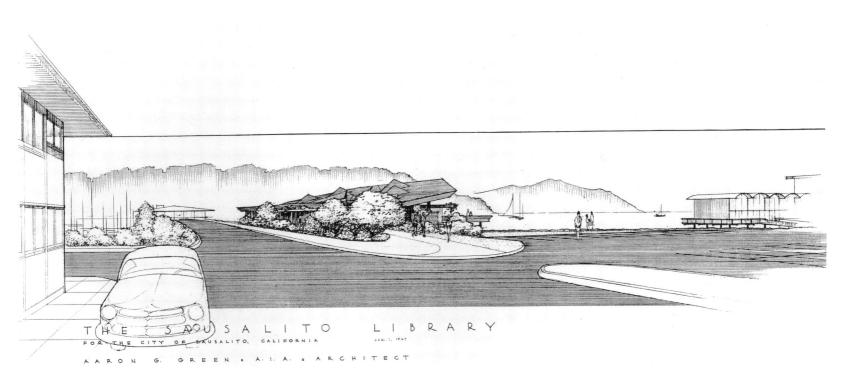

THE SAUSALITO LIBRARY

FOR THE CITY OF SAUSALITO, CALIFORNIA   JAN. 1, 1967

AARON G. GREEN ▫ A.I.A. ▫ ARCHITECT

THE SAUSALITO LIBRARY

FOR THE CITY OF SAUSALITO, CALIFORNIA

AARON G. GREEN ▫ F.A.I.A. ▫ ARCHITECT

THE SAUSALITO LIBRARY

FOR THE CITY OF SAUSALITO, CALIFORNIA

AARON G. GREEN ▫ A.I.A. ▫ ARCHITECT

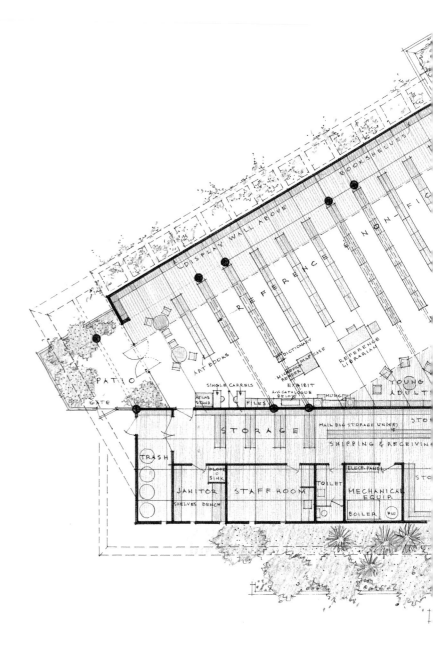

P L A N   SCALE: 1/8" = 1'-0"

T H E   S A U S A L I T O   L I B

FOR THE CITY OF SAUSALITO, CALIFORNIA

A A R O N   G .   G R E E N   ◦   A . I . A .   ◦   A R C H I T E C T

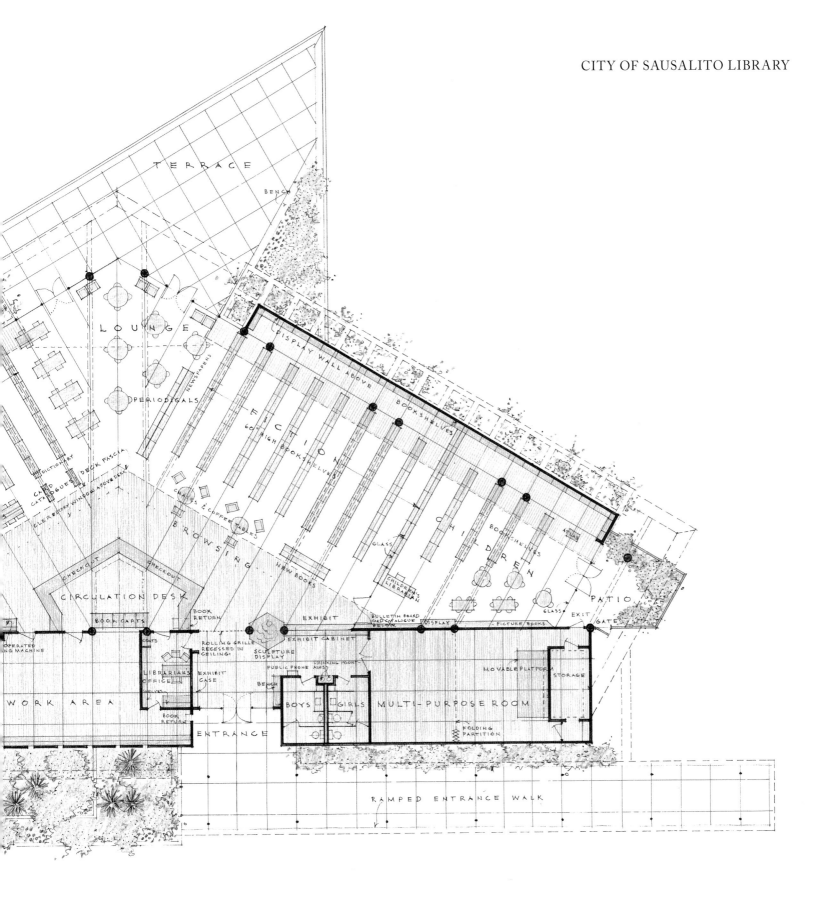

ARY

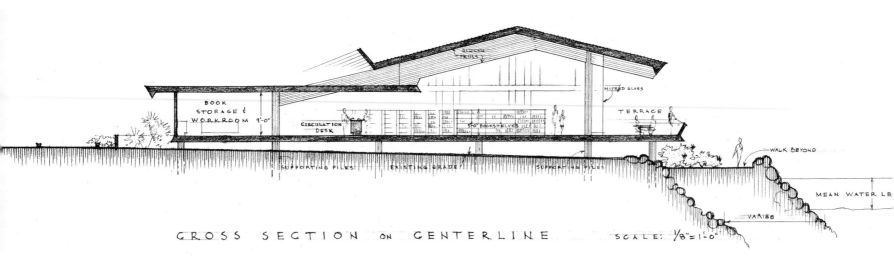

CROSS SECTION ON CENTERLINE   SCALE: ⅛"=1'-0"

BOOK STORAGE & WORKROOM 9'-0"
GENESEE TRUSS
MITRED GLASS
CIRCULATION DESK
5'-0" BOOKSHELVES
TERRACE
SUPPORTING PILES   EXISTING GRADE   SUPPORTING PILES
WALK BEYOND
MEAN WATER LE
VARIES

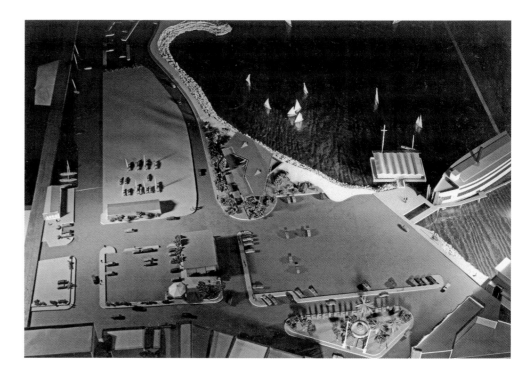

THE SAUSALITO LIBRARY

FOR THE CITY OF SAUSALITO, CALIFORNIA   JAN 1, 1967

AARON G. GREEN ▫ A.I.A. ▫ ARCHITECT

sheltering roof, supported by massive glue laminated wood beams and large wood pole columns, is prominent on both the exterior and interior. Its overhangs protect the floor to ceiling glass walls along the bay front side and the exterior "reading terrace" located at the building's prow, providing patrons an overlook across the expansive views of the Bay.

The interior of the library is essentially one dramatic spatial volume providing bookshelves and reading spaces, all under the watchful supervision of the circulation desk near the entrance. Green purposefully designed five-foot high bookshelves in order to preserve unobstructed views to the Bay beyond. The ancillary support spaces, which are more enclosed and functionally less accessible, are located within an elongated rectangular zone on the side opposite the bay, along the street front, where the building was designed to respond to a more pedestrian scale. At one end of this wing, off the main entrance and usable after library hours, Green located a multi-purpose room for community use. It was Green's intention to vary from the more enclosed library model by providing a more open browsing and reading experience through his spatial response to the incredible vistas from the site.

A large model of the project's design and surrounding context, along with renderings by Jack Howe, were prepared for public viewing prior to the March 7, 1967 referendum vote. The local newspaper came out in favor of the project in an editorial titled "New Sausalito Library—A Worthy Investment." The paper explained, "Aaron Green has designed an imaginative structure ... a center of learning close to the town plaza seems ideally suited to the needs of a city like Sausalito which prides itself on its cultural assets."[67]

It was the site that eventually doomed the project. The bond referendum failed because the citizens, while wholly in favor of the building's design, didn't want the library built in such a prominent place, blocking the open views across the water. The property later became Gabrielson Memorial Park. In 1971 the design was considered for an alternate site nearby but failed to gain the momentum that a project of this nature requires.

■

■

■

■ WAGNER RESIDENCE
■

■ The preliminary design was completed by late 1968 for the proposed home of Wayne H. Wagner, a banker with Wells Fargo, and his wife Mary. Green's focus when siting the project was to accentuate the view over the ravine that the home overlooked in Orinda, California, a community ten miles east of Berkeley, and was designed to nestle into the hillside seamlessly.

Originally intended to be constructed in two phases, the initial phase, containing approximately 1,600 square feet, presented a rotated square-shaped plan slightly elevated above the natural grade with views to the northeast, across the ravine. The northeast corner of the square contained the living room, dining room and open kitchen.

Two bedrooms with a single bathroom were located on the southwest corner. Anchoring the predominantly transparent house into the hillside was a masonry fireplace mass located in the exact center of the square, off of which protruded small, but solid, masonry that extruded out from the square shape on each wall.

The second phase consisted of a master bedroom wing to the southeast, a pool and terrace located to the northwest, and a large, dramatically cantilevered exterior deck expanding the living area of the primary house to the northeast. The elevated deck accomplished double duty as it also served as the roof for a two-car carport below. The master bedroom wing was sixteen steps above the home's main

VIEW FROM RAVINE

level, connected to the main house by a stepped entry gallery glazed on the view side with closets running along the opposite side.

Green's design delineated a well-balanced, nearly symmetrical exterior of glass, horizontal battered bands covered with cedar shakes, and solid masonry all topped with a modified butterfly roof.

Surprisingly, Wagner's own bank refused to loan the money to fund construction of the home because of concerns regarding the site and soils. Green's own hand-drawn thumbnail sketch provides a glimpse at his own intimate understanding of the essential ingredients of the design that would have made this house an

example of Wright's mantra that organic architecture makes the site better.

As a side note, Wayne Wagner's wife Mary was the major force in retaining Green for this project. Seven years later, on July 13, 1975, she became Green's second wife in a ceremony at Taliesin in Wisconsin.

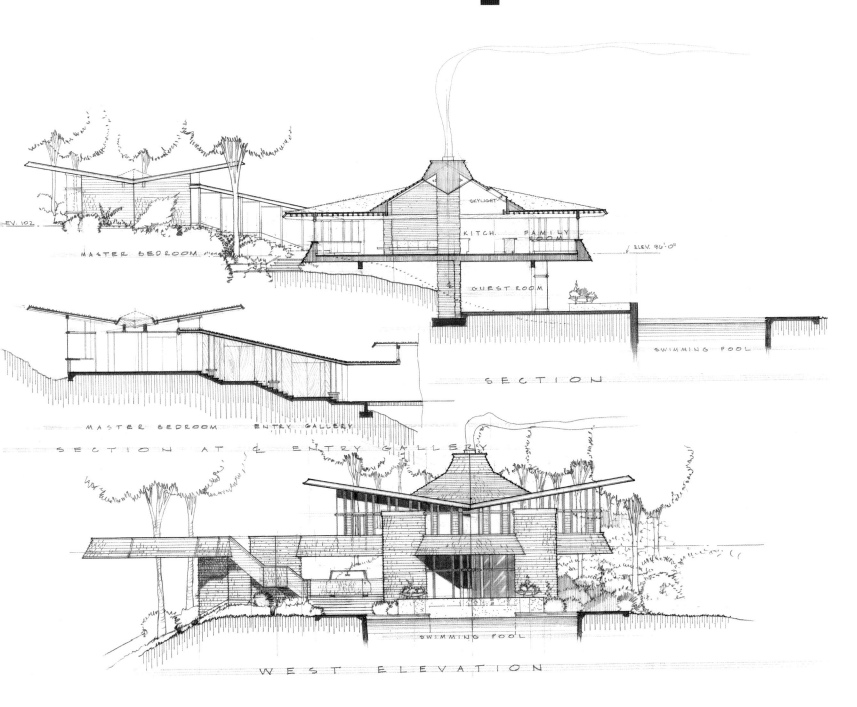

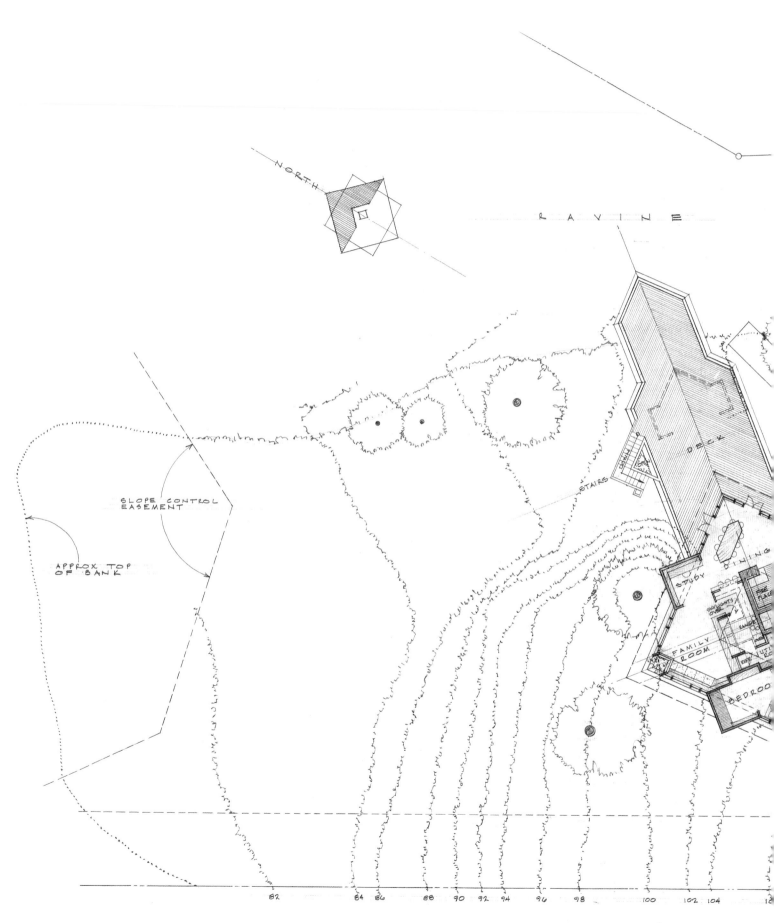

NORTH

RAVINE

SLOPE CONTROL
EASEMENT

APPROX TOP
OF BANK

STAIRS

DECK

DINING

STUDY

FAMILY
ROOM

BEDROOM

82   84 86   88 90 92 94   96   98   100   102 104

RESIDENCE   FOR   MR   &   MRS.
ORINDA · CALIFORNIA
AARON G GREEN · ARCHITECT · 319 G

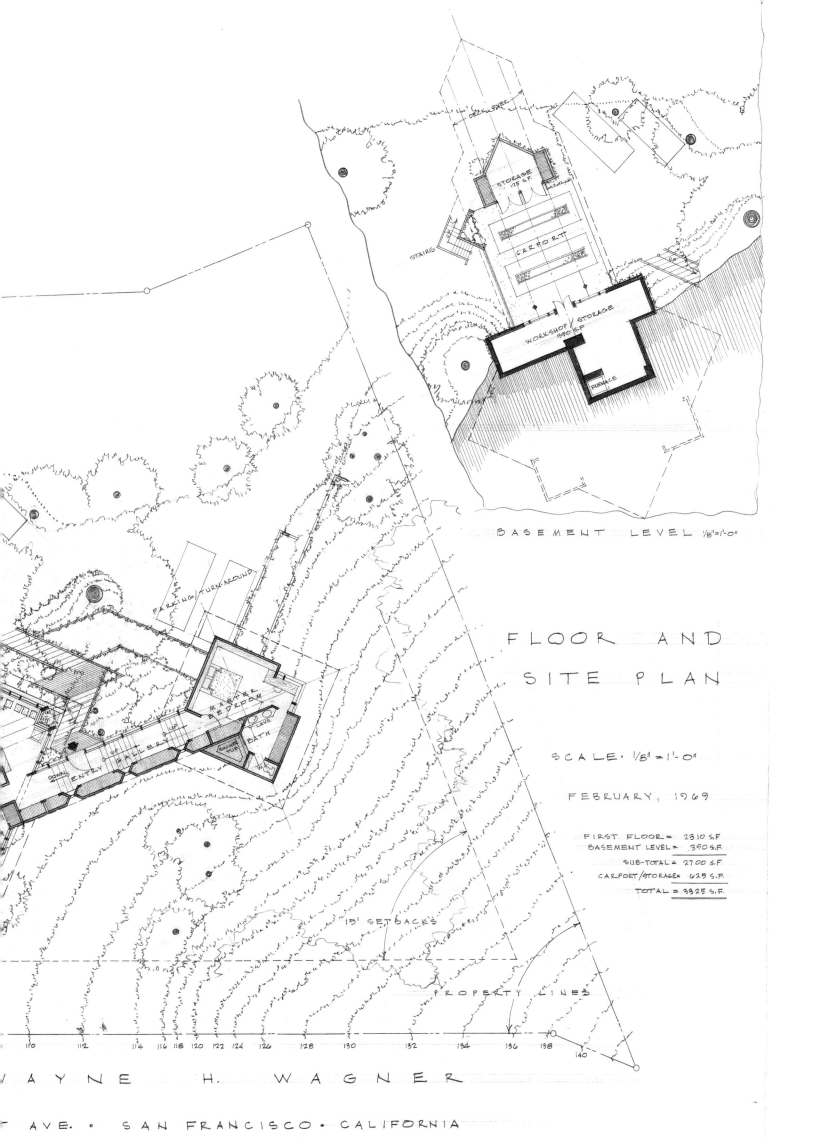

STORAGE
125 S.F.

CARPORT

WORKSHOP / STORAGE
390 S.F.

STAIRS

FURNACE

BASEMENT LEVEL 1/8"=1'-0"

PARKING/TURNAROUND

MASTER BEDROOM

LAVS.

BATH

SHOWER TUB

ENTRY GALLERY UP

FLOOR AND
SITE PLAN

SCALE· 1/8"=1'-0"

FEBRUARY, 1969

FIRST FLOOR = 2310 S.F.
BASEMENT LEVEL = 390 S.F.
SUB-TOTAL = 2700 S.F.
CARPORT/STORAGE = 625 S.F.
TOTAL = 3325 S.F.

15' SETBACKS

PROPERTY LINES

110   112   114 116 118 120 122 124 126   128   130   132   134   136   138   140

WAYNE H. WAGNER

AVE. · SAN FRANCISCO · CALIFORNIA

VIEW FROM DRIVEWAY

RESIDENCE FOR MR. &

ORINDA · CALIFORNIA

AARON G GREEN · ARCHITECT ·

RS. WAYNE H WAGNER

GRANT AVE. · SAN FRANCISCO · CALIFORNIA

■ ST. STEPHEN CATHOLIC CHURCH
■

■ Green had an established relationship with the Catholic Diocese of Oakland through his interment work that began in the mid-1950s, so it is understandable that his name was known to Father Joseph F. Keaveny. Keaveny was the new pastor of the three-year-old Walnut Creek parish, and, in 1969, selected Green as the architect for the design of their new church. St. Stephen Catholic Church was the first of ten church projects Green designed over the final 32 years of his practice.[68]

In the spring of 1969 Green developed a master plan for St. Stephen's sloping ten-acre site just northwest of the center of the fast growing community of Walnut Creek.[69] It included four distinctly separate buildings—the 14,500-square-foot church sanctuary along with a 6,000-square-foot rectory, 6,000-square-foot convent, and 10,000-square-foot parochial school with a 4,000-square-foot Parish Hall attached. Green's master plan also included parking for 200 cars and fourteen quarter-acre residential lots separated from the church property.

The church building was seen as the focal point and was earmarked for the initial phase of construction (this building was the only part of the master plan that was brought to fruition). It was designed to provide for the immediate spiritual, social, and educational needs of the Catholic community in Walnut Creek. Initially designed to seat 500 parishioners, the church building also included six temporary classrooms. Eventually, with the planned construction of the future school building, the non-load bearing partitions delineating the six interim classrooms would be removed allowing the seating capacity of the worship space to increase to 800.

Like many church projects, the biggest challenge was trying to create an innovative design within the owner's budget.[70] Green used four-inch-high custom colored concrete masonry, poured in place concrete, and redwood as the building's primary materials – taking special care to incorporate materials that required minimal maintenance. The asymmetrical fan-shaped plan of the building was a result of the congregation's functional needs, the Catholic

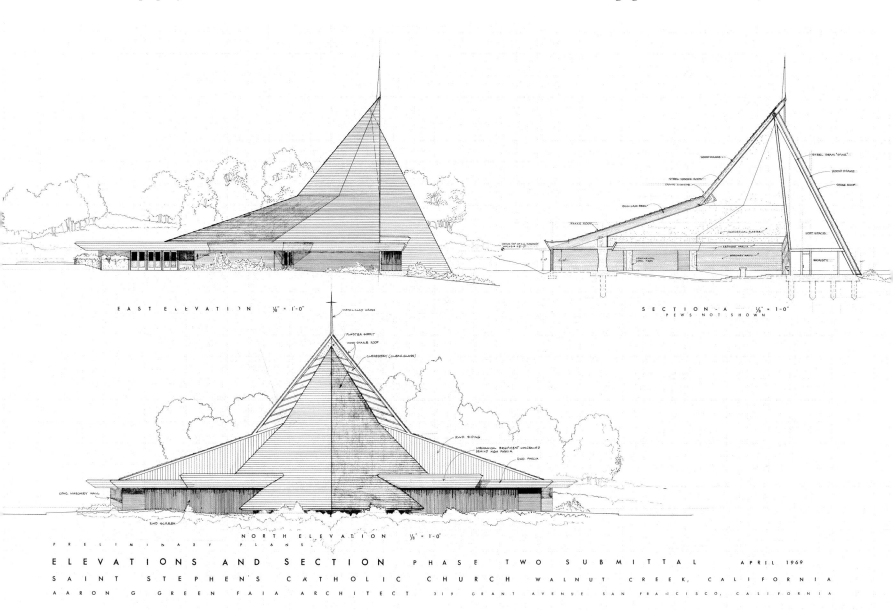

316

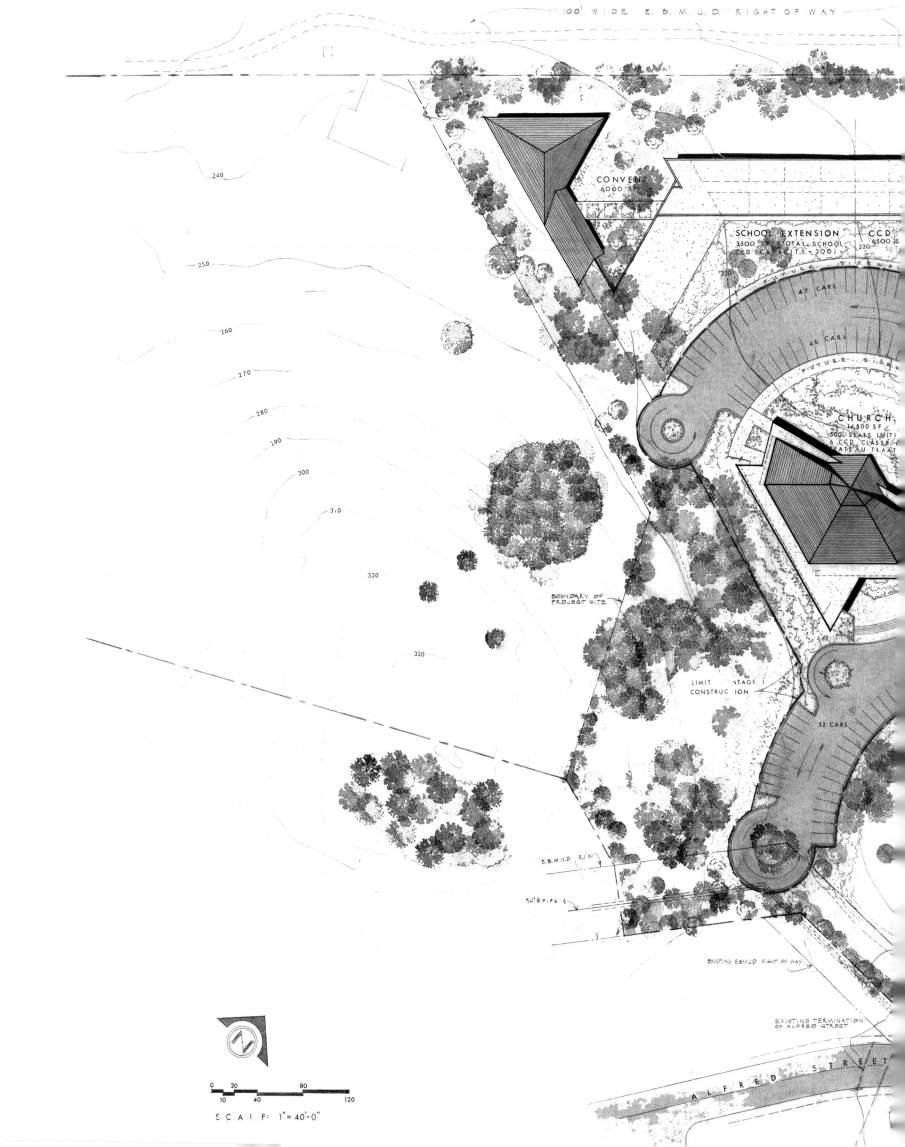

100' WIDE E. B. M. U. D. RIGHT OF WAY

240

250

260

270

280

290

300

310

320

330

CONVENT
4000 SF

SCHOOL EXTENSION   CCD
3500 SF TOTAL SCHOOL   6500 S
CCD CAPACITY - 300

47 CARS

46 CARS

CHURCH
14,500 SF
500 SEATS INITI
6 CCD CLASSR
SEATS ULTIMAT

BOUNDARY OF
PROJECT SITE

LIMIT   STAGE I
CONSTRUCTION

32 CARS

E.B.M.U.D. R/W

54" Ø PIPE

EXISTING E.B.M.U.D. RIGHT OF WAY

EXISTING TERMINATION
OF ALFRED STREET

ALFRED   STREET

0   20   80
10   40   120

SCALE: 1" = 40'-0"

PARISH
HALL
4000 SF

PLAYGROUND & PARKING
81 CARS

210

LIMIT OF STAGE
CONSTRUCTION

2 LOTS AT
10,000 S.F.

7 LOTS AT
10,000 S.F.

RECTORY
6000 SF

270

4 LOTS AT
10,000 S.F.

250

240

230

CONEJO WAY

EXISTING TERMINATION
OF CONEJO WAY

190

50' R.W.

200

210

220

230

270

FIRE HYD.

2,160 SF

DEVELOPMENT OF
SAN LUIS ROAD TO PL
BY DIOCESE

IMPROVEMENT OF EXISTING
SAN LUIS ROAD BY CITY OF WALNUT CREEK

SAN LUIS ROAD

FIRE HYD.

54" Ø PIPE

R/W

EXTG. EBMUD R/W

210

200

190

①②③④⑤⑥⑦⑧⑨⑩⑪⑫⑬⑭

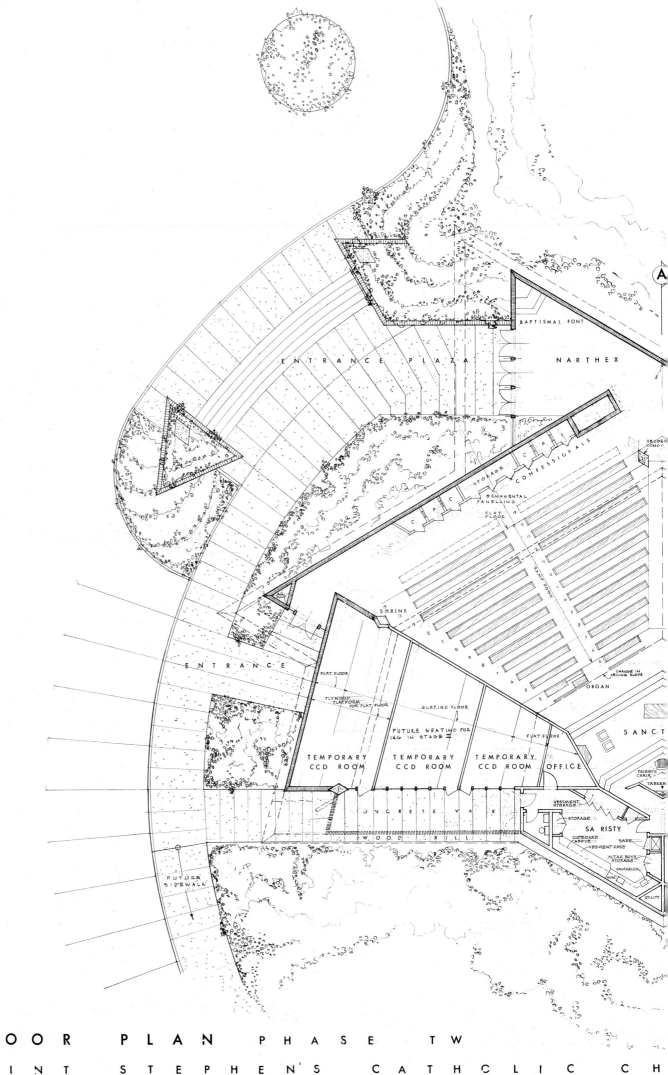

FLOOR PLAN PHASE TW

SAINT STEPHEN'S CATHOLIC CH

AARON G GREEN FAIA ARCHITECT

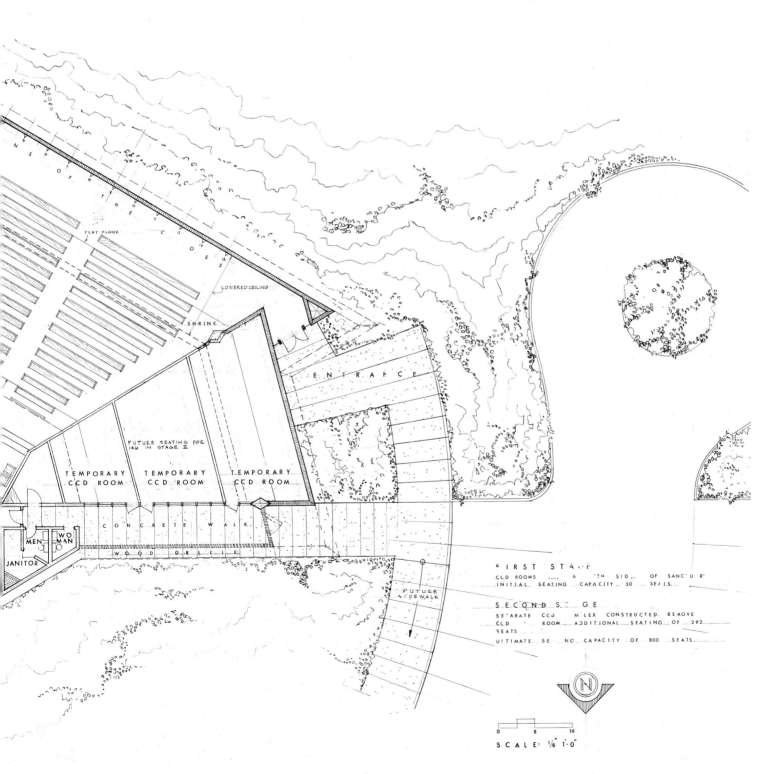

NS OF THE CROSS

FLAT FLOOR

LOWERED CEILING

SHRINE

ENTRANCE

FUTURE SEATING FOR
146 IN STAGE II

TEMPORARY   TEMPORARY   TEMPORARY
CCD ROOM   CCD ROOM   CCD ROOM

MEN WO
MAN

JANITOR

CONCRETE WALK

WOOD GRILLE

FUTURE
SIDEWALK

FIRST STAGE
CCD ROOMS .... BOTH SIDES OF SANCTUARY
INITIAL SEATING CAPACITY 50 SEATS.

SECOND STAGE
SEPARATE CCD COMPLEX CONSTRUCTED. REMOVE
CCD ROOM. ADDITIONAL SEATING OF 292
SEATS.
ULTIMATE SEATING CAPACITY OF 800 SEATS.

N

0   8   16

SCALE: 1/8" 1'-0"

Church's liturgical practices, circulation requirements, and Green's always respectful response to the natural characteristics of the site. Using a characteristic of Wright's architecture at St. Stephen, Green implemented a low sheltering entrance from the exterior entrance plaza into the narthex and the circulation zone at the rear before giving way to a soaring vertical spatial emphasis in the sanctuary. The dominant exterior form of the dramatic interior worship space was influenced by the acoustical requirements and a natural result of the clear span requirements of the structural system of steel and glue laminated wood members. The physical building, liturgical elements, fixtures, furnishings, and landscaping were all designed by Green. Meticulous attention was paid to the fundamentally important altar area, framed by the projected and splayed backdrop wall and high clerestory windows, as well as the geometrically intricate wood framed wall of confessionals.

Construction began in April 1970. The inaugural Mass was celebrated in the new sanctuary on September 11, 1971. Robert Price, an employee of Green's, recalled St. Stephen Catholic Church:

> is an extremely interesting structure created with very modest materials. The exterior is composed of decorative concrete block. The structural concept is that of a tent, with an off-center steel mast, supporting tensile steel cables held in place with glue laminated beams, all in compression. The Arch Diocese of Oakland expressed wonderment, and confided that they had never built a church as inexpensively as St. Stephen.[71]

SKYLAWN MEMORIAL PARK

Perched upon a mountain ridge approximately ten miles southwest of San Mateo, Skylawn Memorial Park overlooks the coastal city of Half Moon Bay and the Pacific Ocean beyond. Skylawn was Green's largest interment and memorial project, completed over a span of more than twenty-five years, which began in 1971. Randy Storer, nationally prominent in the interment industry, was the President of the Skylawn Corporation during much of this period. Storer recognized the importance of quality architecture in his business and quickly developed a deep respect for Green's creative genius. Over the years, as the client/architect partnership of Storer and Green evolved, they became trusted colleagues, kindred spirits, and good friends.

Green designed the master plan around the existing cemetery and mausoleum buildings that had been constructed on the western slope of Cahill Ridge in the 1960s. He expanded the ground burial areas and located additional single- and multi-storied mausoleum buildings, island columbaria, pavilion columbaria tucked into courtyards, garden areas, sculpture and statue elements, religious artifacts and features, fountains, seating, plazas, and terraces. One of the final additions was the design for the Bai Ling Yuan II Chinese garden cemetery.

As with all his interment projects, Green used a mixture of materials, most of which required little or no maintenance. At Skylawn, Green's palette included exposed, plain, and patterned

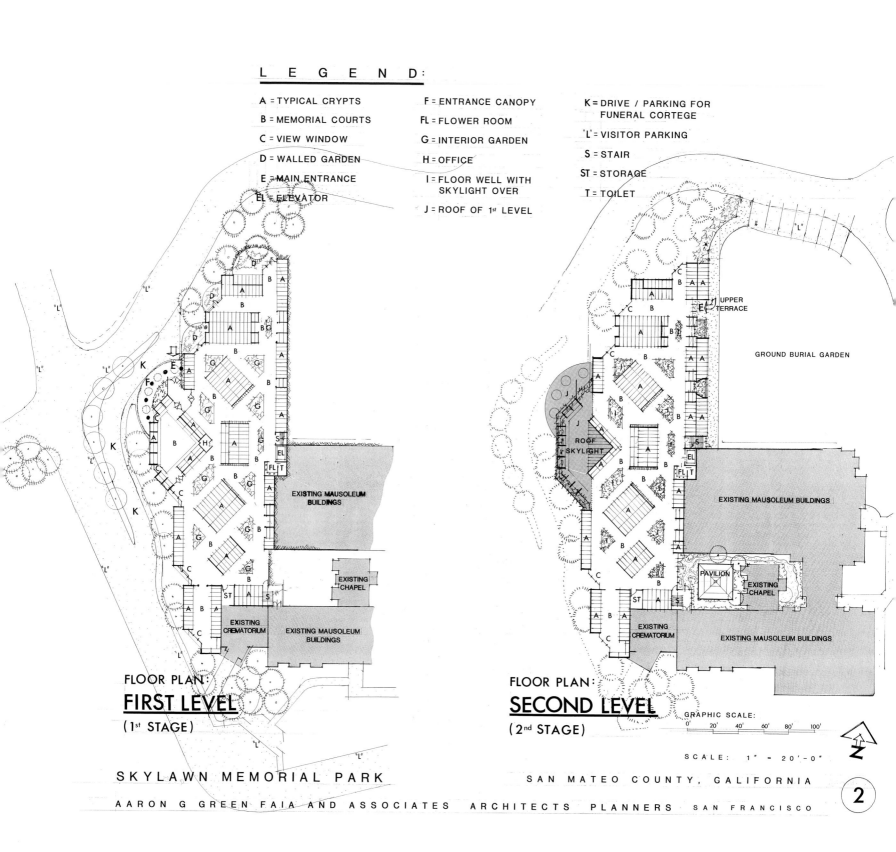

LEGEND:

A = TYPICAL CRYPTS
B = MEMORIAL COURTS
C = VIEW WINDOW
D = WALLED GARDEN
E = MAIN ENTRANCE
EL = ELEVATOR

F = ENTRANCE CANOPY
FL = FLOWER ROOM
G = INTERIOR GARDEN
H = OFFICE
I = FLOOR WELL WITH SKYLIGHT OVER
J = ROOF OF 1st LEVEL

K = DRIVE / PARKING FOR FUNERAL CORTEGE
"L" = VISITOR PARKING
S = STAIR
ST = STORAGE
T = TOILET

EXISTING MAUSOLEUM BUILDINGS

EXISTING CHAPEL

EXISTING CREMATORIUM

EXISTING MAUSOLEUM BUILDINGS

FLOOR PLAN:
FIRST LEVEL
(1st STAGE)

SKYLAWN MEMORIAL PARK

UPPER TERRACE

GROUND BURIAL GARDEN

ROOF SKYLIGHT

EXISTING MAUSOLEUM BUILDINGS

PAVILION

EXISTING CHAPEL

EXISTING CREMATORIUM

EXISTING MAUSOLEUM BUILDINGS

FLOOR PLAN:
SECOND LEVEL
(2nd STAGE)

GRAPHIC SCALE:
0' 20' 40' 60' 80' 100'

SCALE: 1" = 20'-0"

N

SAN MATEO COUNTY, CALIFORNIA

AARON G GREEN FAIA AND ASSOCIATES   ARCHITECTS   PLANNERS   SAN FRANCISCO

2

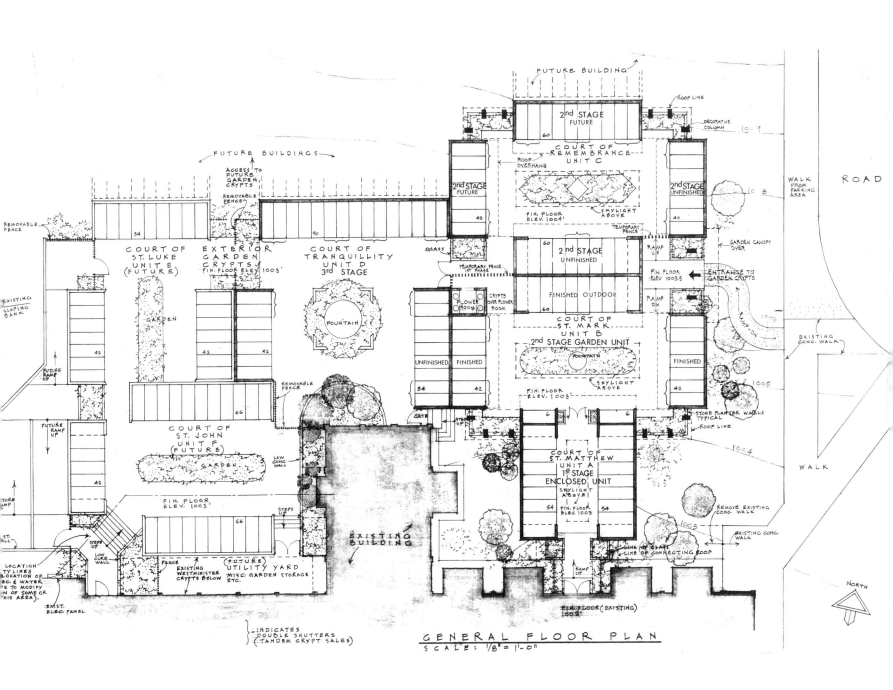

GENERAL FLOOR PLAN
SCALE: 1/8" = 1'-0"

329

SKYLAWN MEMORIAL PARK MAUSOLEUM
AARON G. GREEN F.A.I.A. ARCHITECT

330

AUSOLEUM IN THE SKY

SKYLAWN MEMORIAL PARK   SAN MATEO, CALIFORNIA

AARON G. GREEN, FAIA AND ASSOCIATES   ARCHITECT

MAUSOLEUM IN THE SKY

SKYLAWN MEMORIAL PARK   SAN MATEO, CALIFORNIA

AARON G. GREEN, FAIA AND ASSOCIATES   ARCHITECT

332

AVILION

SKYLAWN MEMORIAL PARK   SAN MATEO, CALIFORNIA
AARON G. GREEN, FAIA AND ASSOCIATES   ARCHITECT

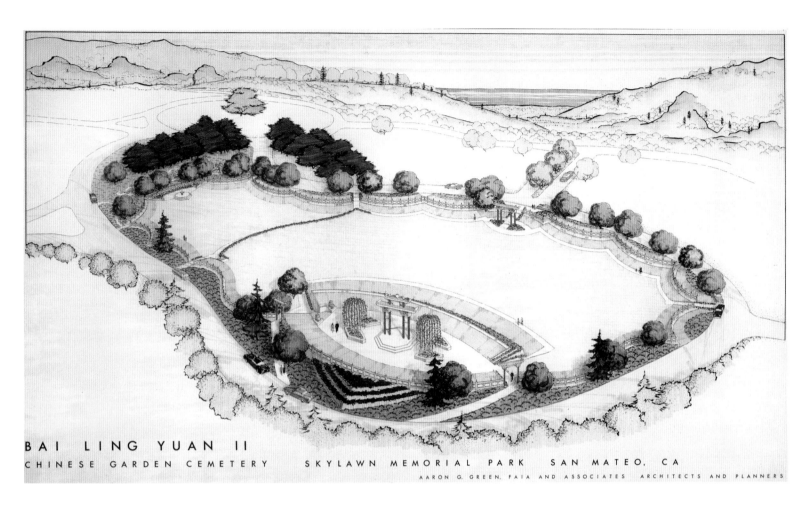

BAI LING YUAN II
CHINESE GARDEN CEMETERY   SKYLAWN MEMORIAL PARK   SAN MATEO, CA
AARON G. GREEN, FAIA AND ASSOCIATES   ARCHITECTS AND PLANNERS

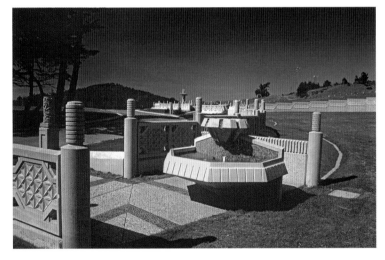

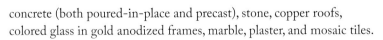

concrete (both poured-in-place and precast), stone, copper roofs, colored glass in gold anodized frames, marble, plaster, and mosaic tiles.

BAI LING YUAN VI

CHINESE CEMETERY

SKYLAWN MEMORIAL PARK

AARON G. GREEN ASSOCIAT

UNION CITY CIVIC CENTER

In early 1974, Green was retained to design a civic activity center for the 29,000 citizens of Union City on a flat, uninteresting, twelve-acre site located on the southern side of Alvarado Niles Road at H Street. Union City was a diverse community with large Latino and Japanese populations. Green sought to reflect this multi-cultural population in the design of the Union City Civic Center, a focal point in the community, fostering a healthy unified community spirit.

Green's master plan consisted of two buildings—a government complex and a public library—with associated parking, and a passive public park. The buildings were to be dignified, informal, and inviting, avoiding any institutional aesthetic. The city desired a modern, up-to-date, progressive image. The park included a lagoon, bridge feature, areas for art exhibitions, small amphitheater, picnic and play areas, and bike and pedestrian pathways, all designed in an informal park-like landscape setting. His successful manipulation of the surrounding area and its integration with the new buildings blended perfectly to create a beautiful and functional site.

The two-story, 35,000-square-foot government complex housed governmental administrative offices and community planning and development staff on the upper floor, and offices and facilities for public safety departments on the lower level. Earth obtained from the excavation for the new lagoon was mounded and sculpted around the building to provide on grade access to both floors while enhancing the project's visual characteristics. The public enters the upper level via an interior sky-lit lobby with a Japanese garden between the city council chambers and the administrative offices. The 40-foot-long skylight rolls open to expose the garden to the natural light when weather allows.

The separate single-story (plus partial mezzanine) public library building enclosed approximately 13,800 square feet, designed to hold 50,000 books, reading areas, offices, work areas, and a small community meeting room. On the exterior Green provided a reading deck that extended into the site's lagoon, linking the building with the site.

Green chose durable materials for the project: concrete (poured-in-place and pre-cast), wood, plaster stucco, and clay barrel tile roofing. The contemporary forms, materials, and colors were intended to express local ethnic traditions. Along with the landscaping and architectural design for the project, Green designed

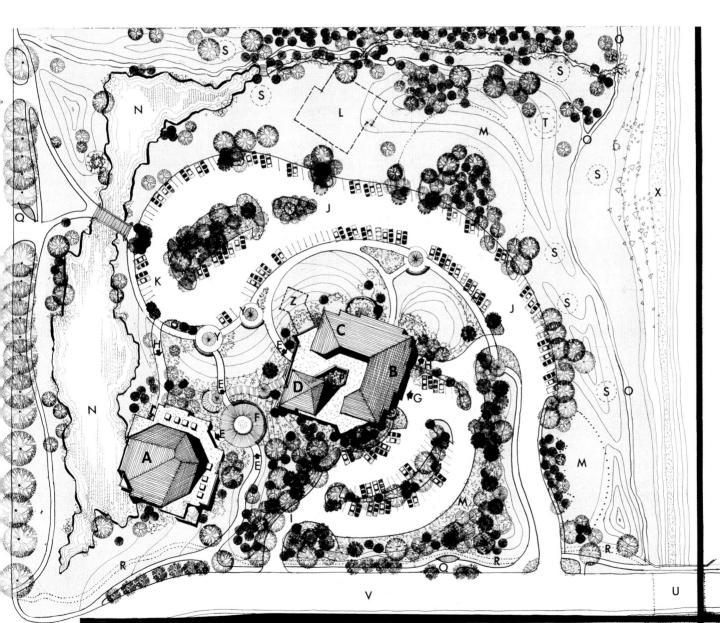

LEGEND

- **A** LIBRARY
- **B** POLICE ADMINISTRATION
- **C** CITY HALL
- **D** CITY COUNCIL CHAMBER
- **E** PEDESTRIAN ENTRANCE
- **F** PASEO ENTRANCE
- **G** VEHICLE ENTRANCE POLICE DEPT
- **H** SERVICE ENTRANCE
- **I** POLICE DEPT PARKING
- **J** GENERAL PARKING
- **K** LIBRARY PARKING AREA
- **L** FUTURE BUILDING SITE
- **M** PARKING EXPANSION
- **N** LAGOON
- **O** TRAIL SYSTEM HIKING PATH
- **P** JAPANESE GARDEN
- **Q** BUS STOP
- **R** WALK AND BICYCLE PATH
- **S** PICNIC SPOTS
- **T** TOTS PLAYGROUND
- **U** PROPOSED BRIDGE
- **V** "H" STREET EXTENSION
- **W** ALVARADO NILES ROAD
- **X** FLOOD CONTROL CHANNEL
- **Y** FLAGPOLE
- **Z** FUTURE ADDITION

CIVIC CENTER FOR THE CITY OF UNION CITY, CALIFORNIA
LIBRARY · POLICE ADMINISTRATION · CITY HALL
AARON G. GREEN, F.A.I.A., & ASSOCIATES · ARCHITECTS/PLANNERS · SAN FRANCISCO

MASTER PLAN

DESIGN DEVELOPMENT PHASE

MAY 5, 1975

LIBRARY — NORTH

LIBRARY — SOUTH

CIVIC CENTER — EAST ELEVATION

SOUTH ELEVATION

WEST ELEVATION

MAIN
ENTRANCE

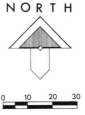

NORTH

0   10   20   30

SALLY PORT
STAFF ENTRANCE

TRUCK DOCK

ENTRANCE

NORTH

0   10   20   30

MEZZANINE

LIBRARY UNION CITY, CALIFORNIA

or selected all interior and exterior fixtures and furnishings, signage, and graphics.

He involved the client and citizenry throughout the process, providing questionnaires to all city employees, the Japanese community, council members, and department heads involved in planting the Japanese garden. Robert Price, an employee of Green's recalled, "Aaron and I personally went to nearby quarries to select the 200 to 300 tons of specimen boulders, rocks, and decorative gravel. When delivered, Aaron assigned me to spend a week with a contract bull-dozer front loader to locate the main boulders, to lift, tilt, spin, partially bury, and to achieve the best overall look."[72] He continued,

"I believe the Union City Civic Center project represented so many of the qualities Aaron brought to his projects and clients. Dedication, vision, client involvement (and appreciation), on budget, attention to detail, architecture as a way of life—all faithfully executed and inherent in Aaron's work."[73]

In 1979, Alan Temko, a local San Francisco architectural critic, expressed about Green's design for Union City, "Green has put the Wrightian philosophy to fresh purpose in a singularly friendly and eloquent civic center for Union City."[74]

349

McANDREWS RESIDENCE

John P. ("Jack") McAndrews and his wife Margaret retired to Pebble Beach after raising their five children and finishing their careers in the Midwest (John was a career executive with DuPont). They requested that Green design a spacious, informal home that would accommodate their new, more relaxed, quiet lifestyle that consisted of occasional small scale entertaining, reading, and study. Their site was an evenly sloped one-acre parcel between Griffin and Spruance Roads, less than two miles from the Pebble Beach golf course. Green placed the linear 4,200-square-foot two-level home parallel to the slope with its primary axis running from the northwest to southeast. The floor plan was based on a rotated four-foot-square unit system.

Green located all the major living areas within a uniquely shaped series of interconnected squares on the uppermost level. Unifying the entire composition is a broad, sheltering, low-sloped, gable roof that flattened into cantilevering eaves with vertically sloped horizontal wood fascias as it extended out. The kitchen, living, and dining areas, linked with the expansive and continuous vaulted ceiling, all have open views overlooking a cantilevered deck that runs the entire length of the southwest side of the house. The deck also serves to protect the lower level, containing two bedrooms and their associated bathrooms and an office, from inclement weather and exposure to the late afternoon sun.

Green located the exterior entrance that flows from grade upwards to the elevated interior foyer between the end of the house and the semi-detached two-car garage. The actual connection of both at the distinctively designed front door, where one finds themselves between the exterior, semi-public space and the interior, semi-private space, is mid-level between the more public living areas above and the more private sleeping areas below. To heighten the three-dimension-

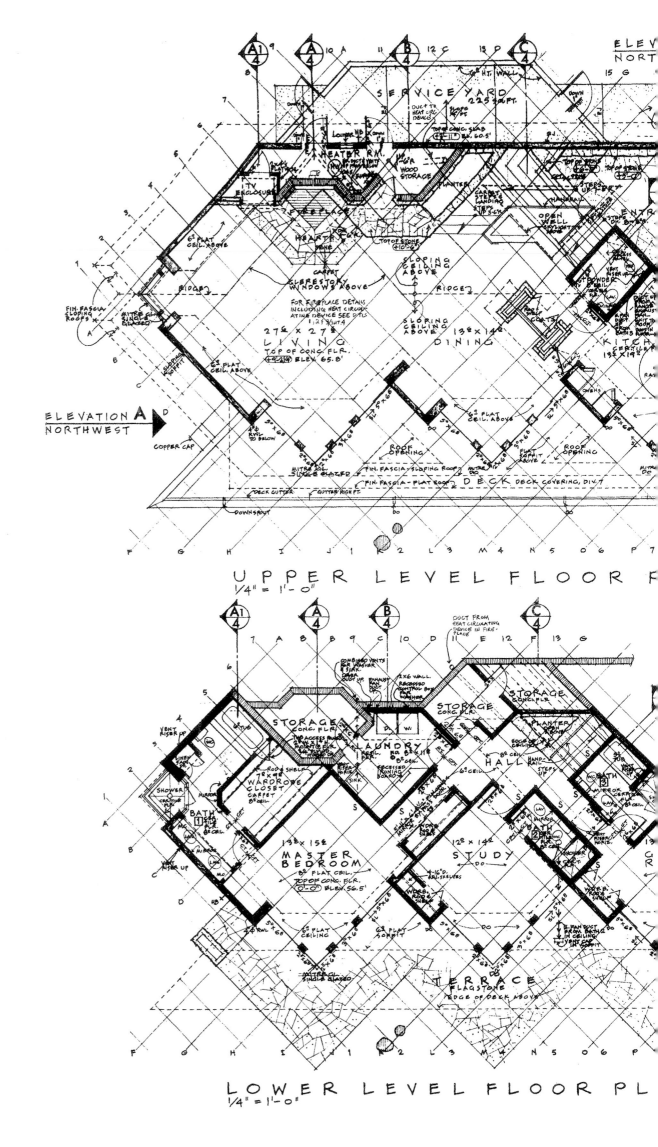

ELEV
NORT

U P P E R   L E V E L   F L O O R   F
1/4" = 1'-0"

L O W E R   L E V E L   F L O O R   P L
1/4" = 1'-0"

ELEVATION A
NORTHWEST

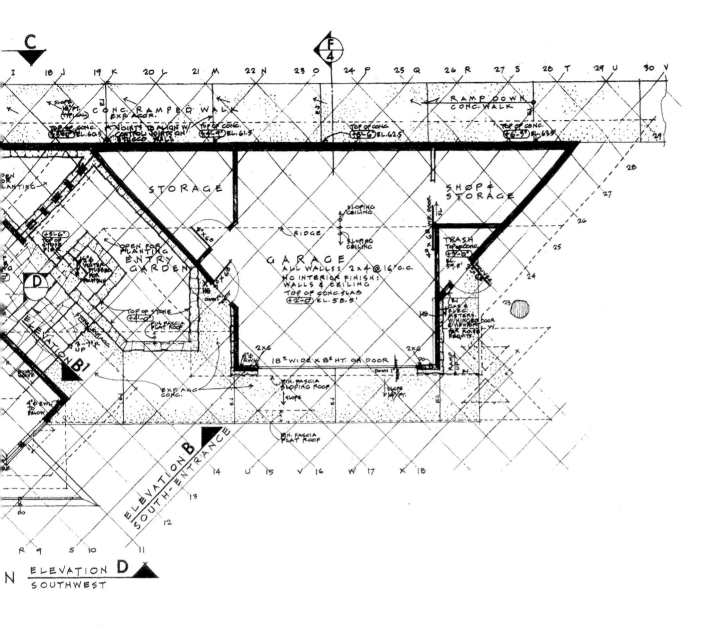

C

F
4

I 18 J 19 K 20 L 21 M 22 N 23 O 24 P 25 Q 26 R 27 S 28 T 29 U 30 V

CONC. RAMPED WALK

RAMP DOWN
CONC. WALK

TOP OF CONC. EL.62.5'

TOP OF CONC. EL.63.5'

TOP OF CONC. EL.61.5'

STORAGE

SHOP &
STORAGE

OPEN FOR
PLANTING
ENTRY
GARDEN

RIDGE

TRASH

GARAGE
ALL WALLS: 2×4 @ 16" O.C.
NO INTERIOR FINISH:
WALLS & CEILING
TOP OF CONC. SLAB
(+2'-0") EL. 58.5'

GAS &
ELEC.
METERS
W/KNOB & DOOR

D

TOP OF STONE

18" WIDE × 8" HT. OH. DOOR

2×6

ELEVATION B
SOUTH ENTRANCE

ELEVATION B1

14 U 15 V 16 W 17 X 18

13

12

R 9 S 10 11

N   ELEVATION D
     SOUTHWEST

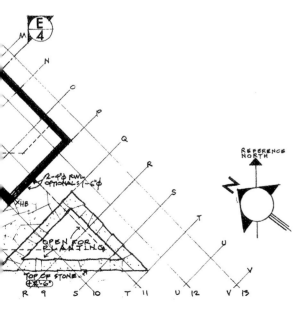

E
4

M

N

O

P

Q

R

S

T

U

V

REFERENCE
NORTH

N

OPEN FOR
PLANTING

TOP OF STONE
(+2'-0")

R 9 S 10 T 11 U 12 V 13

353

al entry sequence that occurs over flagstone pavers, Green provided an interesting, somewhat complex interplay of the protecting and projecting pitched roofs of both the main house and garage. Green incorporated a common planter between the exterior and interior spaces at the front door, separated only by glass, to provide an unexpected garden.

The McAndrews residence is wood framed with a stucco exterior and painted drywall interior. Carmel-type stone masonry was used to provide a material, textual, and color contrast to the otherwise flat surfaces of the stucco and drywall, and redwood and oak trim are incorporated throughout as reliefs, with the whole ensemble capped by the roof which is entirely sheathed with copper. The clients, wanting to divest themselves of their old furniture, requested that

Green design or select all new furnishings for the home, and Green took special care in the design and placement of the built-in furnishings and cabinetry. Corian, a product produced by DuPont, is used throughout the home, a testament to John's lifelong work.

Tom Guice was the builder of the McAndrews house as well as the nearby Haber house, designed by Green the following year. Green made it a point to involve the same builder for the two houses, and used similar details for both projects, which translated into cost savings and quality control for his clients.

HABER RESIDENCE

Charles Pauson Haber (1920-2006), the brother of Green's first wife Jean, and his wife Martha bought a residential lot in Carmel Valley, approximately ten miles east southeast of Carmel-by-the-Sea, in the 1960s and eventually approached Green to design their home. During the design process, Martha became ill and died from cancer in 1985, and the work was abandoned. Two years later the widowed Haber approached Green to move forward with completing the design. Interestingly, even though he was alone, Haber instructed his former brother-in-law to continue to design the house to accommodate both Haber and a future wife. The house was completed in 1990.

Incredibly, as Haber had foreseen, he remarried in 1993 and brought his new wife Candace into the home.

Located at the northwest quadrant of the intersection of Encina Drive and Miramonte Road, the lot allowed for Green's 4,500-square-foot home, decks, and terraces. Green located all of the home's more social living areas within a hexagonally shaped core sheltered by the spreading canopy of an all-encompassing, flat terra cotta colored tile roof. Its central stone masonry fireplace core both anchors this "great room" and serves to separate the various functions that his plan labeled entry, garden room, living room, library, dining,

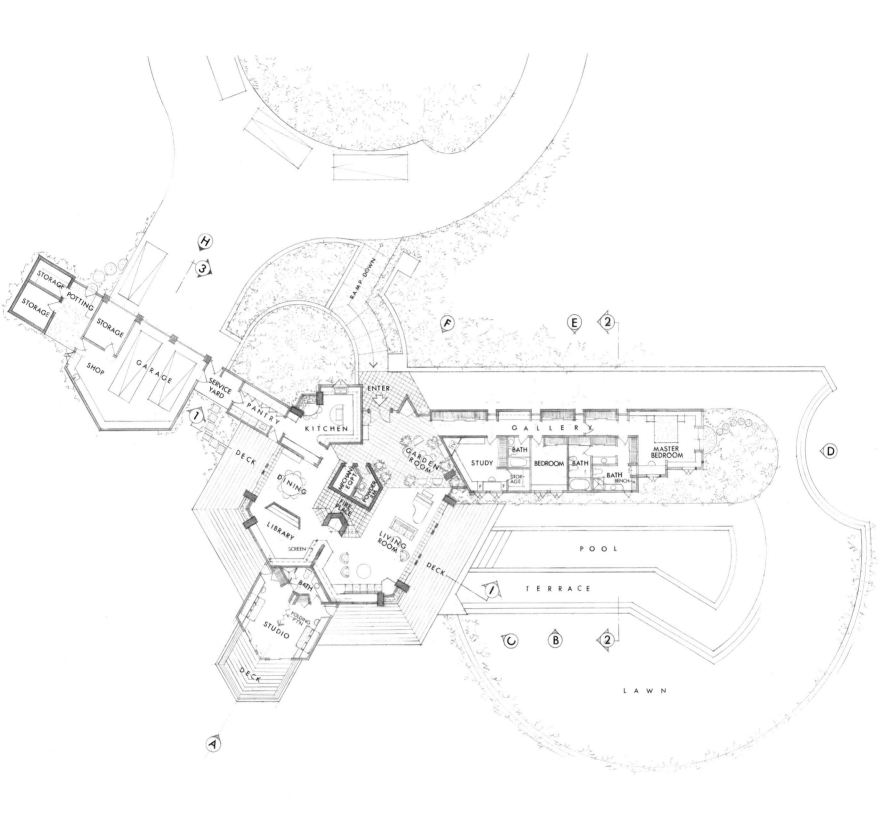

and kitchen. Discreetly attached at the end opposite the entry and garden room, Green located a smaller secondary six-sided studio that protruded from the larger primary hexagonal form. Two wings grew off the hexagonal core – the first towards the north contains a pantry, two-car garage, shop, several storage rooms, and a potting area; the second towards the southeast contains the study, bedroom, two bathrooms, and master suite, all accessed off a gallery.

With the exception of the roofing material, the Haber residence's aesthetic palette is similar to the McAndrews residence in nearby Pebble Beach that Green designed the previous year. The home is wood framed with primarily stucco exterior and painted drywall on the interior. Carmel-type stone masonry is also found both on the exterior and interior to provide a material, textural, and color contrast to the otherwise flat surfaces of the stucco and drywall.

357

Redwood and oak trim is utilized throughout. Green incorporated a continuous clerestory window over the bedroom wing to bring daylight into the rooms below and translucent skylights in the hexagonal roof around the vertical chimney component, allowing soft, diffused light deep into the home's interior.

ST. ELIZABETH SETON CATHOLIC CHURCH

Green's last Catholic church within the Oakland Diocese was the St. Elizabeth Seton Catholic Church in Pleasanton. Pleasanton's single Catholic church, St. Augustine, was built in 1882 and, in 1968, replaced with a larger edifice. As Pleasanton continued to grow (over a span of thirty years, from 1960 to 1990, the population grew from 4,200 to more than 35,000) the Catholic community recognized a real need for a second church. By late 1987 Green completed a Phase 1 and Phase 2 report, and a master plan was created that delineated approximately 70,000 square feet of building area for the congregation's use.

Located two miles north of central Pleasanton, fronting the south side of Stoneridge Drive just east of Rheem Drive, St. Elizabeth Seton Catholic Church was built on approximately twelve acres of uninspiring, relatively flat land within a residential neighborhood. Green's master plan identified two primary structures that he located in the center of the site – pastoral offices and a chapel (phase 1) connected to a larger church edifice (phase 2) encircled by 132 parking spaces. To the east were additional connected buildings designed as classrooms, a multi-purpose gymnasium, and an elementary school plus additional parking. To the west Green identified a parcel for approximately 48,000 square feet of future retail development. Of the master design, only the first two buildings were built.

The initial building, dedicated on October 6, 1991, was a one-level, nearly 12,000-square-foot structure containing a 200 seat worship space with a large sky-lit narthex (planned to accommodate the future larger church addition), administrative offices, and a meeting room. Green estimated the cost to construct phase 1 buildings and site improvements would be close to $3,000,000.

The second phase, a 15,000-square-foot addition built at a cost of approximately $5,000,000, was located northeast and connected to the existing narthex of the original chapel. The symmetrical worship space was designed to seat more than 800. The congregational "theater-in-the-round" seating arrangement responded to the new dictate of the Vatican and was requested by the parish priest; it allowed for clear site-lines and a more intimate connection with each other and the celebrant. The altar is located in the very center of the hexagonal plan directly below a broad translucent skylight. The diffused daylight from above dramatically complements the liturgical service and spiritual experience. The addition was dedicated on June 4, 2000.

While Green's architecture of both phases was generally consistent in three dimensions—its contemporary expression, similar materials, and economical structure—the plans of each phase are uniquely different (the egg shaped chapel as compared to the more

ST. ELIZABETH SETON CATHOLIC CHURCH PLEASANTON, CALIFORNIA
AARON G. GREEN, FAIA AND ASSOCIATES, INC.   ARCHITECTS AND PLANNERS

VIEW LOOKING SOUTH

ST. ELIZABETH SETON CATHOLIC CHURCH   PLEASANTON, CALIFORNIA

AARON G. GREEN, FAIA AND ASSOCIATES, INC.   ARCHITECTS AND PLANNERS

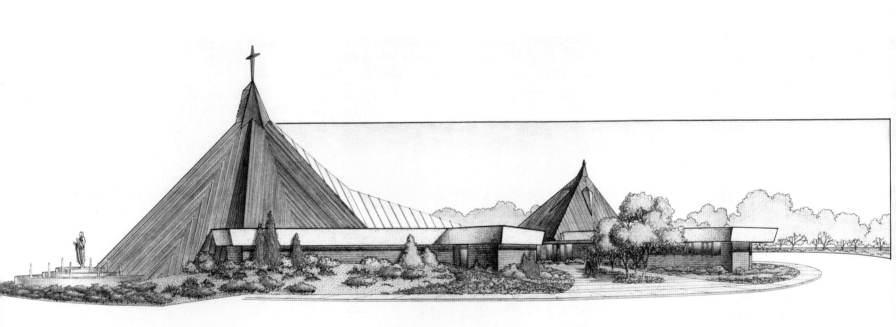

VIEW LOOKING SOUTH

ST. ELIZABETH SETON CATHOLIC CHURCH   PLEASANTON, CALIFORNIA

AARON G. GREEN ASSOCIATES, INC.   ARCHITECTS AND PLANNERS

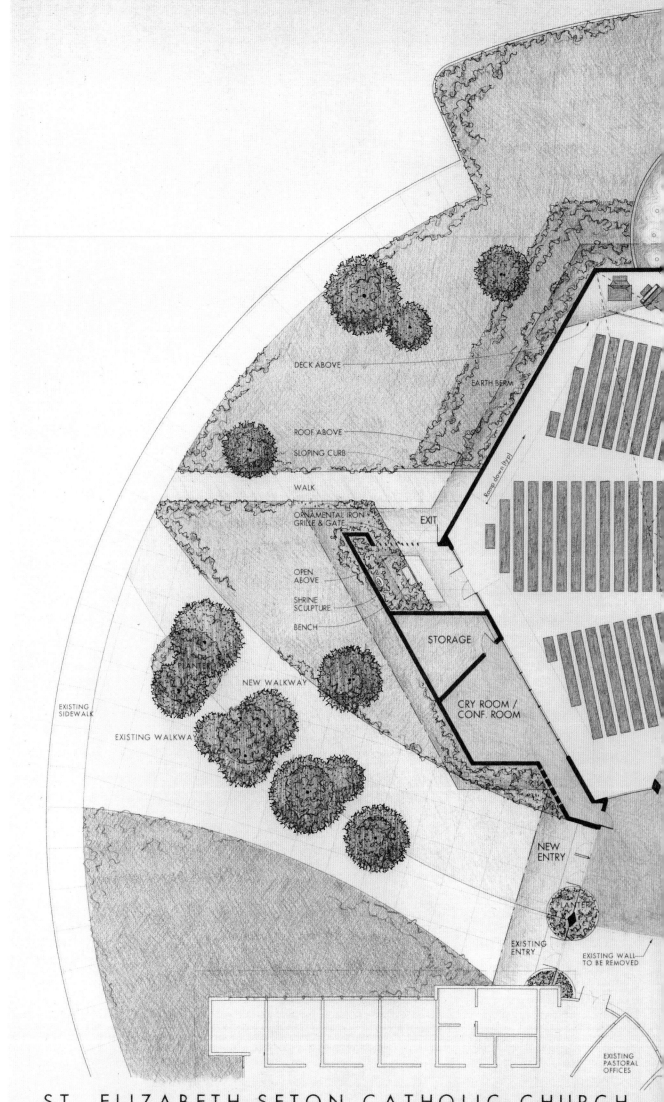

DECK ABOVE

EARTH BERM

ROOF ABOVE

SLOPING CURB

WALK

ORNAMENTAL IRON
GRILLE & GATE

EXIT

OPEN
ABOVE

SHRINE
SCULPTURE

BENCH

STORAGE

CRY ROOM /
CONF. ROOM

NEW WALKWAY

PLANTER

EXISTING
SIDEWALK

EXISTING WALKWAY

NEW
ENTRY

PLANTER

EXISTING
ENTRY

EXISTING WALL
TO BE REMOVED

EXISTING
PASTORAL
OFFICES

Ramp down (typ)

ST. ELIZABETH SETON CATHOLIC CHURCH

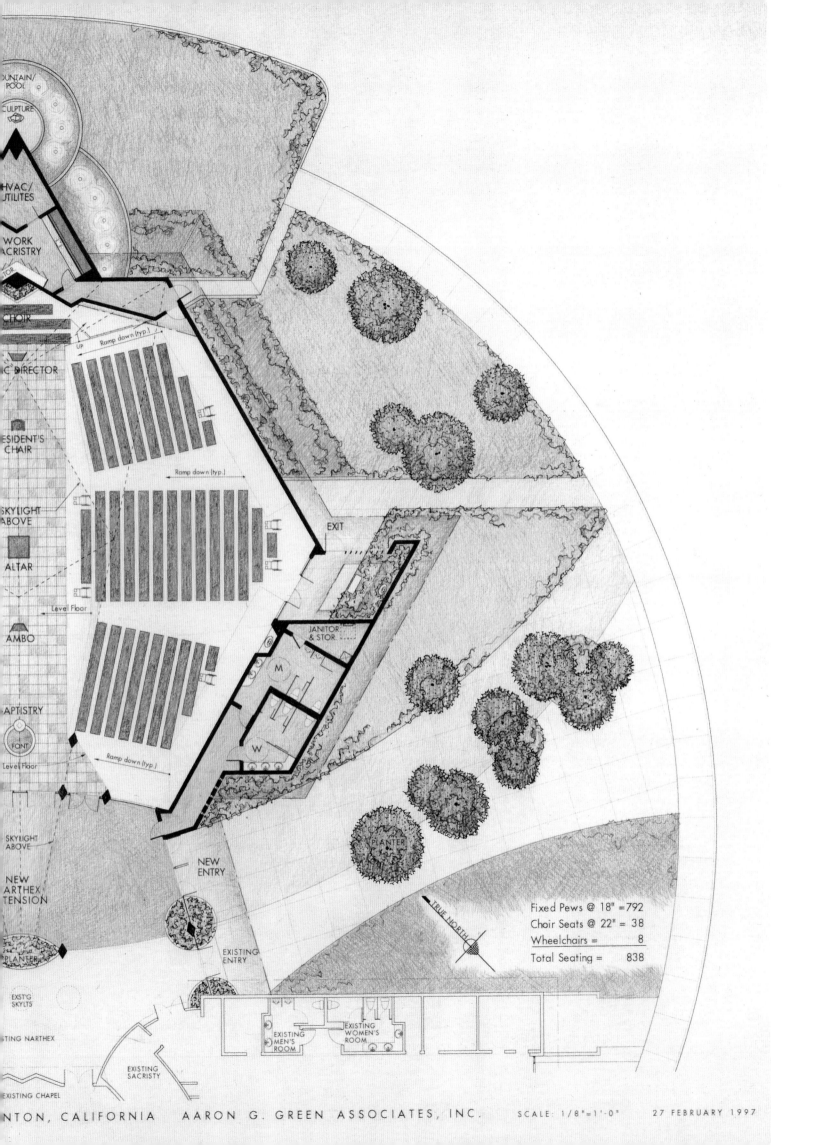

FOUNTAIN/
POOL

SCULPTURE

HVAC/
UTILITES

WORK
SACRISTY

CHOIR

MUSIC DIRECTOR

PRESIDENT'S
CHAIR

SKYLIGHT
ABOVE

ALTAR

AMBO

BAPTISTRY

FONT

Level Floor

SKYLIGHT
ABOVE

NEW
NARTHEX
EXTENSION

PLANTER

EXST'G
SKYLTS

EXISTING NARTHEX

EXISTING
SACRISTY

EXISTING CHAPEL

Up   Ramp down (typ.)

Ramp down (typ.)

Level Floor

Ramp down (typ.)

EXIT

JANITOR
& STOR

M

W

NEW
ENTRY

EXISTING
ENTRY

PLANTER

EXISTING
MEN'S
ROOM

EXISTING
WOMEN'S
ROOM

TRUE NORTH

Fixed Pews @ 18" = 792
Choir Seats @ 22" = 38
Wheelchairs =   8
Total Seating =   838

...NTON, CALIFORNIA   AARON G. GREEN ASSOCIATES, INC.   SCALE: 1/8"=1'-0"   27 FEBRUARY 1997

VIEW   FROM   NARTHEX   ENTRY

ST. ELIZABETH SETON CATHOLIC CHURCH   PLEASANTON, CALIFORNIA

AARON G. GREEN ASSOCIATES, INC.   ARCHITECTS AND PLANNERS

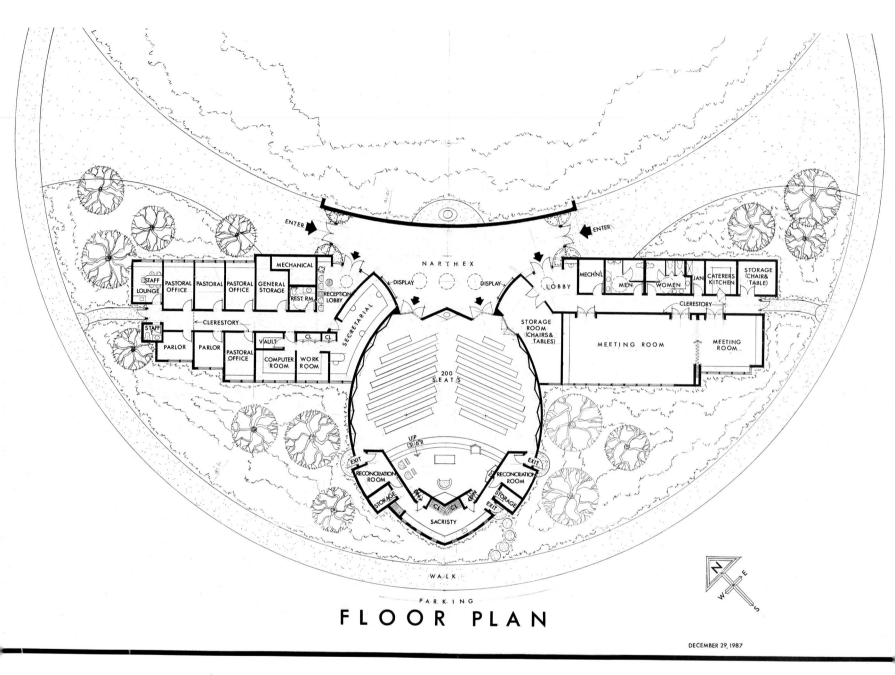

FLOOR PLAN

DECEMBER 29, 1987

CHAPEL AND PASTORAL OFFICES:

SCALE: 1/8" = 1'-0"

angular six-sided church). The faceted, asymmetrical, pyramid roof forms enclosing the worship spaces below aligned with each other axially. While both roofs were sheathed in copper with raised battens arranged in a decorative pattern, they were of differing sizes, with the church roof the larger and more dominant of the two. The materials shared by both phases were economical, low maintenance and of similar nature and color – concrete (both poured-in-place and precast), colored split-faced concrete masonry, plaster, and copper. Like St. Stephen Catholic Church, Green was responsible for the architecture and site landscaping as well as the fixtures, furnishings, liturgical elements, full-immersion baptismal pool, and decorative arts. A

large sculpture depicting St. Elizabeth Seton in a protective embrace of children, commissioned by Green from sculptor Heloise Crista, is prominently placed on the project's primary longitudinal axis over a water pool at the northeast terminus of the final phase (like a period placed at the end of a sentence).

■

■

■

367

MUELLER RESIDENCE

Dr. Gernot Mueller (1955-), a physician with a family practice in Yuba City, and his wife Guinevere Ruth (1939-), an administrator and teacher of the arts in the Fellowship of Friends in Oregon House, California, approached Green after a recommendation from their eventual builder, Stephen Detmold. Detmold himself had been a recent client of Green's and was, at the time of their first meeting, building a Green-designed project on Regent Way in nearby Renaissance, California. Green came to meet with the Muellers over a weekend after which they, in turn, soon traveled to his office and talked about the program for the house for almost eight hours. When told that their budget was a mere $150,000 Green indicated that while it sounded on the low side it only meant that he had to be that much more creative. Still, later Green told them "you got a Mercedes on a Volkswagen budget."[75]

Green's design for the Muellers was to be built in three phases, with the last two additions to appear seamless, as if they had been built with the initial phase.[76] Only the initial approximately 2,500-square-foot phase was realized. It's nestled into a three-acre, sloping site in the foothills of the Sierra Nevada Mountains northeast of Sacramento. Green latched onto a request from Mrs. Mueller – she wanted a retreat for contemplation while looking out over the trees. Green's design expresses that objective with its steeply sloped, tall, pyramidal roof that encloses the spaces stacked vertically within.

The ground floor provides for all the basic functions rotating around a central fireplace and utility core – informal spaces for living and dining, a kitchen, small breakfast area, and an office off the primary entry. The master bedroom suite was above the ground floor and, above the bedroom level and accessible by a circular stair, Green

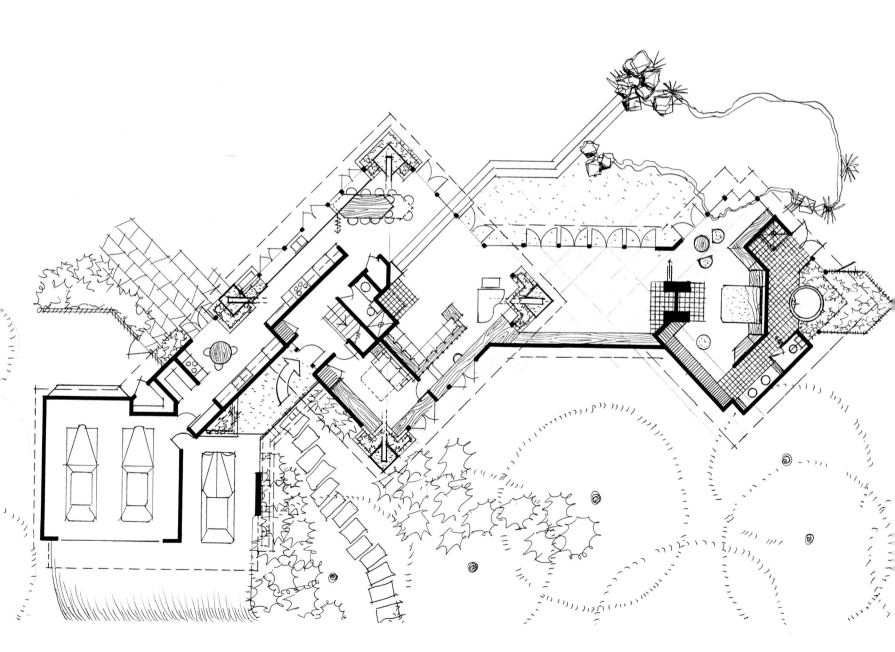

created a small loft-like refuge at the uppermost summit of the roof. This windowed refuge, in amongst the treetops, became the destination space for the desired contemplation and, from its extended balcony, the place to look out over the trees. Both the bedroom and refuge floors were purposefully held back from the exterior walls giving a sense of floating as the space expands vertically under the sloping roof and its supporting glue laminated beams. Completed in the late 1990s, the entire opus was an ingenious, cost effective solution to the site's opportunities and constraints as well as the client's extensive program but limited budget.

ALLAN GREEN RESIDENCE

On May 24, 1949 Green telegraphed his mentor requesting permission to give their just born son the middle name of Wright. Several days later, Wright responded, "Go ahead. Hope it doesn't sink him."[77] Almost forty-five years later, Green's first born, Allan, approached his father for a house to be built on family land in Philo, California. Philo is in Anderson Valley in western Mendocino County, about two and a half hours driving time north of San Francisco. Since the early 1970s Green's first wife Jean and their two sons had been assembling a family compound to escape to in this remote and rural area. Green remodeled two existing structures for his sons in 1973 and 1987 and he designed a small home for Jean in 1975. In 1985 Green designed a tasting room for Allan's wine business, Greenwood Ridge Vineyards.

In 1993 Allan, like any other client, completed a long and detailed client questionnaire that his father had developed over the years to help identify and define his client's needs and desires. Both father and son walked the property to select the suitable site for the home. The design process was deliberate, taking approximately three years. Allan recalled that, "paying clients kept getting in the way of my father finishing this *pro bono* family project."[78] He also recalled that his father designed the home almost entirely in his head before he started to record it on paper (something that his mentor, Wright was known to do). The construction started in 1996 by expert local builder Jim Boudoures of Philo Saw Works, who had built Allan's Greenwood Ridge Vineyards tasting room. Allan moved in two years later, in 1998.

Allan requested a home that required little if no maintenance and was basically fireproof. A bachelor at that time (he married Marianna in 2006), Allan's functional needs were straightforward. James Dixon, an employee at the time, recalled that Green designed the home from the inside out. At the same time the home was designed to be harmonious with the land and environment, Green expertly augmented the area with low maintenance landscaping that blended in with the natural forest. Early on in the design

MAIN FLOOR PLAN

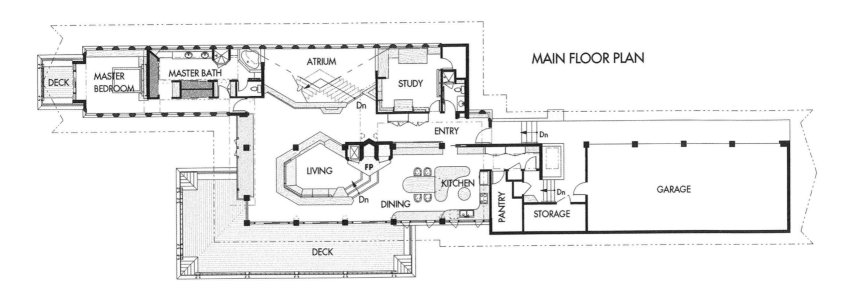

DECK

MASTER BEDROOM

MASTER BATH

ATRIUM

STUDY

Dn

ENTRY

LIVING

FP

Dn

KITCHEN

DINING

PANTRY

STORAGE

Dn

GARAGE

DECK

LOWER FLOOR PLAN

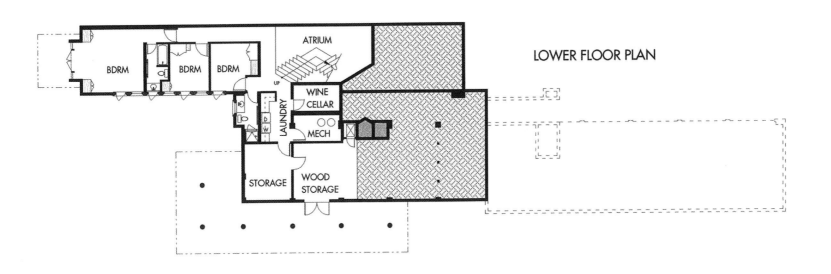

BDRM

BDRM

BDRM

ATRIUM

UP

WINE CELLAR

LAUNDRY

MECH

STORAGE

WOOD STORAGE

process Green actually considered utilizing a sod covered roof for the home.

The built home is unquestionably one of Green's most highly refined masterstrokes of his lengthy career. Like a beautifully built piece of furniture, it is undeniably a well built, finely detailed example of *Gesamtkunstwerk* in architecture. The plan and exterior present a fairly straightforward linear design – low-sloped gabled roofs sheltering ribbon windows (framed with precast concrete) above walls of solid split-faced concrete masonry. There are the requisite cantilevered decks and large clerestory scoop on the roof at the fireplace

chimney. As the house was placed into a hillside, Green located the four-car garage and entry at the upper level along with the living spaces, Allan's master suite and study. The lower level, accessed from cascading stairs within a sky-lit garden atrium, contained three additional bedrooms.

The interior of the home is anything but simple. According to Allan, "In plan it's simple but three dimensionally it's much more complex ... the spatial complexity of the interior is one of the best things about it."[79] The space easily flows throughout the home, reinforced by the continuity of materials (slate flooring, redwood and

sheet rock walls, oak trim and cabinetry) and the varying levels of vaulted sheetrock ceilings. The solid and robust structural square columns, made from locally salvaged redwood logs, are exposed, informing the home's heart. Here Green located an informal seating area that is spatially a part of both the garden atrium and the open dining and kitchen areas. However, the exposed poured-in-place concrete fireplace is the home's *piece de resistance*, the focal point of the open living and dining area.

AMERICAN HEBREW ACADEMY

In 1998, Green was one of ten national architectural firms invited to submit master plan designs for the American Hebrew Academy, a coeducational, pluralistic college preparatory boarding school for the Jewish faith located in Greensboro, North Carolina. Its founder, Maurice "Chico" Sabbah (1929-2006), envisioned an environment where Jewish teens from varied backgrounds could come together to live as a community, enriching their knowledge and experiences of Jewish culture and religion, while pursing their education at the highest level, both secular and Jewish studies. He felt that to support his vision the facilities needed to be state of the art, with advanced technologies and concepts integrated throughout the campus. Overruling his committee's selection of a New York firm, Sabbah chose Green with the only concern being Green's advanced age. Green's solution was that the general overall design of all the buildings depicted in the master plan would be accomplished up front.

It is interesting to note that while Green was born into a Jewish family he wasn't raised in a strict Jewish environment. Before he even started his own practice, his work took center stage. While overseas at war, Green explained to Jean Haber in a letter his feelings

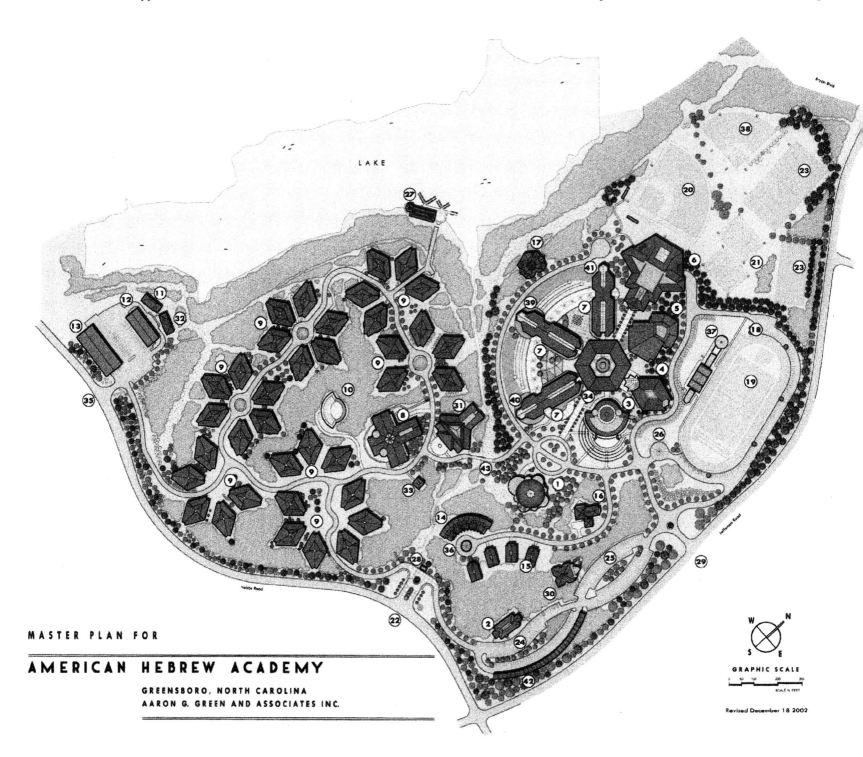

LAKE

MASTER PLAN FOR

AMERICAN HEBREW ACADEMY

GREENSBORO, NORTH CAROLINA
AARON G. GREEN AND ASSOCIATES INC.

GRAPHIC SCALE

Revised December 18 2002

387

about religion, "mine has always been my work and my character, and honesty to myself and others, my religion."[80] He admitted late in life that he was an agnostic. Despite this, Green had more than the basic awareness of the Jewish religion, history, and culture.

The site, bordering a twenty-two-acre lake, was 100 acres of wooded land approximately six miles northwest of downtown Greensboro. Green's master plan provided a multitude of individual building units (approximately seventy-five) grouped in accordance with their function—residential, social, educational, athletic—and located to provide the least disruption to the natural beauty of the wooded property. The aim was to maintain a park-like setting, preserving its natural beauty and maintaining natural buffers around the campus perimeter.

The campus was designed for pedestrians and bicycles with automobile traffic restricted to the peripherals. Sabbah and Green also agreed that the campus buildings would utilize new innovations for teaching, such as Harkness tables and smart boards. They developed a geo-thermal system for heating and cooling the entire campus and also provided wireless internet access throughout the campus. Sabbah's plan was to provide for a total enrollment of 1,000 full-time students.

Like Wright's Florida Southern College in Lakeland, Florida, Green's organically and ecologically designed individual building units displayed differing forms to express their specific function, while using similar materials for cohesiveness and continuity throughout the entire campus. Building exteriors incorporated stone imported from Israel, plaster stucco, pre-patinated copper fascias, and Ludowici clay roof tile, all presenting a statement of solidarity. Sabbah desired that the buildings be designed and detailed to survive a minimum of 100 years. The initial phase contained almost forty buildings, beginning with the construction of two dormitory pods, the dining pavilion, and the initial science lab classroom building, which were all under construction by late 2000. Tragically Green wouldn't live to see the completion of a single building, let alone the entire initial phase of what might be considered his career's masterwork. His successor firm, Aaron G. Green & Associates, oversaw the completion of the project. Green's client Sabbah lived to see his largest philanthropic dream come to fruition when the school opened on September 10, 2001. The school has achieved international recognition, attracting Jewish teens from all over the world. ■

■

■

PROJECT TIMELINE

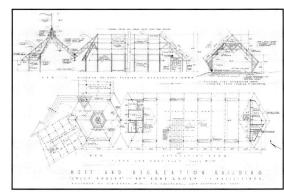

Sterman
Residence

Taliesin Fellowship
Box Project

Jolly Rogers
Mess and Recreation Building

Rosenbaum
Residence

Morris Mitchell Residence
Macedonia Cooperative Community

Aaron Green
Residence

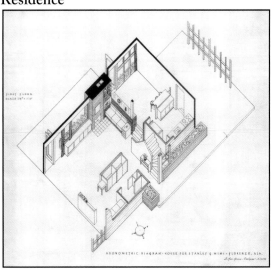

Abraham Green
Residence

New city
for Majaraja B.

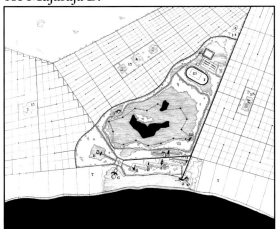

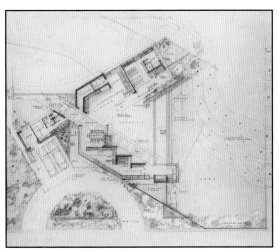

Burakoff Residence
Los Angeles

Burakoff Residence
Palm Springs

Maxwell
Residence

Beasley
Studio

1946

1948

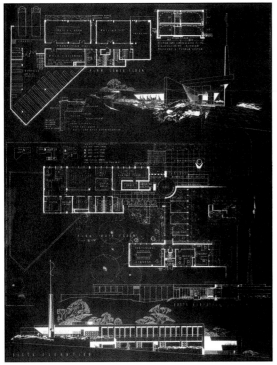

Progressive Architecture Competition
U.S. Junior Chamber of Commerce

Beverly-Wilkins
Apartment Building

Reif
Residence

1949   1950

Chapel of the Chimes
Santa Rosa

Commercial Holding Corporation
Residence

Richmond
Residence

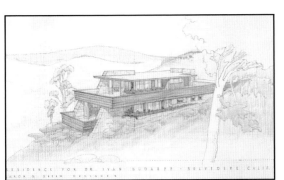

Budaeff
Residence

Paul
Residence

Bartholomew
Residence

1951 **1952** **1953**

Aaron Green / Frank Lloyd Wright
Office Interior

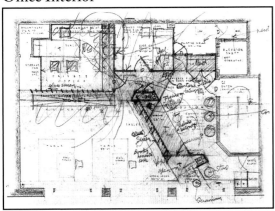

Aaron and Jean Green Residence
San Francisco

Guhl and Richardson
Residence

Hughes
Residence

Goldberg
Residence

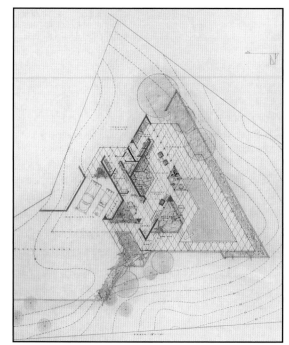

Granger and Mitchell
Residence

1954

Dukes
Residence

Lopes
Residence

Hicks
Residence

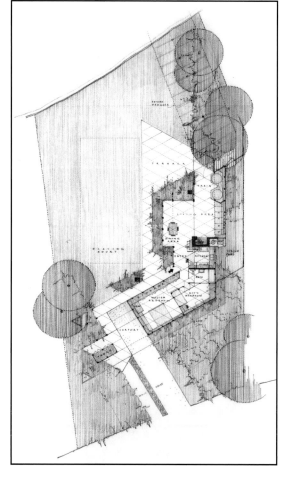

Aaron and Jean Green Residence
Los Altos

Ridley
Residence

Crisofi
Residence

1955

1956

Millman
Residence

Chapel of the Chimes Addition 1
Oakland

Cypress Cemetery Chapel
Hayward

Dorshkind
Residence

Cortelyou
Residence

Villierme
Residence

1956   **1957**

Ives
Residence

Marin City
Low Income Housing

Chapel of the Chimes South Chapel
Hayward

Chapel of the Chimes Mausoleum
Hayward

Anderson
Residence

Lee
Residence

1958　　　　　　　　　　　　　**1959**

Phoenician Splendor
for Leo Mahsoud Carpets

Chapel of the Chimes Addition 2
Oakland

Paul Residence
Studio Addition

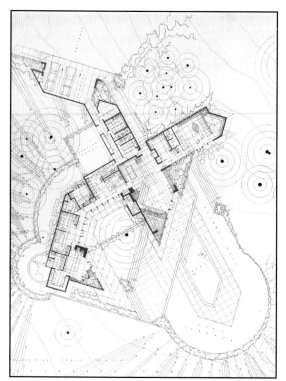

Lennert
Residence

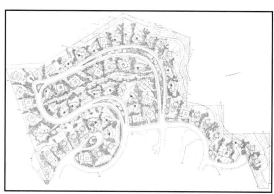

Highlands Residential Development
for Eichler Homes

Chapel of the Chimes Addition 3
Oakland

1960　1961

Forrest
Residence

Paulsen
Residence

Eldred
Residence

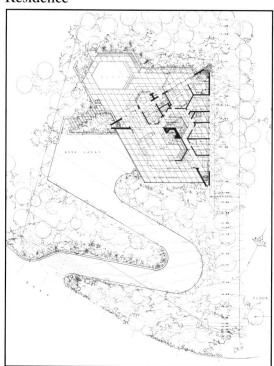

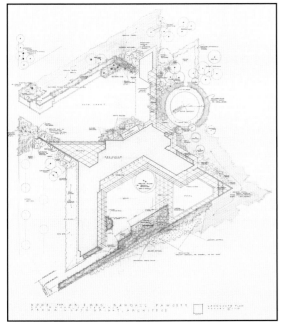

Fawcett Residence
Landscape Plan

Mischel
Residence

Dr. Ives
Dental Office

1962   **1963**

Medical Office Plaza
Santa Cruz

Chapel of the Light, Fresno
Mausoleum Addition

Oriental Gardens
Shopping Center

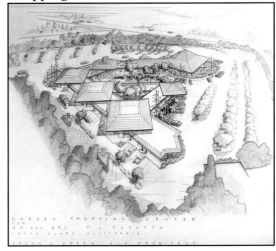

Weir
Office Building

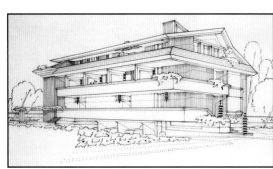

Tousley
Apartment Building

Prototype Housing
San Francisco Housing Authority

1963

1964

Chapel of the Chimes Addition 1
Hayward

Lilienthal
Residence

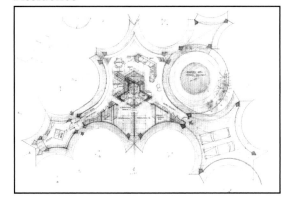

Chapel of the Chimes Oakland
Addition 4 Transition Arch

Chapel of the Chimes Addition 4
Oakland

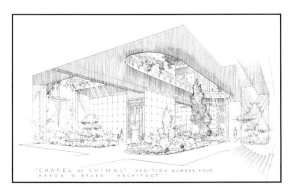

Chapel of the Chimes Hayward
Latter Day Saints Monument

Walker Residence
Palo Alto

1965   **1966**

Ohta
Residence

Lum Yip Kee., Ltd.
Office Building

City of Sausalito Corporation Yard
Office and Shop

411

San Jose State College
Library

Bridge
Townhouses

Woelffel Youth Center
Santa Clara Peace Officers Association

1966   1967

City of Newark
Community Center

City of Sausalito
Library

New Hunter's Point Community
Site 1 Prototype Housing

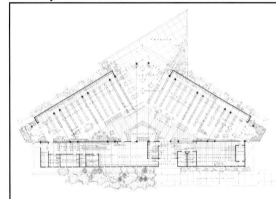

Chapel of the Chimes Hayward
Administration Building

Chapel of the Chimes Hayward
Veteran's Memorial

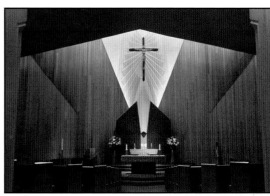

St. Stephen
Catholic Church

1968

1969

New Hunter's Point Community
Original Master Plan

Wagner
Residence

New Hunter's Point Community
Site 3 Master Plan

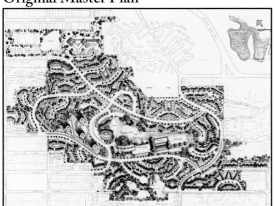

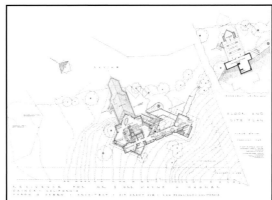

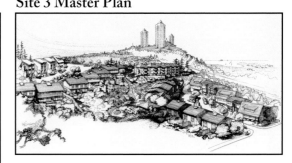

Fire Station Number Six
Hayward

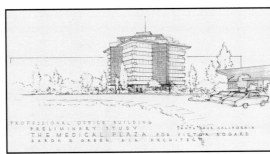

Santa Cruz Professional
Medical Office Building

Skylawn Memorial Park
Mausoleum

1970 — 1971

Judge Haley Memorial Grove
Marin County Civic Center

Wortham and Harper
Residence

Emma Prusch Memorial Park
Master Plan

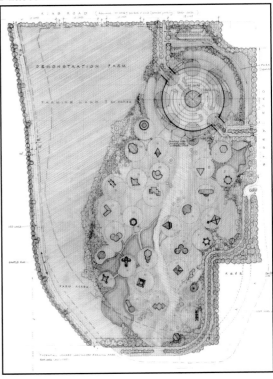

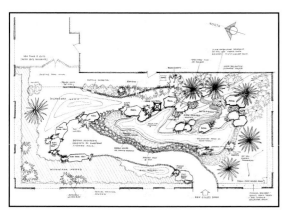

Dr. Victor Ohta
Japanese Garden Memorial

St. Monica's
Catholic Church

St. Monica's Catholic Church
Dove Tabernacle

1972 **1973** **1974**

Calhoun
Residence

Morgan
Residence

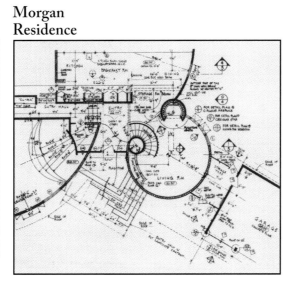

Union City
Civic Center

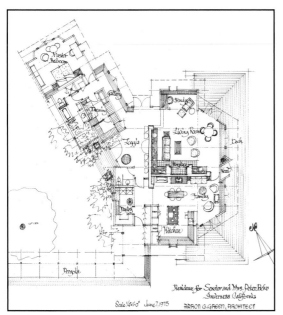

Behr
Residence

St. Joseph's Cemetery
Mausoleum

Stanislaus National Forest Service
Administration Complex

1975   **1976**

Jean Green
Residence

Gates for Prince Faisal al Saud
Unicorn Ranch

C.D.C.
Energy Technology Center

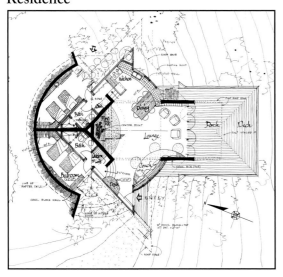

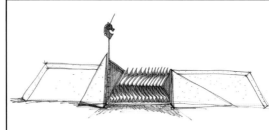

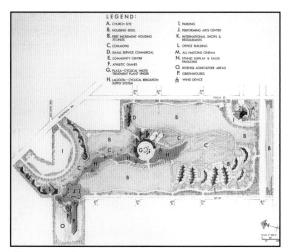

Community
of All Nations

Fung
Residence

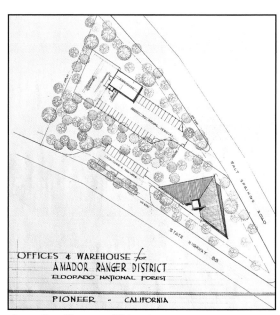

Amador Ranger District
Offices and Warehouse

1978 **1979** **1980**

Klamath National Forest Service
Administration Building

Holy Cross Cemetery
Master Plan and Mausoleum

Skylawn Memorial Park
Master Plan

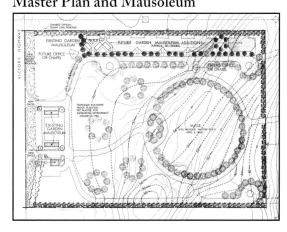

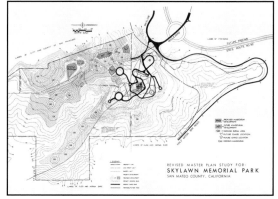

Moss and Rosenbaum
Residence

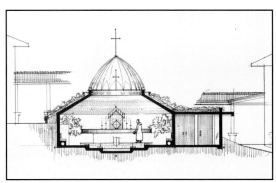

San Damiano
Meditation Chapel

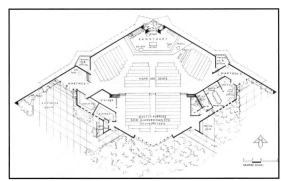

St. Joan of Arc
Catholic Church

1980　　　　　**1981**

Queen of Heaven Cemetery
Garden Mausoleum

City of Newark
Civic Center

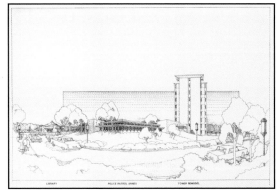

St. Monica's Catholic Church
Rectory and Pastoral Offices

City of Newark
Library

Skylawn Memorial Park
Oceanview Columbarium

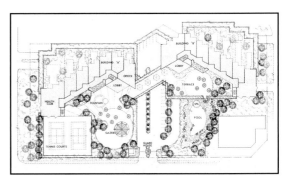

Dallas
City View Towers

1982 · 1983 · 1985

City of Newark
Police Annex

Skylawn Memorial Park
Mausoleum in the Sky Master Plan

Greenwood Ridge Vineyards
Tasting Room

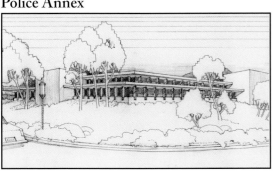

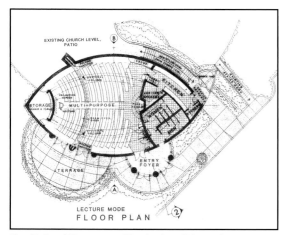

St. John Vianney Catholic Church
Fireside Room

McAndrews
Residence

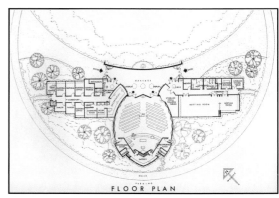

St. Elizabeth Seton Catholic Church
Master Plan, Chapel and Offices

1986   **1987**   **1988**

St. John Vianney Catholic Church
Additions and Pastoral Offices

Haber
Residence

De Nevi
Residence

Marin County
Correctional Facility

St. Joan of Arc Catholic Church
Parish Center

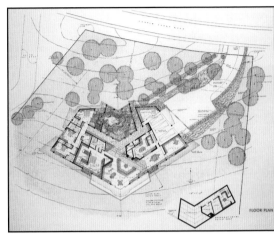

Young
Residence

1989 **1990** **1991**

Harris
Residence

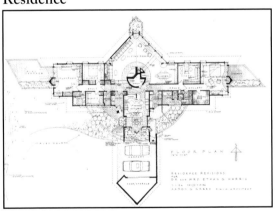

Skylawn Memorial Park
Island East Columbarium

Skylawn Memorial Park
Bai Ling Yuan II Chinese Cemetery

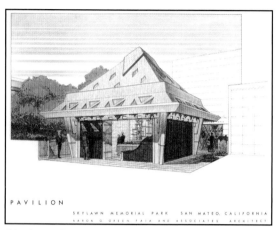

PAVILION

SKYLAWN MEMORIAL PARK   SAN MATEO, CALIFORNIA

AARON G GREEN FAIA AND ASSOCIATES ARCHITECT

Skylawn Memorial Park
Mausoleum in the Sky Pavilion

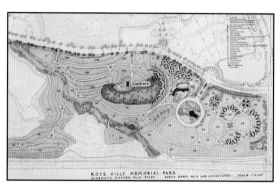

ROSE HILLS MEMORIAL PARK
SCHEMATIC MASTER PLAN STUDY   AARON GREEN FAIA AND ASSOCIATES   SCALE 1"=100'

Rose Hills Memorial Park
Master Plan

Greenwood Ridge Vineyards
Winery Addition

1991   1992   1993

Chapel of the Chimes
Circle of Peace Mausoleum

Mueller
Residence

Allan Green
Residence

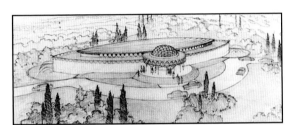

Marin Museum
Adaptation of Frank Lloyd Wright design

Skylawn Memorial Park
Bai Ling Yuan II Extension

Chapel of the Chimes
Mausoleum Addition Number 7

1994　　　　**1995**　　　　**1996**

St. Elizabeth Seton
Catholic Church

Chapel of the Chimes
Bai Ling Yuan

Joyce and Norkett
Residence

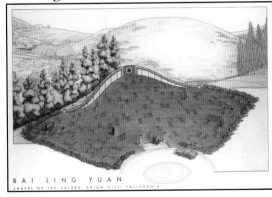

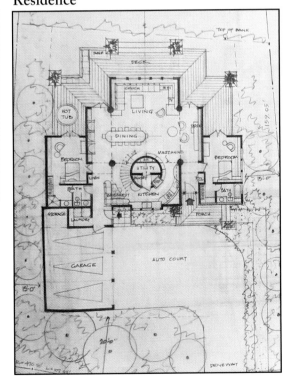

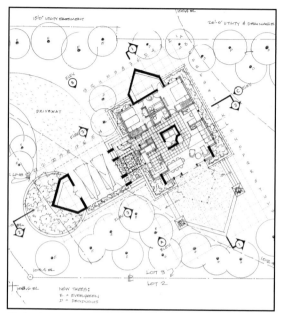

Schultz
Residence

Greenwood Ridge Vineyards
Tasting Room Bridge

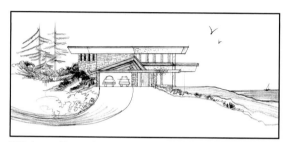

Wilson Residence
New Zealand

1997   **1998**

Walker Residence
Maui, Hawaii

V.C. Morris Shop (Frank Lloyd Wright)
Renovation

American Hebrew Academy
Campus Master Plan

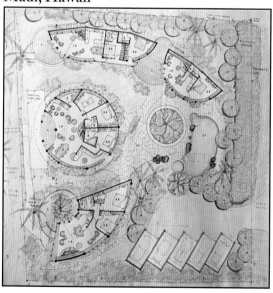

American Hebrew Academy
Classroom Building

American Hebrew Academy
Dining Pavilion

American Hebrew Academy
Fitness Center

American Hebrew Academy
Arboretum Laboratory

American Hebrew Academy
Student Residences

American Hebrew Academy
Boat House

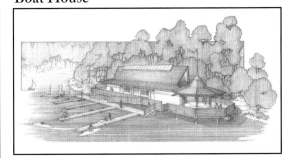

COMPLETE LIST OF PROJECTS

1939

A. P. Campbell Residence Remodeling
Florence, Alabama, *built*

Charles Sterman Residence
Florence, Alabama

Alex Sterman Residence
Fayette, Alabama

Stanley and Mimi Rosenbaum Residence
Florence, Alabama

Abroms Building Remodeling
Sheffield, Alabama

James Lawler Residence
Hodges, Alabama

H. Aizenshtat Residence
Hodges, Alabama

1940

Taliesin Fellowship Box Project

Morris Royal Residence
Red Bay, Alabama

1942

Morris Mitchell Macedonia Cooperative Community Residence
Clarkesville, Georgia

1944

Jolly Rogers Mess and Recreation Building
Philippines

1946

Aaron Green Residence
San Francisco, California

Abraham and Rose Green Residence
Miami, Florida

1947

New City for Maharaja B.
Bay of Baroda, India

1948

H. Aizenshtat Residence Addition
Russellville, Alabama

American League Shop for Joe Rue
Santa Monica, California

B. Burakoff Residence
Los Angeles, California

B. Burakoff Residence
Palm Springs, California

Dr. Alice Maxwell Residence
Los Altos, California, *built*

1949

Mebane Beasley Studio
Los Angeles, California

Dr. Franz Engelmann Cottage
Menlo Park, California

Everett Carlson Kitchen Remodeling
San Francisco, California, *built*

Frank Macintosh Barn Remodeling
Los Altos, California

Golden State Hotel Penthouse Remodeling
San Francisco, California

Chapel of the Light Garden Mausoleum
Fresno, California, *built*

Arthur Gilman Residence
Los Angeles, California, *built*

Sy Levy Residence
Los Angeles, California

U.S. Junior Chamber of Commerce
Progressive Architecture Competition

1950

Beverly – Wilkins Apartment Building
Los Angeles, California

Chapel of the Chimes Garden Mausoleum
Santa Rosa, California, *built*

Commercial Holding Corporation Residence
Mountain View, California

Harry Reif Residence
Los Angeles, California, *built*

Allan Richmond Residence
Bel Air, California, *built*

Pauson's Department Store Remodeling
San Francisco, California, *built*

Dr. Ivan Budaeff Residence
Belvedere, California

1951

Aaron Green / Frank Lloyd Wright Office Interior
San Francisco, California, *built*

1952

Allan and Arlene Paul Residence
Palo Alto, California, *built*

Chapel of the Chimes Addition 1
Santa Rosa, California, *built*

Aaron and Dr. Jean Green Residence
San Francisco, California

1953

M. W. Bartholomew Residence
Los Altos, California, *built*

Loree Guhl and Delores Richardson Residence
Whittier, California, *built*

Dr. Raymond Hughes Residence
Los Altos, California, *built*

Frank Residence Studio Addition
(Frank Lloyd Wright Bazett Residence), Hillsborough, California

1954

Charlton Dukes Residence
Pasadena, California, *built*

Samuel Goldberg Residence
Modesto, California, *built*

George Lopes Residence and Boat House
Mill Valley, California, *built*

Farley Granger and James Mitchell Residence
Hollywood, California

Harry Hicks Residence and Guest House
Oakland, California, *built*

1955

Aaron and Dr. Jean Green Residence
Los Altos, California, *built*

Millman Residence
Denver, Colorado, *built*

Santa Clara Valley Cemetery Master Plan
San Jose, California

Paul Ridley Residence
Malibu, California, *built*

Chapel of the Chimes Addition 2
Santa Rosa, California, *built*

Chapel of the Chimes Addition 1
Oakland, California, *built*

1956

Rudolph and Agnes Boone Crisofi Residence
Westridge Estates, California, *built*

Cypress Cemetery Chapel (Future Chapel of the Chimes)
Hayward, California, *built*

Morris and Sereleen Dorshkind Residence
San Francisco, California, *built*

Dr. Harold Ives Residence
Cloverdale, California, *built*

Peter Cortelyou Residence
Atherton, California, *built*

1957

Marin City Low Income Housing
Marin City, California, *built*

Louis Villierme Residence
Point Richmond, California, *built*

Chapel of the Chimes South Chapel & Mausoleum
Hayward, California, *built*

Chapel of the Memories Mausoleum
Oakland, California, *built*

Phoenician Splendor
Advertising campaign for Leo Mahsoud Carpets

1958

Judge Anderson Residence
Rancho Palos Verdes, California, *built*

Chapel of the Chimes Addition 2
Oakland, California, *built*

1959

Dr. Philip Lee Residence
Portola Valley, California, *built*

Allan and Arlene Paul Studio Addition
Palo Alto, California, *built*

Frank Lennert Residence
Woodside, California, *built*

1960

Terry Forrest Residence
Vancouver, British Columbia, Canada

1961

Highlands Residential Development for Eichler Homes
San Mateo, California

Dr. James Paulsen Residence
Portola Valley, California, *built*

Chapel of the Chimes Pavilion
Hayward, California, *built*

Chapel of the Chimes Addition 3
Oakland, California, *built*

Dr. Roy Eldred Residence
Belvedere, California, *built*

Chapel of the Chimes Master Plan
Hayward, California, *built*

Randal Fawcett Residence Landscape Plan
Los Banos, California, *built*

1962

Santa Cruz Medical Office Plaza
Santa Cruz, California, *built*

Chapel of the Chimes Addition 3
Santa Rosa, California, *built*

Dr. Walter and Harriet Mischel Residence (Eichler "Sunspot")
San Mateo, California, *built*

1963

Blossom Hill Memorial Park
Los Gatos, California

Chapel of the Light Mausoleum Addition
Fresno, California, *built*

Dr. Harold Ives Dental Office
Cloverdale, California, *built*

Oriental Gardens Shopping Center
Santa Clara, California, *built*

Robert Weir Office Building
San Jose, California, *built*

Robert Weir Residence Remodeling
Stanford, California, *built*

Chapel of the Chimes Addition 1
Hayward, California, *built*

Tousley Apartment Building
Alameda, California

Dorothy Lilienthal Residence
Hillsborough, California

Prototype Housing for S.F. Housing Authority
San Francisco, California

1964

Chapel of Memories Addition 2
Oakland, California, *built*

Chapel of the Chimes Addition 4
Oakland, California, *built*

Dr. Victor and Virginia Ohta Residence
Soquel, California, *built*

1965

Chapel of the Chimes Latter Day Saints Monument
Hayward, California, *built*

Lum Yip Kee, Ltd. Office Building
Honolulu, Hawaii

Marin County Civic Center Hall of Justice Courtroom 4
San Rafael, California, *built*

Richard Walker Residence
Palo Alto, California, *built*

Chapel of the Chimes Addition 2
Hayward, California, *built*

Chapel of the Chimes Master Plan
Hayward, California, *built*

1966

City of Sausalito Corporation Yard Office and Shop
Sausalito, California, *built*

Santa Clara Peace Officers Association Woelffel Youth Center
Cupertino, California

City of Newark Community Center
Newark, California, *built*

1967

Mrs. Arthur Bridge Townhouses
Tiburon, California

City of Sausalito Library
Sausalito, California

San Jose State College Library
San Jose, California

New Hunter's Point Community Site 1
San Francisco, California, *built*

1968

Chapel of the Chimes Administration Building
Hayward, California

New Hunter's Point Community Master Plan
San Francisco, California, *built*

New Hunter's Point Community Site 2
San Francisco, California

Ridge Vineyards Winery
Cupertino, California, *built*

Chapel of the Chimes Veteran's Memorial
Hayward, California, *built*

Chapel of the Chimes Master Plan
Oakland, California

Wayne and Mary Wagner Residence
Orinda, California

1969

New Hunter's Point Community Site 3
San Francisco, California, *built*

St. Stephen Catholic Church
Walnut Creek, California, *built*

San Jose State College Master Plan
San Jose, California, *built*

Chapel of the Light Garden Mausoleum Addition
Fresno, California, *built*

1970

Hayward Fire Station Number Six
Hayward, California, *built*

Judge Harold Haley Memorial Grove
Marin County Civic Center, San Rafael, California, *built*

Santa Cruz Professional Medical Office Building
Santa Cruz, California

1971

Mary Wortham and Esther Harper Residence
Groveland, California, *built*

Harriet Mischel Garden Studio Addition
San Mateo, California, *built*

Skylawn Memorial Park Mausoleum and Garden Crypts
San Mateo, California, *built*

Emma Prusch Memorial Park Master Plan
San Jose, California

Dr. Victor Ohta Japanese Garden Memorial
Santa Cruz, California

1972

Ambassador John Calhoun Residence
Mill Valley, California, *built*

Morgan Hill Senior Community
Morgan Hill, California

St. Monica's Catholic Church
Moraga, California, *built*

Robert Weir Residence Master Plan
Los Gatos, California

1973

Casa Del Pueblo for Retail Store Employees Union
San Jose, California

San Jose State University Library Faculty Office
San Jose, California

1974

Chapel of the Chimes Addition 5
Oakland, California, *built*

Joe and Gloria Morgan Residence
Oakland, California, *built*

St. Monica's Catholic Church Dove Tabernacle
Moraga, California, *built*

Union City Civic Center
Union City, California, *built*

Senator Peter Behr Residence and Guest House
Inverness, California

1975

Robert Weir Residence Pool and Dormitory
Los Altos, California, *built*

Dr. Jean Green Residence
Philo, California, *built*

Robert Weir Puerto Vallarta Resort
Puerto Vallarta, Mexico

Chapel of the Chimes Addition 3
Hayward, California, *built*

Chapel of the Light Mausoleum Addition
Fresno, California, *built*

Robert Bush Residence and Studio Addition
Stanford, California

1976

St. Joseph's Cemetery Mausoleum
San Pablo, California, *built*

Gates for Prince Faisal Al Saud
Portola Valley, California

Stanislaus National Forest Service Complex
Sonora, California, *built*

1978

C. D. C. Energy Technology Center
San Bernardino County, California

Chapel of the Chimes Mausoleum and Outdoor Crypts
Hayward, California, *built*

Community of All Nations
Stockton, California

New Hunter's Point Community Bahia Vista
San Francisco, California

Klamath National Forest Administration Building
Yreka, California, *built*

1979

New Hunter's Point Community Phase 3
San Francisco, California

Merced County Court Facility
Los Banos, California, *built*

St. Monica's Catholic Church Remodeling
Moraga, California, *built*

Dr. Daniel and Frances Fung Residence
Hillsborough, California, *built*

Holy Cross Cemetery Master Plan and Mausoleum
Antioch, California, *built*

St. Joseph's Cemetery Master Plan
San Pablo, California, *built*

1980

Amador Ranger District Offices and Warehouse
Pioneer, California, *built*

Skylawn Memorial Park Master Plan
San Mateo, California, *built*

Susan Moss and Alvin Rosenbaum Residence
Washington, D.C., *built*

Queen of Heaven Cemetery Master Plan
Lafayette, California, *built*

Queen of Heaven Cemetery Garden Mausoleum
Lafayette, California, *built*

Tahoe District Ranger Station
Tahoe National Forest, California

San Damiano Meditation Chapel
Danville, California

1981

City of Newark Civic Center
Newark, California, *built*

St. Joan of Arc Catholic Church
San Ramon, California, *built*

Skylawn Memorial Park Amphitheater
San Mateo, California

1982

Chapel of the Chimes Master Plan
Hayward, California, *built*

Roseburg Forest Service Administration Building
Roseburg, California

St. Monica's Catholic Church Rectory and Pastoral Offices Addition
Moraga, California, *built*

City of Newark Library
Newark, California, *built*

Newark Police Annex, Council Chambers and Tower Remodel
Newark, California

1983

Skylawn Memorial Park Oceanview Columbarium
San Mateo, California, *built*

Santa Monica Church Remodeling
Orinda, California

Skylawn Memorial Park Pylon and Niche Garden
San Mateo, California, *built*

Dr. Ethan Harris Residence
Renaissance, California, *built*

Skylawn Memorial Park "Mausoleum in the Sky" Master Plan
San Mateo, California, *built*

Carl and Thea Thorwaldsen Residence Remodeling
San Francisco, California, *built*

1984

Chapel of the Chimes Addition 6 and Renovations
Oakland, California, *built*

Dallas City View Towers
Dallas, Texas

Lee and Estes Residence Addition
Portola Valley, California, *built*

Newark Civic Center Remodeling
Newark, California, *built*

1985

Greenwood Ridge Vineyards Tasting Room
Philo, California, *built*

Wendy's Restaurant for Joe Morgan
Oakland, California, *built*

Skylawn Memorial Park Gan Hazikaron
San Mateo, California, *built*

Grand Avenue Dress Shop for Gloria Morgan
Oakland, California, *built*

1986

St. John Vianney Catholic Church Additions and Offices
Walnut Creek, California, *built*

John and Margaret McAndrews Residence
Pebble Beach, California, *built*

Chapel of the Chimes Mission Terrace Columbarium
Hayward, California, *built*

1987

Charles Haber Residence
Carmel Valley, California, *built*

St. Mary's Cemetery Garden Mausoleum
Oakland, California, *built*

Temple Beth-El Remodeling and New Sanctuary
San Mateo, California, *built*

Lennart and Charlotte Erickson Residence Remodeling
Hillsborough, California

St. Elizabeth Seton Catholic Church Master Plan and Offices
Pleasanton, California, *built*

St. Monica's Catholic Church Master Plan Update
Moraga, California, *built*

1988

Indian Wells Estates Master Plan
Sonoma County, California

Newark Community Center Multi-Use Facility
Newark, California, *built*

Mitch Lelan Residence Remodeling
(Dukes Residence), Pasadena, California, *built*

1989

Donald De Nevi Residence
San Rafael, California, *built*

1990

Marin County Correctional Facility
Marin County Civic Center, San Rafael, California, *built*

St. Stephen Catholic Church Rectory Remodeling
Walnut Creek, California, *built*

Dr. Ethan Harris Residence 2
Renaissance, California

James Peterson Guest House
(Hicks Residence), Oakland, California, *built*

St. Joan of Arc Catholic Church Parish Center
San Ramon, California, *built*

Skylawn Memorial Park Island East Columbarium
San Mateo, California, *built*

Stephen Detmold Residence
Yuba County, California

1991

Kenneth and Ronda Kornfield Residence Addition and Remodeling
Greensboro, North Carolina, *built*

Morley Young Residence
Los Altos, California, *built*

Skylawn Memorial Park Bai Ling Yuan II Chinese Cemetery
San Mateo, California, *built*

Chapel of the Chimes Sanctuary Circle and Bell Tower
Hayward, California, *built*

Chapel of the Chimes Office Remodeling
Oakland, California, *built*

Skylawn Memorial Park Mausoleum in the Sky Phases 2 and 3
San Mateo, California, *built*

Chapel of the Chimes Hillside Master Plan, Fence and Gates
Union City, California, *built*

Skylawn Memorial Park Master Plan
San Mateo, California, *built*

1992

Chapel of the Chimes Circle Of Peace Mausoleum
Union City, California, *built*

Chapel of the Chimes South Chapel Renovations
Union City, California, *built*

Chapel of the Chimes Amador Memorials
Oakland, California, *built*

Rose Hills Memorial Park Master Plan
Whittier, California

Chapel of the Chimes Circular Mausoleum Master Plan
Union City, California

Dr. Gernot and Guinevere Mueller Residence
Renaissance, California, *built*

Greenwood Ridge Vineyards Winery Addition
Philo, California, *built*

1993

St. Monica's Catholic Church Renovation
Moraga, California

Skylawn Memorial Park Fireside Chapel Renovation
San Mateo, California, *built*

Chapel of the Chimes Master Landscape Plan
Union City, California

St. Isidore's Church Master Plan
Danville, California

Allan Green Residence
Philo, California, *built*

1994

Judge Anderson Residence Entrance Gate
Rancho Palos Verdes, California, *built*

St. Elizabeth Seton Catholic Church
Pleasanton, California, *built*

Skylawn Memorial Park Bai Ling Yuan II Extension
San Mateo, California

Skylawn Memorial Park Island North Columbarium
San Mateo, California

Skylawn Memorial Park Mausoleum Renovations
San Mateo, California

Chapel of the Chimes Mausoleum Master Plan and Addition
Oakland, California, *built*

Chapel of Memories Cenotaph
Oakland, California, *built*

Chapel of Memories Martin Luther King, Jr. Memorial
Oakland, California, *built*

Chapel of the Chimes Bai Ling Yuan
Union City, California, *built*

Chapel of Memories Chinese Columbarium
Oakland, California

Marin Museum (adaptation of Frank Lloyd Wright Design)
Marin County Civic Center, San Rafael, California

1995

Skylawn Memorial Park Mausoleum and Columbarium
San Mateo, California

Chapel of the Chimes Columbarium Addition
Oakland, California

Chapel of the Chimes Mausoleum Addition 7
Oakland, California

1996

Forest Lawn Cemetery Mausoleum Addition
Glendale, California

Skygroup / Walter Kim Crematorium
Korea

Skylawn Memorial Park Sunset Terrace
San Mateo, California

Mike Joyce and Mike Norkett Residence
Calaveras County, California

1997

Marin County Civic Center Auditorium Green Room Remodeling
San Rafael, California

Darrell Schultz Residence
Waco, Texas, *built*

Richard Walker Residence
Maui, Hawaii

Taliesin Entrance Landscaping
Spring Green, Wisconsin

Dr. Walter Mischel Apartment Remodeling
New York, New York

William and Lynn Swank Residence Addition and Renovations
(Anderson Residence), Portuguese Bend, California

Greenwood Ridge Vineyards Tasting Room Bridge
Philo, California, *built*

Frank Lloyd Wright V.C. Morris Shop Renovation
San Francisco, California, *built*

Philippine Mausoleum
Philippines

1998

American Hebrew Academy
Greensboro, North Carolina, *built*

John Wilson Residence
New Zealand

Menifee Valley Memorial Park Master Plan
Sun City, California

Toledo Memorial Park & Mausoleum
Toledo, Ohio

1999

Tulocay Memorial Park Master Plan
Napa, California

ORGANIC ARCHITECTURE:
THE PRINCIPLES OF FRANK LLOYD WRIGHT

by Aaron G. Green, FAIA

This essay was originally published in the Winter 2001 issue of the *Frank Lloyd Wright Quarterly* (Volume Number 12, Issue Number 1) and is reprinted herein in its entirety. It provides a personal glimpse of how well the principles of Organic Architecture were understood by Green, as practiced by his mentor, Frank Lloyd Wright. In the issue's introduction, the editor states, "In this essay architect Aaron Green looks beyond a simple definition, or a collection of axioms, and explains how Wright used the term to convey a synthesis of complex ideas."

It is over sixty years since I first encountered Frank Lloyd Wright's concept of organic architecture. For twenty years I had the privilege of a close association with Frank Lloyd Wright, both personal and professional. I began as an apprentice, and during the last eight years of his life was his architectural associate and his West coast representative, working out of a joint office he requested that we opened together in San Francisco in 1951. During that eventful relationship I grew to understand that his integrity as a person and his practice of organic architecture were inextricable. The conduct of his life in its daily details was one and the same with his work as an architect and his devotion to the understanding of nature.

He was constantly moved to demonstrate that the principles of organic architecture were not alone a method of building but contained the elements of a more creative and fuller way of life. In his book *A Testament* (1957) he wrote: "All buildings built should serve the liberation of mankind, liberating the lives of individuals. What amazing beauty would be ours if man's spirit, thus organic, should learn to characterize this new free life of ours in America as natural." The very fundamentals that Wright should demonstrate more directly in buildings than in words were the core of the lectures and writings in which he clarified his views on politics, economics, business, land planning, farming, education and whatever other disciplines, personal or public, claimed his attention.

For the true meaning of Wright's term "organic architecture" one must look beyond a simple definition, or a collection of axioms, or a formula for the design of buildings. To begin with, *organic* can be seen as a convenient one-word reference to the complex synthesis of principles that were most clearly expressed in his earliest writings and evident in his earliest architectural works. The term, as used in those early years, never changed in meaning. For the sake of simplicity one might substitute for *organic* the word *natural*, often used by Wright in conjunction with *logic* ("natural logic," "nature's logic") or the word *rational*, which Wright also often used; but he much preferred *organic.*

For all the efforts of academicians, historians, architectural critics, and others to analyze Wright's work, his own voluminous writings offer the clearest and most direct guide to his thinking. His intent was always educational. His fundamental concerns were with human dignity, with individual freedom and democracy, with

human endeavor on its highest altruistic plane, and with enriching the relationship of the individual to his or her environment. His inner strength and convictions were intensified and matured by constant reference to those he regarded as great creative minds, among them Victor Hugo, William Blake, William Morris, Laotze, Viollet-le-Duc, Jefferson, Emerson, Thoreau, Louis Sullivan, and Dankmar Adler.

The synthesis of the fundamentals inherent in a more meaningful life was so simple and instinctive in Wright's thinking that he had difficulty at times in perceiving the inadequacy of the term *organic* to convey this synthesis to others. Architecture he saw as the Master Art. Also necessary for a full life were music, poetry, and above all nature—the white clouds against the blue sky, the shimmering dew on the morning's grasses, the structural silhouetted form of the oak tree in winter—all freely available to all people, all necessary for life-giving enjoyment. In time, couldn't everyone see this, understand it, and live it? That hope moved Wright to write, to exhort, to criticize, and to demonstrate a more fulfilling way.

Often quoting William Blake's "exuberance is beauty," Wright stressed the joy of understanding nature by observation-nature, which produces the forms of plants, each responsive to the needs of its environment, each with its basic "engineering" structure, its material and color, its form and function evolving in its life's pattern. Carrying the concept "form follows function" a conclusive step further into "form and function are one," Wright threw new light on a major tenet of organic architecture. The building must have its own form, its beauty emergent from its consonance with nature.

In the preface to *Ausgefuhrte Bauten und Entwurfe*, published in Germany in 1910, Wright wrote:

> As we pass along the wayside some blossom with unusually glowing color or prettiness of form attracts us. Held by it we gratefully accept its perfect loveliness. But, seeking the secret of its ineffable charm, we find the blossom whose more obvious claim first arrested our attention as nature intended, intimately related to the texture and shape of the foliage beneath it. We discover peculiar sympathy between the form of this flower and the system upon which leaves are arranged about the stalk. From this we are led on to observe a characteristic habit of growth and discover a resultant pattern of structure having first direction toward form deep down in roots hidden in the warm earth, kept moist there by a conservative covering of leaf-mold. Structure—as now we may observe—proceeds from generals to particulars arriving at the blossom, to attract us, proclaiming in its lines and form the Nature of the structure that bore it. We have here a thing organic. Law and order are the basis of a finished grace and beauty. "Beauty" is the expression of fundamental conditions in line, form, and color true to those conditions and seeming to exist to fulfill them according to some thoughtful original design. Wright's philosophy of organic architecture is not to be confused with his singular style. That

style is unique, his personal form of expression. He often repeated his hope that other architects and students would not imitate him but develop their own individuality. The principles of organic architecture, he believed, were not related to any particular style but were adaptable to all architectural solutions: 'Given similar conditions, similar tools, similar people, similar language, I believe architects will, with proper regard for the organic nature of the thing produced, arrive at greatly varied results; buildings sufficiently harmonious with each other and more and more so with great individuality.'

However many of Wright's building plans and forms we consider, we can always recognize the principles at work. The degree of the relationship of a building to its site and the environment determines the degree of its harmony, the aim being always, as Wright said, "to make the landscape more beautiful than before that building was built."

A superb example is the Marin County Civic Center in San Rafael, California. When he first visited the site, after a twenty-minute review of the hilly terrain in a jeep, Wright turned to me and, making waive-like motions with his hand, declared, "I know what to do here. We will bridge these hills with graceful arches." My voluminous administrative and space-requirement analysis for the project emphasized the need for flexibility to accommodate internal departmental changes. Wright quickly assimilated that information, designed the project, and indicated the forms of the various functional building components requested. Three months later, when I was asked to come to Taliesin to "see what we have done," I was proudly shown the first sketches, which conformed precisely to his initial inspiration for the design. All broad functional aspects of exterior traffic circulation and the relationship of building to topography were beautifully resolved; so also were the basic structural concepts. For interior function Wright had designed a continuous space of two different widths, a space free of column interference and filled with light and air from its internal atrium "mall" and its exterior protected balcony fenestration. Such space would obviously allow the required flexibility for relocating interior partitions, all non-structural. On that occasion at Taliesin, Wright said to me: "Now you can do whatever you want with the inside; it's completely flexible, as you wished." In a speech to the citizens of Marin County prior to construction of the project, Wright said, "Here is a crucial opportunity to open the eyes of the entire country to what officials gathering together might themselves do to broaden and beautify lives." Today, from the interior of the building, each of the graceful arches, large or small, inevitably frames a view, repeating that earlier wave motion of his hand and circumscribing the form of one of the surrounding hills.

Subsequently, a system was developed that allowed partitions, lights, electrical outlets, and so forth, to be located at any place on a grid thirty-two inches square, a remarkably flexible arrangement that has been utilized with great success for many years and is a continuing tribute to his original organic design concept. All state-of-the art technology had been designed into the scheme to create beauty, economy, and rational functional relationships. This skylighted mall concept and form has since directly influenced many copies throughout the contemporary architectural scene.

Contrary to a general misconception, Frank Lloyd Wright was not dictatorial in considering the needs of his clients, nor was he adamant against changes. I have been present on various occasions when he agreed to a client's request for a functional revision, seemingly relishing the opportunity to improve the design. Only if a request appeared frivolous or illogical, or violated his aesthetic principles, would he be steadfast in opposition.

Again and again his creative virtuosity allowed him to resolve all basic functional requirements in his initial concept for the form of a building. Since the plan developed first, the functional concept was the established priority. When I submitted a "bubble diagram" to him to illustrate a client's desired functional relationships for a commercial project, the Degnan-Donohoe Restaurant project for Yosemite National Park, Wright, probably having predetermined a circular scheme, used my diagram directly as the basis for the plan of the building.

Such projects as the Larkin Building in Buffalo in 1904 demonstrated his mastery of functional programs for use by industry and commerce. Many others were to come, among them Monona Terrace for Madison, Wisconsin; the Rogers Lacy Hotel project for Dallas, Texas; the Johnson Administration Building and Research Tower in Racine, Wisconsin; Florida Southern College in Lakeland; the Kalita Humphreys Theatre in Dallas; and the Marin County Civic Center. One of his last commissions was a lyrically beautiful and workable solution for the administration and production of electronic components and systems for the Lenkurt Electric Company building in San Carlos, California, a project with which I was also associated. Unfortunately the building was not built because the company was sold to a less perceptive owner just as construction was about to begin.

Many of Wright's innovations provided a new direction for freedom and logic in architectural design, and all emphasized the importance of an overall sense of unity and harmony. The sense of shelter within the continuous vista of his building-sculptured, as it was, into differentiated functional areas-provided a wholly new experience, visual and sensual, spiritual and emotional, with fresh elements of space, color, and form continuing to surprise and delight.

Wright enjoyed exploring all the characteristics of whatever material he chose to use. In most cases his buildings were predominantly of one basic material or a combination of two primary ones. Most of the early houses were stone or brick masonry in combination with plaster, plus wood as accent material. The Usonian houses were primarily of wood with some masonry. Later there was the unique reinforced concrete and stone masonry combination of Fallingwater, the house for Edgar Kaufmann in Mill Run, Pennsylvania; and the use of reinforced concrete block, usually pattern-textured and earthquake-resistant for California. Several public structures emphasized brick (the Johnson Administration Building) and precast and/or poured concrete (Unity Temple in

Oak Park, Illinois; the Guggenheim Museum in New York; the Greek Orthodox Church in Wauwatosa, Wisconsin; the Marin County Civic Center; and Monona Terrace). In all cases the form was integral with the material. Of his early insight into the nature of materials, Wright wrote: "I began to learn to see brick as brick, I learned to see wood as wood and learned to see concrete or glass or metal each for itself and all as themselves."

The unit system was a very important part of the organic process of design and construction. Just as the warp is discipline for a woven textile, and as the scale and notes are disciplines for the composer of music, so Wright used the unit system as a discipline for design. The choice of the unit system was in harmony with the nature and pattern of the construction, and with the spirit and "grammar" of the design. Later in his career he felt much more free to explore unit systems of circles, hexagons, triangles (occasionally in combination) as well as the square and rectangular units of earlier years.

The unit system not only provided a tool for design, but also unified and simplified the construction process as it developed a modular system for the fabrication of parts, by means of a repetition of sizes of components such as windows and doors, with related dimensions throughout. In practice, the workmen, once they became familiar with the process, were grateful. Since carpentry and masonry tools were designed for ninety-degree angles, and forty-five degree angles, the workmen had to adjust at first to the 120-degree-angle hexagons and sixty-degree-angle equilateral triangles used in many Usonian houses of the later period. However, once they created templates to serve as layout tools for these angles, it became a simplified construction discipline, with all parts related in a direct geometry.

Invariably after completing construction of a Wright building its workmen were awed and proud of what they had produced. Their enthusiasm often bolstered the owner's morale after his experience of the delays and difficulties inherent in varying from a standard building process.

The term "grammar of the building" was frequently used by Wright to indicate the individual characteristics that make a building what it is. Just as the flora and fauna of the sea or the desert develop individual characteristics of color, form, and structure relating directly to their environment, function, and nature—their "grammar"—so also does Frank Lloyd Wright's organic building develop its individual thematic correctness, proper to its environment, while incorporating the special functional needs and/or idiosyncrasies of its user.

Although Wright always emphasized the priority of the plan, in his work the plan and the building forms were inspired simultaneously by his amazing ability to synthesize all factors of environment and need. When he sat down at the drafting table, he had already visualized the project design in its overall aspects. Always the floor plan or plot plan was developed first; it was on the topographical map of the property that he worked, with all the site factors known and generally indicated. He had also absorbed, prior to developing his design sketch, the client's program of needs and desires. Amazingly the full form of the building emerged from his pencil as a flower unfolding, without hesitancy and as a continuous drawing operation from plan to elevation to cross-sections, with some notes and dimensions to denote important aspects; and always drawn in direct relationship to the particular unit system he had chosen as appropriate. Once, when I remarked on how easily and quickly he had developed a solution for a complex project design, he replied, "Yes, but you must realize how much time I spend [mentally] designing before I sit down to draw."

In the next stage, a designated staff member would transfer Wright's original sketch into a more precise line drawing. The original sketch was invariably correct and workable in its engineering, its relationship of functional and structural parts, and its relationship to site. During this stage Wright was always close by to monitor further development of the drawings at the staff member's board, to elaborate with more technical details, and to answer the draftsman's technical design questions – always with spontaneity and the greatest of ease.

Wright's legacy to society includes many things that have become so much a part of our daily life that their origins in his innovation are forgotten. Some of them: indirect lighting, ribbon and corner windows, plate glass commercial entrance doors, steel office furniture, and even the wall-hung toilet used in most commercial buildings.

Always concerned with new technical developments, Wright was quick to incorporate into his creative thinking those he found of particular interest. He also often explored design ideas to improve manufactured objects in daily use. He was fascinated by fine motorcars; and though he often criticized the normal output of Detroit, one of the automobiles he particularly enjoyed was the first model of the Lincoln Continental (1939), a long, sleek convertible, and the following year's Lincoln, a sedan. (He improved its lines by a partial modification, a custom design for the top). He always had his cars painted a rusty red color affectionately called "Taliesin Red." For him, red was the color of life, the most "organic" color. It could be seen on many objects at Taliesin.

In 1957 while on a visit to Taliesin West in Arizona about a project I was associated with, I was asked early one morning to come to Mr. Wright's bedroom. Still in pajamas, he was working at a drawing board near his bed. Saying that his insomnia had generated a desire to get some ideas down on paper during the night, he proudly showed me rough sketches of his designs for a three-wheeled automobile and a vertical-takeoff aircraft. Knowing that I had experience as a pilot, he called me in at such an early hour because he wanted to discuss physics related to the flying machine. I was able to explain the aerodynamic principles of "uplift" as it related to the cross-sectional design of the typical aircraft wing. I recall that very privileged experience whenever I see the published designs for the vehicles accompanying his Broadacre City dissertation in his book *The Living City*. It was all a part of organic architecture.

Another example of organic design in areas not normally invaded by architects was the "Butterfly Wing" bridge in 1949 for a second crossing of San Francisco Bay. The location was under consideration by the State Bridge Authority, and a local structural engineer who wished to participate with calculations for the design asked Wright to develop a design proposal. The concept utilized a variety of advanced engineering and construction techniques such as precast and pre-stressed lightweight concrete and chemical soil solidification. It was of thin-shell monocoque form with cantilevered roadway, using a ribbed cross-section design resembling that of an airplane wing for most of the low-level crossing. At the shipping channel the crossing made a transition to a great arch spanning the required height and width. The arch provided a split roadway, enclosing, in its center, a small park with a fine view of the city skyline. For concrete the structure would be remarkably light in weight. Its basic construction concept included on-shore precasting of major sections, which would then be delivered by barge to the installation point.

The design received little notice. Later, when I showed Wright a picture of the proposed steel "Erector-set" design for the Richmond-San Rafael Bridge (since constructed), he agreed to cooperate with efforts I suggested to publicize his bridge design. "In view of the horrible thing they are about to construct," he said, "it will be in the name of much needed education."

A model of the bridge was constructed, poised on the mirror-covered table sixteen feet in diameter, and was displayed at San Francisco museums and other prominent locations. The media and citizens in general appeared excited by the proposal, but as usual with most of Wright's innovative projects, the engineering fraternity said either "It can't be done" or "It will cost too much." Governor Goodwin Knight felt obligated to request a presentation, which Wright and I jointly made to the governor and a large group of this department heads at a lunch meeting. Few questions were asked; obviously the interest was only token. On the flight back to San Francisco, Wright remarked, "We can't expect politicians and engineers to understand." Yet the San Francisco Bay area did enjoy some residual benefits: the two subsequent bridges constructed as South Bay crossings are low-level reinforced concrete bridges, albeit not as advanced in design or construction techniques.

One of Wright's unflagging hopes was to solve the housing problem for people with limited budgets. He particularly liked prospective clients who came to him with limited funds but with such a perceptive appreciation of the master architect's work that they were ready to construct a Wright building with their own hands if necessary. That kind of person always obtained a design, and several of Wright's residential projects were built in that way.

One in which I participated was a dramatic example of Wright's organic designing: the construction was to be of rammed earth (pise de terre), a method used in many parts of the world dating back to prehistoric times. I was pleased to be the catalyst for the Cooperative Homesteads project and its concept materials. The project was designed in the early 1940s for a site near Detroit. Twenty families had banded together to build their own housing units on a 160-acre farm parcel. They also expected to raise crops on this land as a source of income during periods of unemployment in the auto industry.

After assisting Wright in production drawings and acting as a liaison with the group, I spent several months setting up the project and getting the first prototypical building started. Wartime legislation made it necessary for us to obtain "defense housing" status in order to purchase equipment such as secondhand earth-handling and pneumatic-ramming equipment, and to experiment with bitulithic additives and new techniques for expediting the labor-intensive earth construction. The labor demands of the war effort reduced the work force considerably, but we managed to accomplish enough construction to validate the techniques. When the Army Air Force snatched me away for training, the project drainage system was still under construction. Without a construction superintendent and without the anticipated workers, with the drainage system incomplete, the project became a fatality of the war, literally washing away.

Probably the most successful of the Frank Lloyd Wright designs executed entirely by owners was that for Mr. and Mrs. Don Lovness in Stillwater, Minnesota. Two dwellings—a main house and a guest house—were both exquisitely constructed, together with all furniture, light fixtures, and other accoutrements, as designed by Wright. Virginia Lovness, a gifted artist, personally accomplished a great deal of the construction while her chemist husband was at work. The Lovnesses' family life developed around the construction of their houses and was a true assimilation of Wright's principle of organic architecture as a way of life. Indeed, most clients of his that I have met freely state that the experience of organic architecture, whether or not they had personal contact with the architect himself, has been the most important influence in their lives.

Wright's interest in every detail of building knew no boundaries. After the basic grammar of form and structure must come the detailed items for use and delight, with the same theme of color, texture, contrasts of dark and light, and changes of scale. This involved loving concern for design and harmonious relationships of all furniture, lighting, carpets, textiles, "stained" glass, sculptured or other integral ornamentation, and at times such accessories as china, silverware, and flower vases. In his earlier years, little could be obtained in the marketplace to harmonize with his buildings, residential commercial, or public – and much had to be made by skilled craftsmen to specific orders. In the later years, thanks in part to his growing influence, more acceptable furniture, textiles, hardware, lamps, and so forth began to be available, and this gave him much pleasure. Indeed he had predicted it:

In Organic Architecture then, it is quite impossible to consider the building as one thing, its furnishings another, and setting and environment still another. The Spirit in which these buildings are conceived sees all these together as one thing. The very chairs and tables, cabinets and even musical instruments, where practicable, are of the building itself, never fixtures upon it ... To make these necessary appurtenances elements, themselves sufficiently light, graceful, and flexible features of the informal use of an abode, requires much more time and thought on my part as well as more money to spend than is usually forthcoming in our country at this time. But in time this will be accomplished by improvements in all stock articles. Fortunately, only a few of his clients, or more often their successors in ownership, lacked sensitivity to the importance of the harmonious ensemble.

A large proportion of Wright's buildings were constructed in a hostile environment of ignorance. In most cases building permits were obtained with great difficulty, in some cases ignored entirely; otherwise the construction could not have proceeded. Innovative construction techniques were often ignorantly considered unsafe; many had to be field-tested to convince skeptical building inspectors or structural engineers. The dendriform column of the Johnson Administration Building was test-loaded at the site and proved it would support more than six times its required load; the solid wood. Usonian walls site-tested in various communities proved able to support four times the required load. In Marin County, continuous-arch shell roof slabs supported over twice the design load when tested.

Problems with an unenlightened bureaucracy, which tries to apply formulas still on the books to structural circumstances not anticipated by those formulas, continued to plague Wright's work even after his death. In Marin County, outside engineers called in during building inspection procedures vetoed Wright's articulated structural design for the structure, and thereby lowered its seismic resistance by their insistence on tightly connecting joints that had been designed to be flexible. Wright's design of the Imperial Hotel in Tokyo was also criticized by the engineering profession; but the hotel became one of the few buildings to survive Tokyo's 1923 earthquake, the worst in over a century, thanks to an innovative structure designed to resist seismic forces.

Not only bureaucrats and engineers, but many architects as well have persisted in ignoring the logic of Wright's architectural philosophy. The tenets that appear to accompany the current postmodern architectural style have been developed primarily by academic architects, a group described by Wright as "intellectuals educated beyond their capacity." This superficial proliferation of a pastiche of unrelated mannerisms plucked from history books and utilized without regard to basic functional concerns, climate, or a natural expression of contemporary materials and techniques is the antithesis of organic architecture. Wright's words here are a synthesis of warning and prophecy:

I suggest that a revival, not of the Gothic style but of the Gothic spirit, is needed in the Art and Architecture of the modern life of the world. We all now need interpretation of the best traditions in the world but made to match the great Tradition and our own individual methods. We must repulse every stupid attempt to imitate and fasten ancient forms, however scientific, upon a life that must outgrow

them however great they seem. … But this modern constructive endeavor is being victimized at the start by a certain new aesthetic wherein appearance is made an aim instead of character made a purpose. … Architecture is the very body of civilization itself. It takes time to grow – begins to be architecture only when it is thought and built, that is to say when it is a synthesis completed from a rational beginning and, naturally as breathing, genuinely modern.

■ NOTES

■

■ 1. Interestingly, less than four miles east of Oak Park.

2. Coincidentally, shortly after Green left Chicago and the Chicago Academy, sculptor Alfonso Ianelli and architect Bruce Goff both became instructors for a short period of time under the new leadership of Ruth Van Sickle Ford.

3. AGG oral history interview, October 27, 1991. Frank Lloyd Wright Foundation.

4. Ibid.

5. AGG oral history interview, August 29, 1992. The Frank Lloyd Wright Foundation.

6. Usonia is a word used by Frank Lloyd Wright to describe his vision of the United States; Usonian referred to the appropriate and affordable homes that he designed for the "common people" that were based on his own personal principles and philosophy of an organic architecture.

7. AGG oral history interview, May 11, 1994. Frank Lloyd Wright Foundation.

8. AGG oral history interview, February 21, 1990. Frank Lloyd Wright Foundation.

9. AGG oral history interview, October 27, 1991. Frank Lloyd Wright Foundation.

10. Transcription of AGG talk at Taliesin West, February 21, 1990. Frank Lloyd Wright Foundation.

11. Rosenbaum, Alvin. *Usonia: Frank Lloyd Wright's Design For America*. Washington D.C.: The Preservation Press, 1993. 157.

12. Letter from AGG to FLW, dated September 5, 1940. © 1986 The Frank Lloyd Wright Foundation.

13. AGG oral history interview, October 27, 1991. Frank Lloyd Wright Foundation.

14. Ibid.

15. Ibid.

16. Ibid.

17. Ibid.

18. Ibid.

19. Letter from AGG to OLW, dated April 4, 1943. © 1986 The Frank Lloyd Wright Foundation.

20. AGG oral history interview, August 29, 1992. The Frank Lloyd Wright Foundation.

21. Letter from AGG to FLW, dated December 2, 1945. © 1986 The Frank Lloyd Wright Foundation.

22. Letter from AGG to Jean Haber, dated December 1945. Aaron Green Letters to Jean Haber, Volume 1.

23. Interestingly, this was the location of a restaurant owned by the famous 1930s silent film actress Thelma Todd.

24. While in Los Angeles, Green had assisted Frank Lloyd Wright with Wright's large and expansive Pike residence (1947) that was to have been built in Los Angeles.

25. AGG oral history interview, August 29, 1992. The Frank Lloyd Wright Foundation.

26. Letter dated July 21, 1951 from AGG to FLW. © 1986 The Frank Lloyd Wright Foundation.

27. Letter to AGG from Mary Summers, dated December 20, 1973 (AGG Archives).

28. Letter dated January 28, 1959 from AGG to Elizabeth Gordon. AGG Archives.

29. Ibid.

30. Quoted in article written by Dave Weinstein published in the *San Francisco Chronicle*, March 5, 2005.

31. *Guggenheimer*. "A Taliesin Legacy." New York: Van Nostrand Reinhold, 1995. 134.

32. Alan Hess. "Aaron Green and Organic Architecture in Southern California." Unpublished curator's notes for exhibition dated December 19, 2016, sent by Jan Novie to author on January 20, 2017.

33. *Guggenheimer*. "A Taliesin Legacy." New York: Van Nostrand Reinhold, 1995. 134.

34. Daniel Ruark, email to author, dated January 20, 2017.

35. Dave Weinstein, SF Chronicle, March 5, 2005.

36. Ibid., 38.

37. Ibid.

38. AGG oral history interview. The Frank Lloyd Wright Foundation.

39. Letter dated June 18, 1942 from AGG to Mitchell. MRM Papers (#03832), Southern Historical Collection, The Wilson Library, University of North Carolina at Chapel Hill.

40. Letter dated May 2, 1942 from AGG to Mitchell. MRM Papers (#03832), Southern Historical Collection, The Wilson Library, University of North Carolina at Chapel Hill.

41. Email from Harriet Reif Greenwald to author, dated November 6, 2016.

42. Greenwald, Harriett Reif. Wright Chat, 2006.

43. Barry, Joseph A. "American – Body and Soul." *House Beautiful*, November 1956. 239.

44. Besinger, Curtis. "Shelter That Encloses Without Confining." *House Beautiful*, October 1959. 214.

45. Ibid., 216.

46. Email from Alan Hess, January 24, 2017.

47. Granger. *Include Me Out*. New York: Martin's Press, 2007. 64–5.

48. Delong, James. "This Modern House is Rooted in the Not-So-Distant Past." *House Beautiful*, January 1965. 77, 79.

49. Email from Allan Green to the author dated February 2, 2017.

50. DeLong, James. "This Modern House is Rooted in the Not-So-Distant Past," *House Beautiful*, January 1965. 79.

51. Email from William J. Schwarz to the author dated May 27, 2016.

52. Email from Jan Novie to the author dated May 27, 2016.

53. "Golden Gate Village, Marin City, CA: Historic Resource Evaluation." Garavaglia Architecture, Inc., June 19, 2015. 36.

54. Email from Jan Novie to the author dated January 2, 2017.

55. Besinger, Curtis. "Restraint in the Vastness of Nature." *House Beautiful*, October 1963. 184–86.

56. Ibid., 183–84.

57. Ibid.

58. Besinger, Curtis. "How to Step Up the Loveliness of an Already Lovely Spot." *House Beautiful*, July 1964. 78.

59. Ibid., 80.

60. Romanian born Jacques Schnier (1898–1988) was a prolific sculptor in the Bay Area and became a professor of art at the University of California Berkeley. Lilienthal's daughter Dorothy (1922–1998) was married to Schnier.

61. Lowry, Rich. "Remembering Aaron G. Green, FAIA," unpublished manuscript dated August 22, 2016.

62. The AGG Archives has a single undated drawing drawn by AGG of a service station, circa the late 1940s.

63. Green, Aaron to James DeLong. Rough notes for editing for article on Ohta job dated July 27, 1965.

64. "Aaron Green of San Francisco Designs a Mountain Retreat for a Crest Above Santa Cruz." *House Beautiful*, October 1965. 218.

65. DeSatt, Howard. "Highlights of the Early History of the Santa Clara County Peace Officers Association," undated unpublished manuscript.

66. Email from Jan Novie to the author dated February 2, 2017.

67. "New Sausalito Library – A Worthy Investment." *Daily Independent Journal*, March 3, 1967. 8.

68. These included both Catholic and Lutheran churches.

69. The population of Walnut Creek was less than 10,000 in 1960 but had grown to almost 40,000 in 1970.

70. Email from Harry Rodda, AGG employee in charge of the project, to the author, dated January 12, 2017.

71. Price, Robert L. "Notes Regarding the Aaron Green Experience." Unpublished manuscript dated April 2001.

72. Ibid.

73. Ibid.

74. Ibid.

75. Telephone interview with Gernot and Guinevere Mueller, February 7, 2017.

76. The future phases were two single-story extensions for a two-garage and a ground floor master bedroom suite.

77. Quoted with permission © 1986 Frank Lloyd Wright Foundation.

78. Telephone interview with Allan Green, February 3, 2017.

79. Telephone interview with Allan Green, February 3, 2017.

80. Undated letter from AGG to Jean Haber, 1946. *Aaron Green Letters to Jean Haber, Volume 1*.

PHOTOGRAPHY CREDITS

Aero Photographers, p. 147

American Hebrew Academy, courtesy of, p. 385-94, 396 (top), 397, 398 (top)

Carnegie Museum of Art, courtesy of, p. 20 (five)

John Clouse, p. 78, 84, 86 (right middle), 141 (top), 259 (bottom), 264, 317, 324 (top), 325 (top), 364 (two), 365 (three), 366

Martin Cooney, p. 113 (three), 118-19, 404 (Hicks Residence)

James Dixon, p. 372 (three), 373 (two), 375 (right), 376-79, 382-83, 422 (Mueller and Green residences)

Frank Lloyd Wright Foundation, courtesy of, p.6

Aaron Green, p. 50 (top), 65 (top), 71 (top left), 76, 401 (Maxwell residence)

Frank Green, p. 248-49, 251 (two), 260-61, 263, 265 (bottom), 284-85, 286 (top), 287 (top), 292-93, 295, 342-44 (top), 345 (top), 347 (three), 356 (four), 358-59, 410 (Weir Office), 411 (Ohta residence), 412 (Newark Community Center), 415 (Union City Civic Center), 419 (Newark Library), 420 (Haber residence)

Steve Hanson, p. 165 (bottom two), 168 (two), 169 (bottom), 234 (two), 235 (two), 409 (Mischel residence and Ives office)

Randolph C. Henning, p. 395, 396 (bottom), 398 (bottom two), 425 (five)

Vanessa Kelly, p. 422 (Greenwood Ridge Vineyards addition)

Yehuda Lavee, p. 416 (Stanislaus Forest Service building), 417 (Klamath Forest Service building)

Oren Lavee, p. 216-17 (bottom), 222 (top right and bottom left), 223

Tom Liden, p. 380-81, 424 (Greenwood Ridge Vineyards bridge)

Patrick Mahoney, p. 82-83, 86 (left and bottom right), 87, 137, 140 (thee), 141 (bottom), 254-59 (top), 262, 265 (top)

Ken Molino, p. 148, 150 (bottom two), 151

Jan Novie, p. 407 (Chapel of the Chimes Oakland), 421 (Marin County Correctional Facility)

Bo Parker, jacket (Randolph Henning)

Maynard Parker, p. 48-50 (bottom), 51-54, 58-59, 65 (bottom), 70-71 (bottom), 72-75, 77, 85-86 (top right), 88, 90-103, 154-55,

162 (top, and bottom right), 163-65 (top), 166-67, 169 (top), 170-73, 402 (Reif residence), 403 (Paul and Bartholomew residences), 404 (Hughes and Dukes residences), 407 (Anderson residence)

Gerald Ratto, p. 149-50 (top), 152, 406 (Marin City)

Karl Riek, p. 197, 202-07, 408 (Eldred residence)

Daniel Ruark, p. 41-43, 142 (three), 221 (bottom), 286 (bottom two), 287 (bottom two), 324 (bottom two), 325 (bottom), 335 (bottom), 336-37, 351 (top), 365 (top left), 375 (left), 402 (Chapel of the Chimes, Santa Rosa), 405 (Chapel of the Chimes addition 1), 406 (Chapel of the Chimes South Chapel), 408 (Chapel of the Chimes addition 3), 409 (Chapel of the Light), 410 (Chapel of the Chimes addition 1 and Chapel of the Chimes Transition Arch), 411 (Chapel of the Chimes L.D.S. Monument), 413 (St. Stephen Catholic Church), 415 (St. Monica's Catholic Church), 416 (St. Joseph's Mausoleum), 418 (Queen of Heaven Mausoleum and St. Monica's Rectory), 419 (Skylawn Oceanview Columbarium), 420 (St. John Vianney Offices, McAndrews residence and DeNevi residence), 421 (St. Joan of Arc Catholic Church and Skylawn Bai Ling Yuan II), 422 (Chapel of the Chimes Circle of Peace Mausoleum)

© Ezra Stoller/Esto, p. 120-21, 126-35, 178-83, 189, 192-95, 405 (Green residence), 407 (Lee residence), 408 (Paulsen residence)

Wanda Walker, p. 411 (Walker residence)

Scot Zimmerman, p. 351 (bottom), 354 (three), 355 (two)

All uncredited images appear courtesy of Aaron G. Green Associates. Our thanks and apologies to the unknown photographers whose names were inadvertently omitted.

FRONT IMAGE IDENTIFICATION

Jacket, front: Granger and Mitchell residence
Jacket, back: Reif residence
Half-title page: Dr. Jean Green residence (Philo, California)
Title page: Wagner residence
Copyright page: New Hunter's Point Community

■ ACKNOWLEDGMENTS
■

Albeit short-lived, I was blessed to have worked under Aaron Green's tutelage for the last six months of his long, creative life's journey. He hired me in November 2000 to be his eyes and ears at the American Hebrew Academy. I lived twenty-seven miles from the site; he was more than 2,700 miles away. During my tenure with him as the Associated Architect for Contract Administration, I witnessed his genius and grace, confidence and humility, passion and patience. In the times we spent together his youthful passion and bountiful creative energy for organic architecture was a sight to behold. After Aaron's unexpected death I continued to work with his successor firm in a larger role to complete the initial phase of work at the American Hebrew Academy and had the opportunity to learn more about Aaron Green and his architecture. I was humbled to have been asked to be a part of this book and I have tried to objectively present an architectural biography of a proven body of work representing a pinnacle of organic architecture based upon the philosophy espoused by Green's mentor Frank Lloyd Wright.

As with any endeavor of this nature, while I alone accept responsibility for any and all errors contained herein, I was certainly not alone in my research, and owe a great deal of thanks and gratitude to the people who have assisted me on this journey. Individuals who I reached out to during the research include Frank Green, Dale Allen Gyure, Alan Hess, Patrick J. Mahoney, Eric O'Malley, Bruce Brooks Pfeiffer, William Blair Scott, Jr., Kathryn A. Smith, Brian A. Spencer, and Robert W. Whitten.

Past employees and associates of Aaron Green's architectural practice who assisted me with their recollections and knowledge include James Dixon, Larry Dorshkind, Richard Lowry, Robert Price, Harry Rodda, William J. Schwarz, and David Tirrell. Equally important are the memories of clients, their descendants, and subsequent owners of works designed by Aaron Green, including Harriet Reif Greenwald, Gernot and Guinevere Mueller, Rebecca Schnier, and William and Lynn Swann. And I would be remiss if I did not thank my colleagues in Aaron Green's successor office who were so diligently committed to completing the work at the American Hebrew Academy, all the while sharing with me their stories and recollections of Aaron – Jan Novie, Oren Lavee, Daniel Ruark, Renate Wunschkowski, Armando Solano, James Gallagher, Taisuke Ikegami, Michael Pellis, and Alberto Rivera.

The various institutions that have also equally assisted me in my efforts include the Avery Architectural & Fine Arts Library (Janet Parks, Margaret Smithglass, and Nicole L. Richard), the Frank Lloyd Wright Foundation (Margo Stipe, Indira Berndston, Oskar Munoz, and Elizabeth Dawsari), the California Architects Board (Vickie Mayer), American Institute of Architects (Nancy Hadley), the University of North Carolina – Chapel Hill (Bryan A. Giemza and Tim Hodgen), St. Stephen Catholic Church (Mary Cook), St. Elizabeth Seton Catholic Church (Marilu Radcliff), and the Santa Clara County Peace Officers Association (Howard DeSart and John Tomasetti).

Thanks also to the following organizations for the use of their photographs: Aero Photographers, the American Hebrew Academy (Glenn Drew), the Carnegie Museum of Art, Esto (Erica Stoller), the Frank Lloyd Wright Foundation, and the Huntington Library (Lisa Caprino and Erin Chase). I would also like to thank the other photographers whose work is such an important part of this book: John Clouse, James Dixon, Frank Green, Steve Hanson, Vanessa Kelly, Oren Lavee, Tom Liden, Patrick Mahoney, Ken Molino, Bo Parker, Gerald Ratto,, Karl Riek, Daniel Ruark, Wanda Walker, and Scot Zimmerman.

I owe much to the publisher ORO Editions and especially Gordon Goff and Jake Anderson for their interest, foresight, and commitment in publishing this book and their subsequent trust, assistance, and patience. I knew from the start that ORO Editions was the right publisher to bring this dream into reality.

An individual who deserves special mention and my sincere respect and thanks is Glenn Drew, the Executive Director of the American Hebrew Academy. He was the person charged with keeping the immense project, with all its moving parts and assorted personalities, on track, from its inception in 1996 through to its successful fruition. And he remains tirelessly devoted to protect and foster both Chico Sabbah's dream and Aaron Green's vision. His continued counsel, trust, and faith are appreciated.

Lastly, this project truly would not have been possible without the able assistance and immeasurable enthusiasm of three key people. Each having differing relationships with Aaron Green, never-the-less, they all share the same personal commitment of wanting the legacy of Aaron Green to remain alive through the publication of his work – Allan Wright Green (his elder son), Jan Novie, (his loyal right hand man in the office and the owner of the Aaron G. Green Archives), and Daniel Ruark (a passionate and dedicated associate). I thank them each immensely.

DEDICATION

This book is dedicated to the legacy of Aaron G. Green, to Jan Novie, the custodian of that legacy, to the memory of Maurice "Chico" Sabbah, and, mostly, to my best friend and wife, Maggie.

Randolph C. Henning

■

■

■

ORIENTAL GARDEN SHOPPING CENTER

SANTA CLARA   CALIFORNIA

AARON G GREEN   A·I·A·   ARCHITECT